BOLD AS BRASS

BOLD AS BRASS

My Story

HILARY DEVEY

MACMILLAN

First published 2012 by Macmillan
an imprint of Pan Macmillan, a division of Macmillan Publishers Limited
Pan Macmillan, 20 New Wharf Road, London N1 9RR
Basingstoke and Oxford
Associated companies throughout the world
www.panmacmillan.com

ISBN 978-0-230-76593-1 HB
ISBN 978-0-230-76691-4 TPB

The acknowledgements on page vii constitute an extension of this copyright page.

1 3 5 7 9 8 6 4 2

A CIP catalogue record for this book is available from
the British Library.

Typeset by Ellipsis Digital Limited, Glasgow
Printed and bound by CPI Group (UK) Ltd, Croydon, CR0 4YY

Visit **www.panmacmillan.com** to read more about all our books
and to buy them. You will also find features, author interviews and
news of any author events, and you can sign up for e-newsletters
so that you're always first to hear about our new releases.

I dedicate this book to my beautiful little mum,
to my dad, who played such an important role in
shaping my character in my formative years,
to my stepfather Leonard Cross who played such
an important part in my son's upbringing,
and to my precious son Mevlit.

Acknowledgements

I'd like to thank Megan Lloyd Davies, who is so patient and turned into a very funny friend for life; Adrian Russell, who has been by my side throughout the building of Pall-Ex; Bill Crawford, who was such a source of strength to me in the early days of Pall-Ex and Glenys Hargreaves who was an equal source of strength. Thanks also to Robert Benoist who self-lessly helped me during my recovery from my stroke in 2009 and to all my friends and family. Forgive me if I have missed out individuals but you are all in my heart.

Picture Acknowledgements

All photographs are from the author's collection, with the exception of:
Page 11, bottom © *Sunday Times* / NI Syndication
Page 15, © BBC
Page 16, bottom © *Sunday Times* / NI Syndication

Prologue

I didn't have a Hollywood moment when I decided to become an entrepreneur. You know the kind of thing: a shaft of light shining through the clouds or Scarlett O'Hara scratching at the earth outside Tara. I'm afraid it was far more run-of-the-mill than that. In fact, I was sat on a bloody freezing lino floor when the idea came to me.

I was seven at the time and didn't even know what an entrepreneur was. So I didn't decide to become one because of money (two shillings was a lot to me as a child) or power (my dad was in charge of my world, and it began and ended with him). I just looked at the grown-ups around me and decided that I'd always make sure that I and the people I loved were secure. And had warm chairs to sit on.

My family and I were staying at my grandmother's tiny terraced house in Bolton at the time. How we'd ended up there is another story. For now all you need to know is that weeks before our life had changed in just a few hours, when the bailiffs had arrived at our house. My dad's central heating business had gone bust after his main client went under, owing him thousands, and the house – plus everything in it – was being repossessed. The only place to go was my grandmother

Emily's two-up two-down, and by God I hated it there, because she ruled everything with an iron fist and no velvet glove.

Out back was a dark Tippler toilet, an oblong wooden box with a hole for a seat and a long black waste pipe which plunged into nowhere. Nicknamed the long drop, it was flushed with water from the scullery and stank to high heaven. Meanwhile, inside was a best parlour (which I hardly caught sight of because my grandmother treated it like a holy shrine that no child could enter without getting a clip round the ear) and the living room – the heart of the house because it was the only place with heat, courtesy of the cooking range. Pouring in and out, relatives would sit down at the huge square table in the middle of the living room to soak up the warmth or – if they were really lucky – on the one comfortable chair or tiny sofa that should have sat two but usually had about six people on it.

That's where I was sat on the day a visitor came over and turfed me off the sofa and on to the lino. And it was then, as I watched the adults soaking up the warmth from the range and felt the cold leaching into my bones, that I can remember thinking just one thing: 'I will never end up like this. I will never let this happen to me.'

And I didn't. The drive that was sparked into life in that moment is what's seen me through the last fifty years of ups and downs – with a hell of a lot of hard graft in between. It's helped me build a business with an annual turnover of £100 million in the UK and Ireland alone, providing jobs for 7,500 people across nine countries. It's also seen me through the darkest days of a relationship I thought might break me, and the years when I stared into the abyss of any mother's worst nightmare – my son's heroin addiction. Writing this book has made me remember it all, and I have to say it's one of the hardest things I've ever done.

But this isn't going to be a 'Look what I did so you can too' book, because not everyone can. And not everyone should try. Building a business from scratch brings huge rewards; but there are sacrifices too, and I'm not going to soft-soap what they are. If you're reading this then you should know that I don't do bullshit. So let's start from the beginning, work through to the present day and then, when you know what becoming a successful entrepreneur really takes, you can decide if you're prepared to pay the price.

Chapter 1

It's hard work, all this remembering. Trying to put my child-hood into one neat box is complicated because it was so turbulent. Just like the whole of my life, really. But the first thing you need to understand is this: from the day I was born until now there have been ups, downs, but always lots of laughter. So although there were many aspects of my child-hood that were less than perfect, and others that were never fully explained, I didn't question any of it. I was born in 1957, when people didn't sit children down and tell them every cough and spit of what was going on.

That's why I quickly learned to adapt to whatever was happening around me, which is lucky because, believe me, there was a lot of it. It's a skill that has stood me in good stead, because I honestly believe you're dealt the cards that life thinks you can handle and your job is to just get on with it. I've very seldom sat down and felt sorry for myself. And the few times I have I've soon got up, dusted myself off and carried on again.

So exactly what is the best word to describe my childhood? Unusual. Yes. Very unusual. But whatever I tell you after this, always remember that I knew I was loved, which is all any child really needs. I was so loved in fact that my parents gave me something many kids aren't lucky enough to be given: a sense of myself, a belief in what I could achieve and the capacity to love other people. I was taught how to love and I've done it all my life (although maybe there were a couple of times when I wish I hadn't loved quite so much).

My parents, you see, weren't exactly a conventional couple. My dad, Arthur Channon Brewster, came from a middle-class Chester family. One of his sisters worked as a linguist for the Ministry of Defence, while another opened a string of garages in the Midlands. My dad was eloquent, intelligent, tall, dark and very handsome. With bright blue eyes and well-cut suits, the ladies loved him. But he was married with four children when he met my mum Minnie – she didn't know that at the time, of course. She only found out the truth after my brother Stuart and I had been born, and soon left Dad in a rage. I don't remember a thing about it because I was just a baby, but apparently she took me and Stuart to her Uncle Chris's house in Oxford, although we weren't there long because Dad soon brought us all home.

Minnie left Arthur again and again after that, because theirs was a stormy marriage – packing up suitcases in a fit of rage, she'd head off, usually to my grandmother Emily's house. But it was never for long, and even on that first occasion it was too late for Mum to leave for good, because my parents were quite simply the love of each other's lives. There may have been many times when they couldn't live very well together, but they couldn't live apart either. Arthur and Minnie were drawn to each other like moths to a flame.

However unusual my dad was, well, Minnie wasn't exactly

typical either. She came from a working-class Bolton family and had started at the local cotton mill aged fourteen, before getting married at nineteen and having my older brother Gary. So far, so usual, but then she left her husband after only a few years of marriage because he was a cruel man. By the time she met Dad, she was twenty-seven and living back at home with her mother Emily, who was looking after Gary while Mum went to work in the mill.

I'm afraid the complications don't stop there, though, because the women in my family are like something out of a Barbara Taylor Bradford novel. No wonder I've had my fair share of romantic dramas; even my grandmother Emily was cut off from her wealthy Bolton family, called the Guests, after getting pregnant out of wedlock. I don't know what happened to the father of her baby, but Emily ended up marrying the local window cleaner, Henry Ingerson, who took in her daughter Peggy; and no one ever spoke about Peggy's biological father again. Henry and Emily went on to have another three children – my uncles Chris and Jackie and my mum – and for a while things were good because apparently Henry did quite well financially. But then sadly he fell ill and by the time he died – when he was only in his forties – the family was pretty much penniless.

Emily didn't go out to work though. Her children were old enough to do that, so they were expected to tip up for the income needed to run the house. I'll never forget my parents going off on their first holiday abroad, to Majorca, when I was about eight (I later found out it was their honeymoon, because it must have taken them that long to get their divorces sorted out). Just before they left, my dad bent down to give my brother

Stuart and me each half a crown, but Emily had that money out of my hand the moment they turned the street corner. She even made me wear the same clothes the whole time my parents were away, only changing them the day they were due home. That's why my grandmother was no longer just Emily to me by the time they got back. She was Evil Emily.

I was never surprised at her treatment because I knew she couldn't stand the sight of me. I was far too much like my father, and she couldn't stand him either. But although Mum always said my grandmother was the way she was because she'd had a hard life, I could never quite accept that explanation. Lots of people have hard lives but don't turn out so bloody mean.

However she ended up that way, my grandmother ran her home like a Mafia don and I think that's probably why she didn't like my dad. Arthur Channon Brewster put her nose right out of joint when he appeared, because he was the one person who wasn't scared of her in the slightest. He was way too macho for that.

So all in all I wasn't exactly born into a household straight out of a Doris Day film.

My parents met when Mum went away for a weekend to see the bright lights of Blackpool. Dad, who at forty-two was fifteen years older than her, appeared at a dance at the Grand Hotel and soon swept her off her feet. Within a few weeks, Evil Emily had got so enraged by his constant visits that she bolted the door when Mum was on a night out with Dad and wouldn't let her back in when she got home. My grandmother's plan backfired, though, because the locked door gave my dad the perfect opportunity to come up with a spontaneous plan. What

Mum didn't know then was that he'd spend the next two decades cooking them up.

'Why don't you come to Ireland with me?' Arthur asked, because he was working on a contract there laying pipework for North Sea gas at the time.

I don't know exactly what Minnie said but she must have agreed because they were never apart again. My parents soon settled down together and were Mr and Mrs Brewster to the outside world, even though they hadn't actually married yet. All I can think is that Emily must have had her nose really put out of joint that her daughter had been taken from her, because my dad and her never learned to see eye to eye.

My parents were completely in love. Truly, madly, deeply, and they remained like that throughout their whole lives, however sick of each other they got at times. They would kiss and cuddle even after twenty-five years together, and my dad would say the same thing to me time and again: 'She's the love of my life, our Hils. The love of my life.' So I hope you don't think too badly of him for walking out on his first wife and children, because that's what I'm sure he did.

I know that he tried to do the right thing, however wrong he'd been, because he continued to support them financially. Later, my mum would tell me that even during times when she'd had little money to feed us, she'd still put a postal order into the mail for Dad's other family. He paid a high price for what he did because he lost his family and when he tried to make contact in later years, they didn't want to know.

My mum didn't escape unscathed either, because my father refused to allow my half-brother Gary to live with them, so he stayed with Emily. But I think the fact that Gary didn't live with us was the reason why, however hard Dad tried to get us away from Bolton – because as far as he was concerned it was a town full of peasant northerners who ate chip butties, whereas he came from posh Chester – he never managed to do it. My mum wanted to be close to Gary and went to see him every week to make sure that Evil Emily got enough house-keeping to provide for him. The tug of Gary was always there, which is why, whenever we moved away from Bolton, we always ended up going back again.

While Mum visited Gary regularly, I didn't see much of him growing up. It's only in more recent years that I've got to know him and discovered that my brother is larger than life, full of intelligence and pragmatism. But while my grandmother adored him (because she wasn't evil to everyone, you see), I don't think Gary ever quite forgave Mum for leaving him and to be honest I don't blame him for feeling as he did. I could never have picked a man over my child.

But Minnie did, and I won't judge her for it because what kind of life was she going to have without my dad? Working her fingers to the bone in a cotton mill for a pittance as a single mother was pretty much it. She fell deeply in love with Dad and he cared for her in a way that men did back then – by doing absolutely everything. So much so that when he died years later, my mother didn't even know what a chequebook was. And that was how she wanted her life to be.

The reason my dad didn't want Gary to live with him was simple: he wasn't going to bring up another man's child. I can't soft-soap it. Arthur was lovely, but a typical northern misogynist all the same. Later on he thought nothing of keeping me off school far more than I went to it because why did I need to be educated? I was a girl and so I was going to get married one day and didn't need proper schooling. In the mean time, I could work.

My brother Stuart was born in June 1955, and I arrived just under two years later, in March 1957. Apparently Dad's first words when he came to see me in hospital were: 'Is she really mine? She's so ugly.'

'Yes,' my mum said. 'But hasn't she got beautiful feet?'

'Well let's just hope her face grows as beautiful as her feet then, shall we?' my dad replied.

It didn't. I was about three when I developed Bell's palsy, which made the left side of my face droop. Some of my earliest memories are of making the long journey to have electric shock treatment, which doctors hoped would get my nerves feeling again and bring my face back to life. Every Monday and Wednesday my mum and I would catch the first of the two buses we took to get to Bolton District General Hospital, where I'd sit as pads were put on my face to give me tiny electric shocks to stimulate the nerves. I used to hate the pain, but at least I was given a boiled sweet at the end of every session.

The treatment worked and my face recovered, so I don't know what my mum must have thought when the other side went. Once again Bell's palsy had affected my face and it didn't fully clear up until I was about eight. Maybe that's why Minnie was so determined to make me into the picture-perfect daughter, which didn't exactly come naturally. You see, as well as the Bell's palsy, I was much more at home playing in the dirt than keeping dresses clean.

The day Mum loved most every year – and I hated in equal measure – was Singer's Day. It was held around Easter time each year and organized by the local church. I haven't got a clue now exactly why the local kids had to parade through the streets. But whatever the reason, Mum would spend weeks preparing for the moment when she'd put me in a white dress and best shoes.

'Don't touch!' she would cry if I so much as looked at the white dress she'd got ready and pressed for me to put on.

I never quite understood why I had to take part in Singer's Day – or go to church in fact – because my parents never went with us. I'm sure the only reason they sent Stuart and me was so that they could have a bit of peace and quiet together. But for one precious day each year I lived up to Mum's mental image of me looking perfect in a pretty dress with short white socks and Mary Janes.

That's how Minnie was, though. She loved things to look nice – herself and me in particular. She'd scrimp and save out of the housekeeping she was given each week just to make sure I was always well dressed because, like my dad said, 'If you look like shit then you'll be treated like it.' Back then, I wasn't so sure, but those lessons learned young gave me the love of fashion I still have today. I'm not a slave to trends, because what's the point of looking like everyone else? But one of my greatest pleasures now is the clothes I treat myself to: I couldn't believe what a stir my cream jacket caused after I first hit the screen on *Dragons' Den*, for instance. But it's fashion, I like it, and if people take the piss then I say: Sod them. I've worked hard for those shoulder pads.

Minnie was gorgeous: small, dainty, the kind of woman that men want to look after. Later my dad made sure the glamour factor was turned up another notch after boasting to a business associate that his wife was a blonde bombshell. Just in the nick of time for their next dinner, Dad made sure that Mum's naturally brown hair was dyed platinum blond, and bought her a beautiful fox-fur coat to wear. As perfectly turned out as Don and Betty Draper, they must have turned all sorts of heads when they headed down to London to go to the kind of clubs where the Krays hung out, which they did every now and again when I was very young.

Take our poodle Timmy. Even the dog was an accessory to my mum's outfit when she took him out for a walk. Now Timmy was a tiny thing who must have thought he was a German shepherd because he was forever squaring up to other dogs. But that didn't put my mum off from walking him because she got to leave the house looking immaculate in boots with brown fur peeping over the top that matched Timmy's, a brown bouclé coat and a fur stole.

That's just how she was though and Mum could afford the clothes when I was a small child because we'd yet to get on to the rollercoaster that would see us living anywhere from a big comfortable house to a caravan. Life was good when I was young. In fact, Dad was doing so well that my cousin Janet thought we were millionaires because we always rolled up in a Jag.

The reason we were flush was because Dad's central heating business was making good money – with plenty more left over. He'd set it up after meeting Mum and it boomed as he took on contracts to put heating into some of the houses that were being built as England well and truly got back on its feet after the Second World War. At one time he apparently employed more than a hundred engineers.

But things obviously started to go wrong when we were living in Hulton Lane, a 'nice' road full of big houses and only a short bus ride from the centre of Bolton. Ours had four bedrooms, a big front and back garden, carpets throughout, central heating, hot water and all the mod cons. We were very lucky considering that lots of people were still living in freezing, mice-infested terraces. But Stuart and I were too young to realize how good we'd got it because, like most kids, we just took it for granted.

We left the big house in Hulton Lane when I was about five and I think that by then Dad's business must have been having problems because we moved to a two-up two-down in Ruby Street, where I started at Wolfenden Primary. Nevertheless, with central heating and carpet throughout, our house was still a cut above many. It was a lovely, cosy home and however tight money was, Minnie didn't let her standards drop: it wasn't long after we got to Ruby Street that she decided to tame my wild mane of curls with a demi-wave perm. Yes. You heard that right. A perm. Aged five.

Now I wasn't happy about this. Not happy at all. But after taking me for my first perm, Mum made a fatal mistake the second time I had it done because she sent me alone to the Embassy Hair Salon on Blackburn Road. Sitting in the hairdresser's chair, I was told that I mustn't get my hair wet for at least twenty-four hours to allow the lotion to take properly, and knew I'd found a get-out clause when it started to pour on my way home. Slowing down to a snail's pace, I stood against a wall in a back street to make sure I was absolutely dripping.

Mum was livid when she saw my hair was ruined by the time I got home. But at least she gave up giving me perms after that, and even abandoned her attempts to put my hair into a bun because I'd always pull it out.

'Leave our Hils alone,' Dad would say. 'She's not a bloody doll.'

Life changed for ever though when I was seven. It was May 1964 when Stuart and I heard a knock at the door as we sat in the living room one day. A minute later, two massive men walked into the room and without so much as a look in our direction or a smile to soften the blow, grabbed the chairs we were sitting on before carrying them outside. Then they came back for the sofa. Next to go was the television, followed by the pictures on the walls. Bit by bit, they stripped our entire house – mattresses off the beds, crockery from the kitchen and the cooker – as we stood and watched. Mum was silent throughout the whole thing, but as she watched the bailiffs bring the beds downstairs, she finally slid down the wall and started to howl.

I tried to comfort her but she was inconsolable, and I was too young to really have a clue about what was going on. I wished my dad was there to stop these men, but he was away in Germany on business. Looking back, I think he must have gone there in some desperate attempt to drum up more work. Whatever the reason, he wasn't there as the bailiffs swept through our home like locusts, taking absolutely everything with them. They left us just two Jaffa orange crates to sit on.

Our neighbour Clarice Baxter, who'd seen what was happening, soon came to scoop us all up and take us back to her house. There, the first of a thousand cups of tea was served and a telegram was sent to my dad. But it was a few days before he could get home and by the time he did I'd heard enough of my mum shouting down the phone and all the conversations with the neighbours to understand that we'd lost everything.

I didn't feel scared. In fact, I just carried on playing as usual with Clarice's daughter Audrey, because I knew Dad would look after us like he always did. I don't remember any sense of shame in front of the neighbours either. People understood that Arthur hadn't done wrong. His bankruptcy was one of those blows that life so regularly dealt in a place where most people worked incredibly hard just to make ends meet.

But we couldn't stay at Clarice's for ever, which is why we had to go and stay with Evil Emily – and believe me when I tell you that she was truly horrible. Even so, I might have been able to stand the Tippler toilet, the freezing cold and the mice running through the house, the stodgy meat and potato pies she served up with far more potato in them than meat, and even the sharp switches with a stick that she always seemed to be giving me. I could also have just about managed to stop the anger which boiled up whenever I heard her snarl about me to my mother: 'That girl has far too much to say, Minnie.' But what did for me were her false teeth. Two chomping great rows of them that she'd put in a glass by her bed each night.

Mum, Dad and Stuart were in the big back room, and Gary had the box bedroom, which meant I had to share the front bedroom with Evil Emily. Each night without fail, I'd stare in horror as she got into bed beside me and took out her teeth before settling down for sleep. I swear I didn't get a wink. Lying in the dark, I'd cling on to the side of the mattress as I imagined the teeth climbing out of the glass and scuttling across the floorboards to come and get me.

I was exhausted by the time we left that house, about two months after we'd arrived. My dad must have been too because he'd worked day and night to find some sort of solution to the disaster that had beset us and had come up with a plan he thought would get us out of Bolton and make us some money. Now ultimately it didn't do either. But at the time it must have seemed like a sure-fire money-making scheme. And if anyone deserves a medal for dreaming up those, then it was Arthur Channon Brewster.

Chapter 2

Picture the scene: I've gone from a poshed-up terrace that was the equivalent of the *Dynasty* mansion in 1960s Bolton – complete with my mother looking not a million miles away from Krystle Carrington – to Evil Emily's. So where did I find myself next? In a run-down Manchester street with Myra Hindley a few doors up. I swear. It was during the time that she and Ian Brady were committing the Moors murders, a thought that still chills me.

My dad needed to do two things: maximize our income to get us back on our feet, and find us a place to live. The answer to both came in the form of a corner shop in Gorton, a run-down area of Manchester, because we could live above the shop, which my mum would run while Dad went back to work as a one-man band fitting central heating. I'm not sure how he got the money together to buy the shop, but he can't have needed much because Gorton must have been cheap. No wonder. It was used as a location for the TV drama *Shameless*, where it looks posh in comparison to how it did back then.

Dad's plan was perfectly well intentioned but there were two big problems with it. The first was that everyone in Gorton was so poor that many of them wanted to shop on tick, so the list of our neighbourly creditors grew longer and longer by the day.

'I'm a bit short today, Minnie,' a worn-out mother would say. 'Can you put this ham on tick?'

'Go on then,' Mum would reply, because she could never refuse, no matter how angry my dad got about it.

'They should be paying their way,' he'd tell her when he got in at night and looked at the lengthening credit list. 'We're not a bloody charity.'

'But what can I do, Arthur? I knew that quarter of ham was going to feed three kids their tea. How could I say no?'

The other problem was that my mum hated being away from Bolton almost as much as she hated running the shop. In fact, she'd often just close it up so she could nip back to Evil Emily's for the day, which enraged my dad almost as much as the growing list of credit.

Meanwhile, I think I must have been in a state of shock. I mean, I took what was happening on the chin because that was my nature, even when I was young. But I can't imagine now that any child could have experienced so much change and not been shocked. I think it's probably why I learned to cope so well in later life with whatever was thrown at me. I realized early on that you have to be adaptable, bend to whatever direction life takes you, which is a quality you need to succeed in business because nothing is ever as straightforward as you think it's going to be. Aged seven, I was already learning the lessons that would make me the businesswoman I am today.

Gorton was a world away from what I'd known though. I'm not sure if there were actually kids on the corner of the street that wore sparking clogs. But there were certainly families rammed in tiny terraces, kids all over the place and mangy dogs running everywhere. I didn't like it at all and there wasn't even the comfort of being guaranteed a constant supply of sweets, because if our parents went out on a Saturday night they made sure to lock the door of our flat so that Stuart and I couldn't go downstairs and do a raid on the shop. What were they thinking? God knows what would have happened to us if there had been a fire.

It wasn't just the area that was rough, though. Some of the people were too. Of course there would have been nice families in Gorton because there always are in any neighbourhood, rich or poor. It isn't money that makes you decent, is it? But the only vivid memory I have of the people of Gorton is a pretty unpleasant one. After meeting a girl at my new school called Mandy, I was invited back to her house one afternoon and arrived to find it tiny, dirty and full of kids. Then we walked in to find her dad in the kitchen.

'Can we have some money for sweets please?' Mandy asked him.

'You know what you have to do,' he said.

With that Mandy reached her hand into her dad's trousers. I watched, not knowing what on earth was going on until that dirty old bastard turned to me.

'Do you want some money for sweets too?' he asked.

All I knew was that I had to run and I belted out of that house as fast as my legs could carry me. Kids are clever like that though, aren't they? They trust their instinct, while adults are too busy listening to all the noise rattling around inside their heads instead of what their guts are telling them. Women are even more blessed in that department, thanks to feminine intuition, and it's one of the greatest assets we have. We should listen to it more.

So that afternoon I turned tail and ran back home, where I breathlessly told my mother what I'd seen. She told my dad the moment he got home and he, being pretty handy with his fists, went round and knocked seven shades of shit out of Mandy's dad, who disappeared for a few weeks after that.

It wasn't long before we left the area too, so we can only have been in Gorton a few months. The last straw came when Dad got so sick of everyone buying on credit that he put up a list of the worst offenders' names in the window. Of course everyone boycotted the shop, and we had to leave.

Somehow Arthur must have got some money together though because it was then that my parents started in the business that was to define my childhood: the sometimes heady, never glamorous and always bloody-hard-graft world of pubs, working men's clubs and hotels.

Arthur had bought a pub tenancy and I'm sure Evil Emily must have been involved in planting the idea in his head because the Crompton's Monument just happened to be five minutes' walk from her house back in Bolton. My dad wasn't stupid though. In fact, he was a true entrepreneur at heart, always on the lookout for the next opportunity, and knew when he bought the tenancy for the Crompton's that the pub would not only provide an income and a home but also an exit strategy that would maximize his profit.

You see, back then St Peter's Way – the dual carriageway that would eventually link the M61 to the centre of Bolton – was being built and Dad knew it would have to go slap bang across the bottom of Mill Hill Street. Where was the Crompton's Monument? Mill Hill Street, of course. Sooner or later a compulsory purchase order would be issued on the pub and Dad knew he'd get a good price for it – not just for the building but for the business as a going concern. With a bit of creative accounting, he'd do well because Dad was never shy of sailing close to the wind. In the mean time, Arthur was going to maximize his profit by making sure that every Irish road digger within a five-mile radius drank at his pub.

It wasn't exactly a huge step up from the corner shop. A lot of the terraced houses on Mill Hill Street had already been knocked down by the time we moved into the old Victorian pub and the place was infested with the rats and mice that were scurrying to find new homes as each new foot of the foundations of St Peter's Way was dug. It was so overrun in fact that the council pest controllers were out almost every day. But those rats and mice still won every battle in the war we fought against them. The traps and boxes of poison scattered everywhere had such little effect that I'd sit in the living room and watch mice racing out when the fire went on, boldly licking themselves clean in front of the heat. Or I'd lie in the bath watching them scurrying about on the bathroom floor and see them dashing across the kitchen worktop.

There was no way those vermin were going to leave a place full of nice dark corners to hide in – especially when they could feast on a constant supply of crumbs from the pies that were kept warm behind the bar before being served to hungry road diggers. In fact we'd sometimes find toasted mice in the pie warmers, after they got really cocky and started pushing their battle lines forward in the search for an even better supply of crumbs.

Our living accommodation at the Crompton's could not have been more different from our cosy terrace or the big house. With a cramped kitchen-cum-living room downstairs behind the bar and small bedrooms on the first floor, there were no creature comforts – just lino floors and bare walls. It was in the bar where life in all its shades unfolded, because, just as Arthur had hoped, the place was packed. The main room, which was filled with wooden chairs and tables, was always heaving and off it was the 'vault', a tiny room where all the diggers used to sit playing cards and dominoes. Pubs didn't open all day then and so the Irish workers would be thirsting for a pint whenever the doors opened – be it midday or evening.

Mum worked the bar alone during the day while Dad went out to fit central heating before the two of them did the evening session. Maybe Mum, who continued to make sure that she always looked her best however much she'd gone down in the world, was the reason why the workers liked the Crompton's Monument so much. But I suspect it also had something to do with the 'Arthur's Mild' my dad soon started brewing. Once again, he maximized his profit (albeit in a slightly question-able way) because there wasn't a drop of leftover whisky or gin, a splash from the bitter or slop trays, that didn't get recycled to make his brew.

'Slop bucket!' my dad would shout if it looked as if anyone was about to throw out the dregs after collecting up some glasses.

Throughout the night, Dad would disappear every so often with his precious bucket and go down to the cellar, where all the wooden beer barrels were housed. Then he'd pour his booty into the one containing his 'mild', add yeast and sugar and return now and again to lovingly tap the barrel. It was never emptied. Instead, it was endlessly topped up with all the leftovers as anything and everything went in. Most precious of all was Gold Label barley wine, and Dad would think all his Christmases had come at once if anyone left a mouthful at the bottom of their bottle because it was so alcoholic that it gave the mild an extra good kick.

A few pints of Arthur's Mild and all the Irish diggers were guaranteed a good night.

'That's a good pint, for sure it is, Art'ur,' they'd cry as they asked for another.

I'm still not sure to this day if they'd have cared even if they'd known where that mild came from.

The other way my dad maximized his profit was by doing regular lock-ins. If the diggers looked as if they were getting a bit rowdy one night then Dad would promise them a lock-in on the next if they behaved, before cleaning up by charging everyone a flat – and inflated – price whatever they drank. Word must have got around because soon the local police turned up.

'Whose is this?' they asked as they pointed at a pint after they'd battered at the door and got Arthur to let them in.

'It's mine of course,' he said.

'And this one?'

'Mine too.'

'And this?'

'Mine.'

'And this?'

'What can I say? I was thirsty.'

There was nothing they could do because apparently every drink in the pub was my dad's so he wasn't breaking any law, and none of the diggers were going to contradict him. The police knew when they were beaten and were soon piling in on lock-in nights, when my dad happily kept the till ringing after he'd bolted the doors shut.

Night after night I'd sit in the living room with Stuart, listening to the roar from the bar. There'd be the hum of voices which got louder as the evening went on, Irish songs being sung, and always the rumble of laughter. There was usually a fight too but I was never scared by them. In fact I think I must have enjoyed them because whenever I heard a tussle spilling out on to the street, which it usually did, I'd put a chair by the window, climb up on to it and make sure I got a good view.

The best fight I ever saw had to be the one Dad got into after one of the diggers had got a bit fresh with Mum or something. When Stuart and I heard shouting one night, we raced over to the window with our chairs and got up to look outside. Now the Crompton's Monument was at the top of a long hill and we stared in wonder as we watched Dad pick up a man and throw him on to a car roof. As the man bounced off and on to the road, the diggers who'd poured out the pub to watch started cheering as he rolled down the hill.

'Dad won!' I cried to my brother. 'He won!'

Nothing made me afraid back then and it was a good job too because there were always fights breaking out. Every so often my dad would bar a workman who had got out of hand. But they'd usually turn up the next day, having forgotten what they'd done after sobering up, and he'd let them back in. The only time the diggers were better-behaved was on Saturday nights, when they brought their wives in for a brandy and Babycham or a schooner of sherry. But those weekday fights never worried me too much. It was only later that I learned to be afraid of violence.

In those first few months at the Crompton's Monument my parents worked every hour God sent, so it meant that Stuart and I were left to fend for ourselves a lot more than we'd been used to. We hadn't spent much time together before because my brother and I just never hit it off. Some siblings don't, do they? Mum once told me that Stuart scratched out the eyes in a photo of me when I was a baby, and I'd say that was a sign of how things were headed. It wasn't that we fought or argued. We were just so different. I was the feisty, difficult one and Stuart was far more malleable. In fact, my dad always said I should have been the boy. (It's that misogynist streak again I'm afraid.) To him, men were men and women were women, whereas Stuart and I didn't play to type. I wonder now if all Dad's talk was one of the reasons why Stuart and me never stood much of a chance of getting on.

When we'd lived in the posh house and in Ruby Street, Mum had put meals on the table, shooed us off to school and run the home. But now she didn't do nearly so much for us so we started to make our own tea, do our homework and put ourselves to bed. In fact, if I'm being honest then I'd have to say that Mum didn't do much for us at all after we went into the pub trade.

'Is it beans and egg tonight or egg and beans?' we'd joke if she said she was going to cook tea, because those were the only two things she ever made.

A few years later, when the advert came out saying that a million housewives every day picked up a tin of beans and said, 'Beanz Meanz Heinz,' we'd laugh that she was a mum in a trillion because she loved them so much. If we were lucky we got a few chips with our egg and beans but it was such a rare treat that I soon learned how to cook them myself. The best nights were when Dad had gone out because then Mum would let us dip stonking great butties made of doorstep slices of white bread and thick yellow best butter into our bean juice.

My dad would never have allowed us to do such a thing because even though we were as working-class as they come, he held on to his middle-class roots. That's why he'd never allow us to have butties with our tea or say 'grass' instead of 'graaarse', 'baff' instead of 'baaarth'.

'There's no 'f' in baaaarth,' he'd tell me in his perfect Queen's English.

Dad was an articulate and well-educated man who wanted us to speak properly, so woe betide me if I ever uttered something as common as 'Flippin' 'eck' – even though it was what all the kids I knew were saying. If he ever heard me say it, he'd send me straight upstairs for the *Oxford English Dictionary*.

'Now, can we find "flippin' 'eck" in here?' he'd boom at me.

One look from him was enough to tell me never to dare speak those awful words again. All that trouble he went to didn't really pay off though, did it? I mean absolutely nothing could get rid of my Bolton twang.

So Mum didn't do what many other mums did at the time, and occupy herself with all things domestic. In fact, when it came to most things related to work Minnie wasn't that interested. Dad was the one who humped barrels, stacked shelves, rang up the tills and ordered stock. Mum was simply born to stand behind the bar and look gorgeous.

'Evening, Minnie, you're looking lovely tonight,' the diggers would say.

'Do I?' she'd reply, as if butter wouldn't melt.

Mum adored every minute because she was demure, charming – and boy, did she love to talk. So much in fact that even after all that chatting in the pub, she still spent every Saturday lunchtime talking nineteen to the dozen with Evil Emily and her sister Peggy. Leaving my dad to run the pub and knowing that he'd settle down in front of the racing on TV with Stuart once they'd closed, she'd cart me off to the Pack Horse in Bolton, where the women of my family would order a bottle or two of Mackeson Stout, light up their Benson & Hedges and start putting the world to rights.

'She's a sour-faced old cow,' Evil Emily would snarl about Uncle Jackie's wife Lily. 'I don't know what he sees in her.'

Uncle Chris's wife Betty didn't get off any more lightly either, and my Auntie Peggy would try to stand up to her mum as Evil Emily moaned on.

'Come on, Mum,' she'd say. 'Lily's all right.'

'No she's not!' Evil Emily would snap.

I think Evil Emily just took against the people her children were married to because they were outsiders to her – and so were some of their children. There was no logic to her preferences, though, because while Evil Emily adored my brothers Stuart and Gary, she hated my cousins Alan and Janet almost as much as she did me. Maybe that's why Janet and I became the best friends as kids that we still are today.

Back then, Stuart, our cousins and me all went to St John's Church of England Primary School, which was just up the road from Evil Emily's. Each dinnertime, we'd troop down to her house to eat the bread and jam that she served up most days. She always gave the boys more food than the girls and never ever served seconds (Mr Bumble had nothing on Evil

Emily when Oliver asked for more). Neither would she ask where the red marks that I regularly appeared with had come from. I swear I was clonked on the head that many times when my teacher Mr Woods threw the blackboard rubber at me for being a chatterbox that I've wondered recently if it was one of the reasons why I had a stroke a few years ago. But my grandmother was only interested in getting us round the dinner table, feeding us the basics and getting us out again. After all, she got well paid for her trouble by our parents.

Sitting in the Pack Horse listening to her moan on, I'd think that Evil Emily looked like a sparrow sat between two peacocks. How my grandmother managed to produce two such glamorous daughters I'll never know. By then my mum's hair was dyed platinum blond and French-pleated so she really did look a million dollars. But with her shock of always beautifully curled red hair, Peggy was possibly even more glam than Minnie.

Tiny, just like all the women in my family were until I came along and inherited my father's height, Peggy would always arrive wearing a two-piece suit, high-heeled court shoes and a slick of red lipstick. She could afford to look good because she and her husband, Jack Tunnah, had done quite well for themselves. Jack ran his own plumbing business and Peggy managed the shop attached to it. Sadly, though, she died in her forties of thrombosis so I never got to know Peggy that well – I couldn't get a word in edgeways during those afternoons in the Pack Horse. And if all that chatting over stout bottles wasn't enough, Minnie would then drag me round Bolton Market, where she'd stop to talk to every stallholder in the place.

But that's who she was, and I loved her because I knew I was the apple of my mother's eye. Certainly, she didn't sit down to read books with us and God forbid either Stuart or I made a peep after the first notes of the *Corrie* theme tune played because if so the wrath of Minnie would rain down on us. But Mum did the stuff that really mattered, like traipsing on all those buses to get me to hospital when I was small and being endlessly patient with all my questions. Then there was the day when I was knocked off my bike after a moped clipped me and the man who was riding it carried me home. I was badly bruised and had a big lump on my head from falling on to the concrete. After screaming at the reckless driver, Minnie put me to bed and showered me with kisses.

My dad was just as loving too. When I was little I would sit on the floor between his legs as we watched TV, with my arms slung over his knees and his arm around my neck. He was always joking with me, because I laughed so much as a child that he'd sometimes say: 'What on earth's funny, our Hils?' which would make me giggle even more. But like he always said: 'If you can laugh all your life as you laugh as a child then you won't go far wrong, my girl.'

I loved his jokes and the way he'd spit on his hands before giving me a smile as he tried to smooth down my hair before I left for school. Or the ditty he'd repeat whenever he caught me out of bed too late.

'I don't like your face, Mr Moon,' he'd cry. 'It is round, fat and white like the moon.'

So however much our life had changed, we remained a close family, knitted so tightly into each other's lives that I felt secure. I didn't sit in front of computer consoles or TVs like kids do nowadays, missing out on family life because technology kept us apart, lost in little computer worlds and not interacting with each other. I *lived* life every day.

I've also worked for almost as long as I can remember. Not full-time, mind you, until later. But even at the age of seven, I realized that I'd have to get involved in pub life if I wanted to see my parents now they were working so much. So while Stuart, who was always happy with his own company, sat in the lounge and read his astronomy books, I went into the bar to help with clearing glasses and emptying ashtrays at the weekends when there was no school to occupy me.

Looking back, I think I must have overshadowed my brother a bit because I was always so full of beans and he was probably closer to Mum than I was then. Our Hils was a bit of a daddy's girl, to be honest, and Arthur would roar with laugher as he taught me how to pull a pint when I was hardly tall enough to see over the top of the beer tap. I loved being in the thick of things. But the feeling didn't last too long, because soon something happened that changed everything.

Chapter 3

I've told you I wasn't scared of anything when I was a child, but that's not strictly true. The one thing guaranteed to make my skin creep were the rats and mice crawling all over the Crompton's Monument. But my natural fear turned into a full-blown phobia about a year after we got there.

By then my mum was heavily pregnant, about eight months I think, and one day I heard a scream and ran to find her lying at the bottom of the stairs covered in blood. She was just as scared of the rats as I was, and had tripped down the stairs after seeing one bolt out and stare up at her. Screaming for my dad, I could see the bright red flush of blood on Mum's dress grow ever darker. Fear scratched at the back of my throat as we waited for the ambulance to come, and then I watched as she was put into a wheelchair, covered in a blanket and taken away.

Mum came home a few days later looking like she'd always done, but I soon realized something had changed. She'd lost the baby that would have been a sister to me and, looking back, I think she must have suffered badly with depression after that. All I knew then though was that Mum became increasingly short-tempered with us and started constantly rowing with my dad. The hard-working but happy atmosphere in our home had changed, and I missed it.

Mum was always in bed when we got up to leave for school, and getting ready for work behind the bar when we got back from it. Meanwhile, Dad was fitting central heating by day and running the pub by night, so he was always busy. All this meant that I started getting used to my own company at a very young age, and I have to say that I'm still the same today.

I might know hundreds of people and get invited to posh parties and functions all the time, but I only have a few close friends. The loner was bred into me as a child because our nomadic lifestyle meant that we moved around far too much for me to ever learn how to make good, lasting friends easily. Strange as it might sound though – because I know lots of women who have more friends than fingers – I'm happy that way. It's how I've always been and I've never felt short of love.

Putting times and dates to all this is hard. Why? Because when we left the Crompton's Monument we started moving around so much that I don't even remember some of the places we lived. Janet still laughs about the tricks we got up to when she came to stay at a hotel we once ran in Stockport. By then she had a boyfriend called George, who her parents disapproved of so we of course did all we could to make sure they stayed together. He can't have been that bad because Janet recently celebrated her thirty-third wedding anniversary with George. But while I *can* remember helping to make the path of Janet's true love run smooth, I can't recall even living in that particular hotel in Stockport – or some of the other places I lived – and I think I went to thirteen different schools over the years but can't be entirely sure.

My mother hated the Crompton's Monument after losing the baby, and all this must have coincided with the compulsory purchase order being issued because we soon moved on to the Railway Hotel in Farnworth, another area of Bolton. And it was there that what little of our family's fortune my dad had managed to rebuild began to slip through his fingers.

You see, Arthur did what so many people do when a small business is going well: he upsized it. But like many people he didn't anticipate the problems this would bring because the Railway was a far bigger pub than the Crompton's. If a hundred diggers had been able to cram into the old pub, then the Railway could fit two hundred and fifty-plus on a good night.

A smaller business is easier to control and a bigger one can bring unexpected challenges – often related to human resources. Dad's was no different because he discovered there was a lot of staff thieving at the Railway. Later he'd tell me that to catch a thief you needed to set one, which is why he'd deliberately not sack someone for a while after discovering they had light fingers, so that he had time to watch and learn their tricks. Giving out free drinks, failing to ring up rounds properly, or making 'mistakes' with change – there are so many ways in which someone can relieve you of your profit margins in a pub environment, which is high-volume, low-margin and hard to keep track of until you stock-take. Even the cleaners were nicking bottles at the Railway, by stashing them in their laundry baskets.

That wasn't the only problem either. Dad didn't keep as tight a rein on the Railway as he should have done because Nat Lofthouse, the legendary Bolton Wanderers player who was by then the club's assistant trainer, drank in our pub with other footballers. It meant that a sprinkling of glamour was dusted over the place and my mum in particular got a bit star-struck.

Swept away by it all, the head she'd never had for business got even more turned, and so my dad had yet more on his shoulders. Make no mistake: there was money to be made. But as things started to slip out of Dad's grasp, he began to drink heavily. Some mornings before we left for school I'd see him gulp a tot of whisky, on other nights his eyes would blur and he'd slur his speech when he spoke to us.

Arthur was drunk in fact the night he decided he'd finally had enough of it all. Hearing him shouting, I ran to find him leaning out of the window on the first-floor landing. But after trying my best to drag Dad back in, I gave up and screamed for Mum.

'What are you doing, Arthur?' she shouted when she came running. 'Not in front of the children!'

I'm not sure if it was my mum's admonition or the fresh air that sobered Dad up enough to convince him not to jump. But the drama didn't end there because the next day Minnie decided she'd had enough of him, and left with us. We'd only got about ten minutes down the road though when my dad found us.

'Come home, Win,' he said, using his pet name for her. 'Please come home.'

'No, Arthur! I've had enough. I really have.'

'Things will be better, I promise they will,' my dad pleaded. It took just a few more minutes of his coaxing to persuade Mum to relent.

She always did, and the packing of suitcases, flights back

to Evil Emily's or hurried walks to train station platforms were never explained to us kids. We just got on with it all and didn't ask too many questions.

I think Dad drank as a way to release pressure. My mum was bloody helpless, to be honest, and he allowed her to be because it was the macho thing to do. In addition to running the pub and doing central heating jobs to earn extra, Arthur did a fair bit of cooking, cleaning, washing and ironing too. Don't forget that he had seven kids to support – four from his first marriage plus Stuart, Gary and me – so the pressure on him must have felt unbearable at times. And while my mum had at first relished the chance of being more than a stay-at-home trophy wife, she never quite put down the trophy and got her hands dirty.

Anxious to help out, I started doing more around the house, and one of the first jobs I mastered was the Sunday dinner. Each week at the Railway, I'd peel the potatoes and cook them a bit before calling Dad to come upstairs to lower them into the hot fat. Then I'd smash up the swede after it had been boiled to within a hair's breadth of sludge, and call my father when I thought the joint was done. Coming upstairs, he'd lift the meat out of the oven, peer at it and either cover the joint with tin foil and put it on the side, or tell me to call him in another fifteen minutes.

It was the one time of the week when we ate together – even if it was on our laps – and I loved that we did because on every other day family life got forgotten in the hard business of running a pub. I can't remember sitting down to a Christmas lunch together after we went into pubs because it was such a busy time of year that my mum had to take purple hearts just to get through it. Can you imagine? All the sixties

Mods were using them to get high and there was Minnie taking them to get through to New Year's Day, like *Valley of the Dolls* meets Annie Walker.

It all sailed straight over my head, of course. The only thing I was really aware of was the intense loneliness I felt for the first time in my life when we were at the Railway. It was a big building and gone was the comforting roar of the diggers at the Crompton's or the sound of my mum or dad's feet occasionally clipping down the lino to come and check on us. It felt as if they were a million miles away as I sat upstairs at the Railway, hating the eerie silence.

I didn't make friends at my new school either because our attendance started to slip. I think the school must have been a way away from the pub, because there were lots of days when we didn't go in if Dad wasn't doing a central heating job and didn't get up in time to take us. When the headmaster came to complain, Arthur got him so drunk that he never said a word about it again.

That was fast becoming Dad's answer to problems, and things obviously spiralled out of control because we'd moved on from the Railway by the time I was about nine. When I was older, my dad would tell me again and again that money couldn't be chased. But I know now that he never took his own advice – although, to be fair, he usually made it for a while as he chased it, before losing it again.

Money ran through Dad's fingers because he was always generous, the first to buy a round and the last to leave anyone else to foot the bill. Cash flow was such a problem in fact after we left the Railway that my parents couldn't afford to buy a new pub tenancy, so a new era in our lives was ushered in: pub relief management. And what did that mean? A new pub every month or two if we were lucky, and with it a new school.

For the next year or so we moved around all over the Bolton and Manchester area, and wherever we ended up, Mum simply walked me and Stuart to the nearest school and signed us on to the register. I hated most of them and was always the new kid, the girl without any friends. But I quickly learned how to read a roomful of children and work out who I should steer well clear of, where I'd fit in the pecking order and whose ego needed soothing with placatory words or buttoning down with a quip.

Even so, I felt just as lonely at school as I did at home and didn't make friends because we were always moving on, so what was the point? We just didn't have a life in which I'd have been able to invite a girl from my class home for tea. Between the odd purple heart, regular screaming rows and plentiful whisky shots, it wasn't exactly an average family home, was it?

But when my parents had got together enough extra money from the relief management, it was time to make our next move and this time we went to a house in Lostock, a few miles outside of Bolton town centre – a *bona fide* home complete with three bedrooms, a garden and Axminster carpets through-out (cream in the best parlour, red in the living room). I bloody loved it. For the next year or so, my mum cooked the odd thing other than a plate of baked beans, I went to the same school for a while, and the arguments seemed to melt away now that there wasn't a limitless supply of alcohol in the house to tempt my dad.

It was then that my love affair with horses began, after I started visiting a farm just up the road from our house. It was owned by a couple called the Cockers and they had two horses which had belonged to their daughter who'd tragically died. Jimmy was a chestnut Shetland pony with a white flash on his nose, while Simon was a big grey gelding, and the Cockers told me that I could ride the horses in return for mucking them out. I didn't know how to ride, of course, but soon taught myself and got so good that I'd stand Simon in front of the stable, climb up on to the half-door and jump onto his back like something out of a John Wayne film.

He had an unfortunate habit of bolting, though, and I was usually left clinging on to his back for dear life – sometimes not nearly tight enough. I came home again and again with bruises and one day even got stuck in a mud hole after Simon threw me in a field. Some kids who were playing near by pulled me out but my school shoes got left behind and I got a good hiding when I got home.

'You're not handling him properly, our Hils,' Dad told me one day. 'I think I need to come and show him what's what.'

Now as far as I know my dad had never even got on a horse before. But that wasn't going to stop Arthur, was it? The next time I went to see the horses he came with me, and as I led Simon out of the stables into the field, Dad shouted at me from where he was leaning on the fence.

'You've got to be firm with him. Now look at what I do.'

Climbing over the fence to where I'd come to a halt with Simon, he stood behind the horse and slapped him heavily on the backside. Now if there's one golden rule about horses, it's this: never stand behind them – particularly when you've just clouted them on the arse. Simon's leg shot back and my dad got kicked so hard that he had a hoofprint on his shin for weeks to come. After that he hated Simon even more and soon started telling me that if I was thrown off again I wouldn't be allowed to ride him any more.

That's why I didn't breathe a word when Simon did inevitably chuck me off again because this time I knew I'd really hurt myself. My arm was throbbing good and proper by the time I got home but I didn't dare tell my parents. It was only a few days later when my mum touched me and I flinched that she realized something was up and took me to hospital, where I was told I had a broken arm.

I loved those horses so much that when I found out they were for sale I did every job I could – from washing glasses in the local pub and doing a paper round to helping out on the travelling fruit-and-veg van – to try and save up enough to buy them. I continued to look after them even after we moved up in the world, into a large, fancy house in Chorley New Road near Queen's Park. My dad's central heating business must have been going well again and Mum had got a factory job so there were two incomes coming into the house. Even so, the costs of running such a big house must have quickly become too high because we soon moved on again, to a smaller place in nearby Ernest Street. I was devastated when my parents told me shortly after that I couldn't keep looking after the horses. Then the Crockers sold the farm and so Simon and Jimmy got sold on.

The new house needed work, which meant another golden opportunity for Arthur to make some money. Most of the many houses we lived in were usually in a state and Dad would rip them apart, do every bit of DIY imaginable, and then sell them on at a profit. In fact, it wasn't unusual to go to bed at night and come down in the morning to find that he'd knocked a wall down because he was always so full of ideas – and impatient to bring them to life.

With secondary school approaching, I got a place at Bolton School Girls' Division because I'd done well on the eleven-plus. It was a private school but provided a lot of free places to students from poorer backgrounds and somehow I'd always done well at my exams, however little I'd actually been in class. I soon realized though that my parents were struggling to find the money to send me because Bolton School was where all the posh kids went and, as well as a regular uniform, I would need a hockey kit, tennis whites and all that caboodle.

To help out, I got a job on Pot Bailey's stall in Bolton Market – the only place to go if you wanted a job lot of cheap china.

'Come on, ladies and gentlemen,' I'd shout to the punters as they walked by. 'Who'll give me a fiver for this? No one? So who'll give me four quid then? OK, I know I should be selling this for at least ten pounds but who'll give me three?'

Soon a crowd would form around me and slowly but surely I worked out how to get the best price – usually by cracking jokes and shouting loudly.

'How about this for your wife, sir? No? Not feeling generous today? Don't worry. You don't look like you'll suit this box of china anyway. But you, madam, you look like you've got some class. How about a couple of quid for the lot?'

My favourite trick was the reverse sell, giving customers a glimpse of something and then hiding it away – which only made them want it more.

'Now I was going to show you this gorgeous basket and auction it off,' I'd say as I lifted up a box of china. 'But no, I'll put it back. This might be more your thing, ladies and gentlemen. It's a little bit cheaper.'

Bending down to put the box back under the stall, someone would invariably make me a bid, and soon there'd be that many wanting to buy, they'd all be bidding against each other.

It was there on Pot Bailey's that I first learned just how much I loved the banter, chatting and joking with customers that came with sales. I was a natural. But as the weeks passed, it became more and more obvious that I had one big failing: I was forever dropping the pots. In fact it got so bad that Alf, the man who ran the stall, sent me home without pay one day.

'We'll see about that,' Dad exclaimed when I told him what had happened, and he marched me back down to the market to claim my wages.

'I love her, Arthur, I really do,' Alf insisted. 'And one day your girl will be a millionaire because she's that good at selling. But I just can't keep her on.'

'Why not?' my dad roared, ready to pitch in and fight my corner.

'Because she's costing me a fortune in pots.'

In the end, even Dad could see that it didn't make good business sense to leave me on the crockery stall, but I left with my head held high and my wages in my pocket.

'Oh, Hils,' Arthur said with a roar of laughter as we got back in the car. 'I guess we'll just have to find you something that you can't break.'

After giving me a massive hug and taking me home, Dad was as good as his word. He found a job for me on the textile stall at the market, where neither of us thought I could do much damage. We were wrong. Do you know how much water fabric rolls can suck up if you leave them in the driving Bolton rain? I might have been a good salesgirl, but I was always a bit accident-prone.

In the end my parents realized that what with the uniform and the extras, they just couldn't afford to send me to Bolton School so I got a place at White Croft, the local comprehensive, instead. Dad got the money for my uniform the Friday before I started by selling his old Imperial typewriter for £20.

I loved it at White Croft, and fitted into secondary school in a way that I'd never done in primary because we'd moved around so much. For the first term I lapped up all I was being taught, loved my lessons and even the homework. I felt like I had a purpose and a structure to my days and learning really inspired me.

But then what happened? Just as you might have guessed, my parents decided to move on again and I have no idea whether my dad's itchy feet or just the need to make money from another scheme was to blame. But one afternoon my parents drove us to Accrington and pulled up the car outside a place called the Richmond Hotel. It was slap bang opposite a wall that seemed to go on forever, with a huge mill behind, and I remember thinking how depressing this place was with its long cobbled streets and grey skies.

I must have tried hard to let the conversation wash over me as I sat in the pub. I was happy in our house and enjoying school; I'd made friends and was doing well. But when we got outside and opened the car doors to find that the dog had crapped everywhere, Dad cleared the mess up uncharacteristically calmly.

'It's a sign,' he said as he turned to Stuart and me with a broad smile. 'Where there's muck there's luck.'

My heart sank. We were going back into the pub game.

Chapter 4

'Is Sandra ready yet?'

'No.'

'I want to go.'

'Relax.'

'I have to go.'

'Why don't you sit down?'

'Where is she?'

'Busy.'

'Is she ready yet?'

'No. Sit down. Have a drink.'

I looked at the man, unsure of what to do. The sound of grunts and groans was seeping through the kitchen wall next to the doorway I was standing in. I thought it was sex but wasn't sure.

I wanted to leave the flat, go back to the Richmond, to my mum and dad. They didn't even know I was out. I'd sneaked out without telling them because I knew Dad wouldn't let me go out with Sandra. He didn't like me hanging round with some of the older girls who were friends with the boys who drank in the pub. They were a bad lot, he said.

But I wanted to say yes when Sandra asked me out for ice

cream. I'd met her as she sat on the bottom of the steps outside the back door to the pub, smoking cigarettes and talking to me while I sat up top. Sandra was a couple of years older, and wore make-up and short skirts when all I ever had on was jeans and T-shirts.

I didn't know that her Italian boyfriend Luigi and one of his friends would be coming out with us for ice cream. But I couldn't say no when Sandra said we should go to their flat afterwards for a drink. Then she disappeared with Luigi and I felt sure it was them making the noises next door. Something just didn't feel right. I wanted to run – just as I had that day in Gorton when Mandy's dad had asked me to touch him.

But I didn't. Instead I stood in the doorway, not knowing what to do, as Luigi's friend sat on the bed in the corner of the living room in front of me. I didn't want to look stupid in front of Sandra by running off. She might tell me that she didn't want to hang around with me any more if I did that, and however much I'd told myself since arriving in Accrington that it didn't matter if I didn't have any friends, deep down I knew it did. No one wanted to come near me at school and Sandra was the first friend I'd even tried to make for so long. The only people I usually spoke to were my parents or pub customers, which is why I couldn't run off now. I had to wait. Sandra would be back soon.

'Want a glass of pop?' Luigi's friend said.

I looked at him, unsure of what to do.

'Go on,' he said. 'Sit down.'

'OK.'

And so I sat down next to the man on the bed in the house I didn't know.

I've never told anyone about that night when I was twelve

years old. It was shut away tight inside me and I didn't breathe a word about it. I didn't know how to. Until now.

I quickly fell back into pub life after we got to the Richmond, however much I didn't want to leave behind the school in Bolton that I'd loved and the days of living together like any other family in a house. All that quickly melted away after my dad interpreted the dog crap as divine intervention, because I was back in a familiar world. Just one thing had changed: I was expected to work now far more than I had ever done before. Gone were the days when I had wandered in and out of whatever pub we were running as a kid and done as I pleased by emptying ashtrays or pulling pints. From the day we got to the Richmond, I had to pull my weight and soon learned to order stock, bottle up, clean the mirrors behind the optics, wash down the bottles and dry up glasses.

Otherwise, I was soaking the labels off Smirnoff bottles so that my dad could stick them on to cheaper vodka, or watching him tinker with the optics like a brain surgeon making a delicate life-or-death incision. Such was the look of complete concentration on Arthur's face that I'd hold my breath in fear until he finally smiled. Then I knew he'd get twenty-eight measures out of the bottle that night instead of twenty-six.

Not everyone had to work like I did, mind. Mum spent more and more time sitting at a table in the pub with her new friends, while Stuart continued to keep himself to himself in our living accommodation. But I enjoyed the hard work at the Richmond and knew that whatever I did, Dad did a hundred times more. The Richmond was a big place, you see, with a jukebox room, a 'vault' where the men played cards, and a room with a piano in it that was packed every Saturday night; there was also a big bar with walls covered in red flock paper.

Soon I was running the pub each Wednesday while my parents had the day off to go back to Bolton. Can you imagine walking into a boozer and seeing a twelve-year-old running the place alone? There were no other bar staff because the pub was quiet on weekdays and my parents only employed a barmaid to help us at the weekends. I never gave it a second thought though as I opened up the pub, served drinks and announced last orders. Once time had been called, I'd cash up the tills, wipe down the bar, do the glasses and sweep the floor.

I never heard a peep out of the drinkers when I rang the bell and shouted, 'Last orders' in my most booming voice ten minutes before closing. Then, after calling, 'Time, gentlemen, please,' they'd all shuffle out the door and I'd get on with the list of jobs I'd been given to get the pub ready for the evening. After all, I'd learned early on to give as good as I got during our years at the Crompton's, and Arthur Channon Brewster had done what he always did after arriving in Accrington: quickly built himself a reputation for being handy with his fists, which meant that no one dared play him – or me – up.

I enjoyed those Wednesdays. In fact, I thought that running a pub was easy compared to the new school I'd been sent to, which I hated so much I was glad of every minute away from it. The trouble had started on my first day, when I'd had a drink from the toilet tap and a teacher had decided the water I'd spilled down my skirt was something else.

'You dirty girl,' she'd roared at me in front of the whole class. 'Now stand on that chair and learn your lesson.'

Nasty old cow. I didn't stand a chance because everyone

thought I was the new girl who'd peed herself. After all those years of melting into the background at the many schools I'd gone to, there was now no escape from the bullies and I was targeted good and proper. It was miserable.

'You can get us fags,' some girls told me after finding out that my parents ran a pub.

'No I can't.'

'Well find a way, because if not you're going to get some real trouble.'

Knowing that I couldn't talk to my parents because they were too busy, and also reluctant to be labelled a sneak, I started doing as I was told. Smuggling out fag packets from behind the bar, I'd hide them in my cat Snowy's basket before putting them into my schoolbag and handing them over to the girls. I knew it was wrong but I had to do it: my parents couldn't help and giving in was the only way I'd ever get any peace.

Not that I was the only one on the rob, mind you. For every decent punter who walked through the doors of the Richmond, there were a good deal more who were unlike anyone else I'd ever met. As rough and ready as some of the drinkers I'd known before had been, the customers at the Richmond were in a different league. In fact, I can safely say that it was the only den of actual iniquity I've ever lived in.

The young people who drank in the Richmond were led by a long-haired guy called Jim, who looked like Jesus and sat listening to the jukebox every hour the pub was open. Sitting in the room where the music was played, he and his friends would smoke marijuana as my parents wondered where the strange herbal smell filling the pub was coming from. They had no idea about that kind of thing and were far too busy anyway, keeping their eyes peeled for the rogue punters who'd worked out how to play the fruit machine for free.

I knew even less about drugs than Arthur and Minnie but was still sure that our customers weren't exactly stand-up citizens. Whatever they were like, though, I was just happy to be busy working because it kept my mind off school. A few months after we got to Accrington, I'd been invited to a bonfire party by some girls in my class, who set on me the moment I arrived to meet them. I was wearing my new school coat and it was so badly ripped by the time I got home that I got yet another good clout. I have no idea why I was picked on. Why does any kid decide another's good for bullying? I suppose that I was a bit of a loner, new to the area, and bullies find strength in numbers.

As ever, I found comfort in animals and Snowy my cat was my pride and joy. I'd got him after a customer offered him to me as a kitten during one of those lunchtimes when I was working alone and I couldn't resist – even though I knew that Mum hated cats. To put off the inevitable moment when I'd have to give up my kitten, I hid him in a cardboard box, but my secret was soon out when Dad heard him mewing. Convinced that Snowy would soon be homeless, I was overjoyed when Dad persuaded Minnie to let me keep him.

I adored Snowy, which is why I was horrified when the white fur on his face started to go browner by the day when he was a few months old. I just couldn't understand it. What on earth was happening? For weeks, I was at a loss as to why Snowy was losing his looks but eventually realized that he'd been following Dad down into the cellar and licking all the yeast off the beer barrels. That was what was discolouring the fur around his mouth and I swear that cat was an alcoholic.

Some nights Dad would lock Snowy in the cellar by accident and he'd stagger out the next morning rolling like a sailor who's just got dockside after months at sea.

I was determined to do something, but what? Snowy had proved he was a clever cat, and I had no idea how to outwit him. Luckily inspiration came when I saw an advert for Ariel washing powder, which promised that it could get any white whiter than white. What can I say? Snowy got a good wash and Ariel delivered on its promise: he was as pure as his driven namesake again. Only trouble was that Snowy also soon developed bald patches. Poor cat. I'm not sure he ever forgave me for what I did.

Even so, I wasn't public enemy number one. That accolade was reserved for Dad, because Snowy and Arthur couldn't stand each other. Their mutual hatred had been sparked into life after I forgot to wrap the Sunday joint in foil one afternoon. Unbeknown to me, Snowy – who we already know was an opportunist kind of cat – made off with the juicy meat and Dad blew a gasket when he came up to carve after the pub was finally closed.

'Where's the roast?' he yelled. 'Who's got it?'

I didn't understand. The leg of lamb couldn't have just disappeared into thin air. Convinced that one of the pub regulars must have nipped up and nicked it, because most of them were stealing whatever wasn't bolted down, I started to hunt high and low with Dad. Then he went into the back yard and I shuddered as I heard him scream.

'That effing cat!' he roared, because however much of a stickler he was for how his children spoke, Arthur could swear with the best of them when he wanted to.

Running outside, I saw Dad advancing on poor Snowy as

the cat tried to drag the roast away as quick as his legs could carry him. He didn't stand a chance. Dad picked up Snowy, slung him through the air, and I stood rooted to the spot as I watched him hit the clothes line. Clinging on for dear life, he spun around in circles while I could only watch helplessly.

'That will teach him not to steal,' Arthur roared as he scooped up the joint.

Snowy never dared touch the roast again but even my love for him couldn't cure my hatred of Accrington. That's why I took my chance for escape when a coachload of friends and family came over to visit from Bolton one night. While everyone drank and chatted in the pub, I hid myself on the coach and no one was any the wiser until it arrived back in Bolton. Sauntering off, pleased as Punch to be home, I was sent back with my tail between my legs when the empty coach made the journey back to Accrington that night.

My parents must have realized just how unhappy I was, though, because they decided to send me back to Bolton and White Croft, the school I'd loved. Only trouble was that I had to live with Evil Emily again, and it wasn't any better than it had been the first time. What that woman didn't know about being bloody vile just wasn't worth knowing: Emily was soon pocketing my dinner money and even made me buy clogs when Mum sent money for new shoes so that she could keep the rest. When my classmates laughed at me, I realized I was now just as out of place now at White Croft as I was in Accrington. By then my half-brother Gary was studying to be a welder and tried to stand up for me. But however many times he told Evil Emily to leave me alone, she just wouldn't listen.

Within a few weeks, my parents had realized that I was

far too homesick to be away from them so I went back to the Richmond, where I was as isolated as ever. I think the reason I didn't make friends was six of one, half a dozen of the other. I was the new kid and so people were wary of me. Then I was bullied and became even more of a loner. That's why I wanted to be Sandra's friend when I met her sitting on the back steps. She alone seemed to understand how much I hated school.

And so I agreed to sneak out for an ice cream and ended up in a room with a man I didn't know, wondering when I'd be able to go home, hoping it would be soon.

He kept talking to me. He wouldn't stop trying to wheedle his way into a conversation. But I couldn't understand most of what he said because the man had a thick Italian accent which I couldn't make head or tail of. So I stared at the glass of orange he'd brought me as I sat on the bed beside him, hoping that Sandra would hurry up.

'What are they doing?' I kept asking but he didn't tell me.

I wished I could leave. Why couldn't Sandra come and get me? We could walk back to the pub together and I could sneak us a couple of Cokes or something.

But then the man started to touch me, playfully at first and then more and more insistently. He just wouldn't stop and however much I kept trying to push him away, he didn't take any notice. Spots covered his face and he stank of something that I would later learn was garlic. Knowing I should go but unable to leave, I felt fear rise inside me when the man started pulling at the school shirt I'd left on after changing my skirt for jeans.

'Please don't,' I cried.

But the man didn't listen as he pushed me back on to the bed, throwing his weight on top of me.

'Get off me,' I sobbed as I started to cry. 'Let me go!'

But the man said nothing as he ripped my shirt open. Terror now made my stomach roll inside me. I couldn't move. I was trapped. Still crying as I tried to get away, I pleaded with him.

'No. Please. Don't.'

But when he threw his weight on top of me and I knew I would never be able to escape, my body went slack. Too afraid to move or even cry out any more, all I remember is the pain which filled me then, a pain so violent that I wondered if I would die. I just wanted to disappear, close myself down inside until I was a tiny speck, too small to be hurt by what was happening to me.

The most vivid thing I can remember of that night is seeing my glass of orange tip over and staring as it slowly seeped into the bedspread. I wanted to lose myself in the stain, forget everything else. I couldn't think about how the man was hurting me, how afraid I felt. I was so scared that I couldn't move, scream or stop him from taking what he wanted. Even if I'd been able to fight back, I'm not sure I could have stopped him anyway. I didn't even know what the man was taking because I was too young to properly understand what it was.

He kept me there with him all night. The bastard who thought that raping a child was his due at the end of the night. He did it again and again and Sandra never came back to get me. I didn't see her again and I've always wondered if she'd cooked up a plan for that night with her friends. I can't be sure. All I know is that when the man finally let me leave the house, early the next morning, he told me that if I ever told anyone about what had happened, he'd make sure he found me.

I walked numbly back to the pub along silent streets and sat on the step outside as I waited for Dad to open up for the brewery delivery. I was too shocked to think about what would happen when he did but the moment he caught sight of me, Arthur exploded.

'What are you doing?' he screamed. 'Why aren't you upstairs in bed? Have you been out all night? Get in, girl, and upstairs NOW!'

He followed me as I walked into the pub and up to my bedroom, slapping me round the head again and again.

'What have you been up to?' he kept shouting. 'Have you been out all night? What kind of dirty little whore are you?'

Dad had never spoken to me like that and his words cut through me like a knife. I knew I was dirty, just as he said, and so I didn't say a word to defend myself. I didn't cry or sob, try to explain or beg to be forgiven. It was as if there was a screen between Dad and me and although I could hear him shouting, feel his words strike me like blows, it also felt so far away.

'Out all night?' Arthur roared. 'You've obviously been with a boy. What kind of slut are you? How dare you?'

When he finally went back downstairs to sort out the delivery, I walked into the bathroom, turned on the taps, undressed and got into the water. All I wanted to do was wash myself clean.

'What's this?' Mum asked as she walked into the bathroom and picked up my knickers from the floor. There was blood on them and she stared in disgust.

'I hope you haven't been doing anything you shouldn't,' she

said. 'Because you'll be out of this door if you bring any trouble to it.'

I knew my world had changed for ever as I stared down into the water. I'd lived a sheltered life in many ways, however unusual it had been in others. I'd been kept close to my parents, I hadn't gone out and made friends like other kids, played and laughed, learned how to get along in the rough-and-ready world of children. All I'd really done was work, and it was only now that I'd discovered the world wasn't as safe as I'd always thought it had been.

I was so innocent, you see, that I didn't even really know what sex was. I knew it existed, of course. I'd heard the word and understood that sex got you pregnant. But I didn't know what it actually was or what it meant. I felt sure though that it must have had happened to me – just as I knew that I could never talk to my parents about it. Sex was so taboo in our house that when I'd started at secondary school, I'd read the word 'period' on a medical form I'd brought home for my parents to sign and wondered what the word meant. Then I'd sat at the top of the stairs and listened to my parents talk.

'Have you seen this, Arthur?' Mum said in a low voice.

'Yes I have, Win, and you're going to have to tell her.'

'But I can't.'

'Well if you don't then I'm going to have to. And do you really want that?'

My mum never did explain it all to me and that's why I knew I couldn't tell my parents about what that man had done to me, how he'd pushed me down and raped me again and again. All I felt as I sat in the bath and washed myself was shame.

Dad continued to berate me for the next few days.

'I can't even look at you,' he'd say as he walked into the lounge.

Mum didn't speak to me either. In fact, neither she nor Dad ever asked me where I'd been. They simply assumed that I'd willingly been with a boy and I didn't contradict them. The two of them were disgusted by me and I understood why. I was disgusted by myself. And so I closed down inside and was filled with nothing as my body and brain slowly froze in the weeks and months after I was raped. Becoming more and more withdrawn, I didn't laugh like I used to or joke with customers. I kept myself to myself as I got on with my work and the only time I ever cried about that night was when Dad came into my bedroom one evening.

'I want to talk to you,' he said gently as he sat down beside me. 'What's wrong, our Hils?'

Dad had never come into my bedroom like this before. I looked at him as the muffled talk and laughter seeped up from the bar below. How could I tell him what had happened? How could I put it into words? I couldn't bear it if Dad hated me. I'd rather anything than that. He'd kill the bloke if I told him, and then where would we all be?

'You don't laugh like you used to, Hils,' Dad said softly. 'Come back to me.'

I didn't say a word as he got up and left. But after the door had closed, I finally cried for the first time. Then I dried my tears and knew I would never be scared of anything again.

Chapter 5

We left Accrington a few months after that night because my parents were so worried about the change in me. Completely unaware of what had happened, they decided that the bad types who drank at the Richmond must be what had caused me to withdraw into myself, and so we moved back to Bolton, where they got jobs as steward and stewardess of the Tonge Ward Labour Club. Fast-forward eighteen months, though, and the child who'd been too scared to fight back was now an almost-woman with a gob on her like the Mersey Tunnel. I'd always been stroppy and headstrong, but teenage hormones nearly did for my dad and me when I started to defy him.

I'm not sure if it was because I was so unafraid after what had happened in Accrington, or whether it was just growing up and realising that my dad could be a tyrant when he wanted to be. It happens to lots of teenage girls, doesn't it? The halo worn by the dad they idolize starts to slip as they get older. Whatever the reason, I started to find my own voice after we left Accrington, and it got louder. And louder.

Make no mistake, that night in Accrington was still with me and would be for years to come. Wounds might heal but scars leave a mark for ever. I was learning though that whatever happens in life, you have to blot out the bad memories and I learned to be happy again when we moved to Tonge Ward by focusing on my two main talents: pulling pints and shouting the odds with Arthur.

'Can't I leave you two alone for five minutes?' Mum would cry when she came into the room to find us fighting again.

The answer was no. If I went into the garden to cool off after an argument, Dad would lock the door and refuse to let me back in. If he grounded me after a row, I'd sneak down to the kitchen in the house we lived in around the corner from Tonge Ward, climb through the window, over the shed roof and out, because I'd finally made some friends back in Bolton. They were the girls who lived in the streets around mine and I was happy to have friends. I wouldn't go near the local lads, though, and would usually go home if they started to hang around us. The only time I chatted with the boys was if everyone was sitting on the wall just a few feet in front of my house. Otherwise, I kept my distance.

Even so, Dad didn't like my growing independence at all and it was like a rock meeting an immovable object as I was determined to defy him. I'd wanted to have friends for a long time and all we did was go to the park to share a John Player's if we were lucky. Dad didn't have much to worry about.

Maybe, just like me, he hadn't forgotten that night in Accrington, though, because the moment I started to show signs of life again, Arthur made it clear that he wanted to keep me locked up like Rapunzel. All I could do was play him at his own tricks, because Evil Emily had been right: I was indeed my father's daughter. Soon, I'd started to tap the barrels of cider kept in the Tonge Ward cellar before sneaking out with it, much to the delight of my friends. What can I say? I'd learned from a master.

It meant that our house was like a World War One battle-field: Dad on one side, me on the other, with both of us regularly sticking our heads over the top of our trenches to snipe at each other.

'Stop shouting at her,' I'd scream at him when he had a go at Mum.

I was sick of him laying into her but my poor dad just didn't understand where his cheery – and obedient – girl had gone. Then when he realized I wasn't going to get back in line, he did what you might expect a northern misogynist to do: he started clouting me pretty regularly.

Now I'd always known the back of my parents' hands but I decided that enough was enough on the day Dad belted me around the ear so hard that my Bell's palsy temporarily returned. I'd been told since I was a child that my nerves were sensitive and I had to make sure not to sit in draughts or bang my face. But when Dad walloped me, he must have literally hit a nerve or something. As stars danced in front of my eyes, I picked up one of Mum's precious brass ornaments.

'If you ever hit me again, you'll be sorry,' I screamed as I wielded the brass eagle like a machete.

We stared at each other like a bull and a matador facing each other off. He never touched me again.

It wasn't just my dad, though, who I found the strength to stand up to. When a massive girl called Denise, who was a few years above me at school, started picking on me, I knew there was no way I was going to allow myself to be bullied again. Notorious for being bigger than most of the boys, Denise was the only girl I'd ever heard swear.

'I'm gonna get you, bitch,' she'd scream when she caught sight of me in one of the back streets as I walked home from school.

I didn't feel afraid though. I just felt angry and had soon battered Denise in the back street – plus a few of her mates too – to let her know that I'd had enough of all her taunting. She never came near me again. Then when Stuart started insisting we walked miles out of our way to school each day to avoid some boys who were picking on him, I got stuck into them too. No one dared come near me or my brother again.

Meanwhile, at home, I was shouting the odds with Dad every chance I got.

'You're not going out dressed like that,' he'd roar when I came downstairs in the denim dungarees I'd personalized with a big felt picture of a poodle on the bib after developing a passion for fashion.

'Yes I am!' I'd cry. 'It's my money and I earned it.'

It was true. I was finally getting paid at Tonge Ward, and worked hard all weekend to earn enough money to go shopping on Saturday afternoons with Mum. My favourite places were C&A, Vera Modal and Hilary Anne's, where I bought myself not just the denim dungarees but a maxi-dress and a pair of high-waisted flares – the first time they were fashionable. My pride and joy though were my blue and white platform clogs, which I insisted on wearing even though I fell off them every time I put them on.

'You've left nothing to the imagination,' my dad would grumble as I walked into the Labour Club ready for another night pulling pints.

To be fair, he had a point. Between the playsuit, the clogs and the make-up I'd started to plaster my face with, I must have looked like a drunken clown. Weaving about, I'd stare in the mirror to admire my bright blue eye shadow, pink lipstick and the shiny white highlighter slathered across my cheeks like Red Indian stripes. The only thing I didn't bother trying to do anything with was my hair, because it still had a will of its own.

I might not have been nearly so brave about standing up to my dad though if it wasn't for the Tonge Ward Management Committee. From the moment we arrived, they loved me because I was the best barmaid they had and I loved them because they were such characters, real salt-of-the-earth people who worked hard all week and wanted a few pints and a chat on a Saturday night. There was Stan, who had the biggest head I'd ever seen and always drank bitter; Reg, who never said anything in less than an ear-splitting shout and was partial to a Bell's; and Iris, who had a shock of pillarbox-red hair and loved a Drambuie. The only one I couldn't make head or tail of was the priest from the Irish church down the road. I'd never known a Catholic before and was convinced for years afterwards that all of them were piss-artists because their priest was always three sheets to the wind.

Saturday nights were the highlight at Tonge Ward as comedians like Benny Hill and Les Dawson came to warm up the crowd before a band played. I can even remember Rod Stewart performing 'Maggie May' but couldn't stop to take much notice because the place fitted hundreds on a busy weekend and I was always rushed off my feet.

The club was so big in fact that Dad had to run it like a military operation to keep on top of staff thieving. He'd learned his lesson by the time we got to Tonge Ward and each of the seven bars was divided into stations with a barmaid on each who had her own till to ring up so that Arthur could spot if 'mistakes' had been made. While he was always on the top bar, I was on the other busiest one which was all the way down at the other end of the club.

It was the hardest bar for Dad to keep an eye on but he knew he was safe with me and not just because I was his daughter. I could have given Carol Vorderman a run for her money if *Countdown* had been on back then, because even if the customers were ten deep at the bar, I could still serve up a round of twenty drinks *and* keep track of every penny as I added it up in my head. But it meant I had to concentrate so hard that one day I made a mistake, which gave Dad the excuse he was always looking for to come down on me like a ton of bricks.

The Tonge Ward was so huge that Dad used to call time over a microphone, because it was the only way he could ensure all the barmaids heard him. The moment we heard Arthur's cry, we were supposed to pull down the shutters on our bar and stop serving. But I hadn't heard a thing when Dad marched up to me one night with a face like thunder.

'I've called time,' he roared.

'But I'm still serving. I'm in the middle of a round. I won't be a minute.'

'You won't be another five seconds!' he thundered. 'Pull those shutters down NOW!'

'Just let me finish this.'

'No.'

'But I didn't hear you call time, Dad. I can't stop now. I'm in the middle of these drinks.'

'STOP!'

'Can't you see how busy it is?'

'Don't backchat me, my girl.'

'I'm not. I'm just saying.'

'Well stop staying.'

'But . . .'

'I mean it, Hilary. How dare you . . .'

'DAD! Will you listen? I've . . .'

'And I've had enough. You're sacked.'

I stared at Dad. I was his best barmaid and he was sacking me?

'Now get out,' he roared.

'Fine,' I screamed back. 'I'll get my coat and go.'

'Good!'

We didn't speak for days as I licked my wounds and Dad insisted he'd been right to inflict them. The mood at home was nothing less than Arctic and I'm not sure it would ever have thawed if Mum hadn't broken the deadlock after being given a helping hand by the committee.

'They've demanded that your father reinstates you,' she told me. 'They want you back. The place isn't the same without you.'

As much as I wanted to crow, I stopped myself. But forgiving was one thing, forgetting was another. A few months later, when Dad demanded that I work the whole of Christmas for him, I refused. By then I'd got a second job at the Swan pub in Bolton town centre (because no one seemed to worry too much about legal working ages in the early seventies) and they were willing to pay me far more than the going rate at Tonge Ward for Christmas shifts. There was no way I was going to lose wages.

'You can't say no!' Dad screamed. 'It's our busiest time of the year. I need you at the club.'

'So match my wages then!' I told him. 'I'm getting paid quadruple time at the Swan. I'm not going to miss out for you.'

'But I can't! The committee would never allow it.'

'Well I won't work then. I've earned my keep all my life and you've already sacked me once so I'm not going to miss out now.'

Off he stormed and once again we were deadlocked until Arthur told me that the Tonge Ward committee had agreed to match my wages. I might have lost the battle but it felt like I'd won the war.

Believe me when I say that I didn't mean to take revenge. I'd just stood my ground when Dad had tried to order me around because I was just like him – bloody stubborn. But let's face it: teenage girls can be evil if they want to be, can't they?

We left Tonge Ward after about eighteen months following one too many fallings-out between Arthur and the committee; before starting his next job, Dad decided to take us on our first holiday abroad.

'We're going to the Continent,' he cried after waking Stuart and me up in the middle of the night.

'But they need to go to school, Arthur!' Mum remonstrated.

'No they don't, Win! They'll learn far more with us than they will there.'

So off we went to France, where Dad and I had a ball tucking in to every bit of French food put in front of us. Stuart and Mum though turned up their noses at everything and I got so sick of my brother in the end that I didn't breathe a word when my parents set off from a petrol station without realizing that he was still in the loo.

66

'Where's your brother?' Mum shrieked when she finally turned around a few miles down the *autoroute*.

'I don't know,' I said innocently.

'What do you mean, you don't know?' my dad shouted. 'What have you been up to, young lady?'

'Nothing!' I insisted.

'So where's Stuart?'

'Still in the toilet, I suppose,' I replied.

'You little swine!' Dad exclaimed.

I still feel guilty about it today because even if my brother and I were like chalk and cheese, he didn't deserve to be abandoned in a French motorway khazi. But we were saved from too much more of *la belle vie* together because a few days later Dad decided he'd had enough of France. It was too expensive, he said, as he drove us back to the ferry. After touching down on British soil again, he took us to Butlins in Bognor Regis and we had a ball.

Next stop was the High View Hotel in Salford, which my parents were going to manage for the owner, an orthodox Jewish man called Mr Weiss. Dad soon worked out how to make sure his new employer didn't get too involved – or find out that he had a few more guests staying than he told him he did – by letting our dogs loose every time he heard that Mr Weiss was on his way. He was so afraid of them that he didn't come near the place and Dad was left to get on with running it undisturbed.

Meanwhile, Mum had decided that whatever dalliance she'd had with hard graft was well and truly over. She'd never been on the best terms with it, after all, so I was the one who took her place. It meant I didn't go back to school after leaving Tonge Ward, even though at fourteen and a half I was six months short of the leaving age. No one noticed though. I think I must have slipped through the net because I'd been to that many schools. I didn't mind. Granted, the endless conversations about Mum's health complaints got to me from time to time. (When someone once commented that Mum was ill, I quite truthfully told them that she'd been ill for nearly forty years.) But I also knew that my mum just didn't enjoy work like me and Dad.

I didn't miss school at all because once my formal education had ceased, my business learning started. Dad had gone back to doing central heating during the day to make a bit extra and so I did a lot of the running of the High View. First off, Arthur taught me shorthand (which he'd learned from his sister during a long spell in hospital as a child) and then I taught myself to type. Soon I was doing all his secretarial work – typing up quotes and letters – as well as running reception, doing the bar at night, stock-taking and ordering, making sure the rooms got cleaned and the sheets laundered properly, keeping an eye on the staff and bottling up in the bar.

However responsible I had to be, though, Dad wasn't going to let me become any more independent. In fact, there was a new enemy to protect me from now that I was getting older: boys. He needn't have bothered. I wasn't at all interested in them after what had happened in Accrington. But if I so much as spoke to a man who came into the bar, my dad would sidle up to me.

'You've got a bit of green in your eye, our Hils,' he'd say, warning me that I knew nothing about men and was bound to make mistakes.

One poor Liverpudlian lad must have wondered what he'd done so wrong when he asked to take me to the cinema. To be honest, I thought it was a strange thing to do because I'd never been to see a film in my life. But I enjoyed it and would have gone again when the boy suggested it if Dad hadn't put a stop to it.

More and more, I felt hemmed in by his over-protectiveness and how close he wanted to keep me to him. But then something happened which explained it all, after Mr Weiss asked us to move on from the High View to run a bigger hotel he owned called the Mancunian. I'd turned fifteen by now and didn't like the look of a woman who came to stay with her young daughter one night. She looked like trouble to me, the kind that might disappear without paying the next morning. That's why I kept a close eye on her when she came down alone to the bar that evening after leaving her daughter upstairs asleep.

As I served some soldiers who were staying with us, I could see the woman and Dad getting cosier by the minute. Arthur was getting more and more pissed and I heard the woman telling him that her boyfriend had dumped her. I knew Dad of old: he loved wine, women and a sob story. He might have been in his late fifties by now but he was still a very handsome man and vain enough to know it. He never could resist a bit of gentle flirting and women were always happy to oblige because they loved the twinkle in his eye.

By the time I'd called last orders, the two of them had disappeared and the hotel was quiet as I cleared up before starting to lock all the doors for the night. And it was then, when I couldn't find one of the keys, that I went looking for Dad and somehow knew where I'd find him.

I didn't knock on the door of the room I knew should be empty for the night. I just opened it and saw Dad lying asleep in the bed with her next to him.

'You bastard,' I shouted, rage filling me up as I saw him there – middle-aged, flattered and making a fool of himself.

I looked at the woman. 'You can get back to your own room,' I hissed at her.

The woman could stay in her own room for the night because I wasn't going to kick out her little girl into the street. Tomorrow morning she could go.

'Don't tell your mother,' Dad pleaded as he got up and started pulling on his trousers.

I didn't say a word as I turned on my heel and went back downstairs. What was I going to say to Mum? How could I tell her? I'd heard the arguments through the years, been there on the nights when Dad had gone on benders and not come home again, followed by the mornings when he finally did and Mum would scream at him loud enough to shake the china. But I had never thought he'd actually do anything to betray her.

'Please don't tell your mother,' Dad kept saying again and again when he came to find me in the bar.

He sat with his head in his hands, as if surprised that he'd been found out. I didn't say a word. I was too angry to speak. He'd always been so jealous of my mother, and look at the way he treated me. All I wanted was some of the independence that other girls my age had. But now I finally understood why he was so possessive. He knew exactly what might be going through men's minds when they looked at me and Mum because it was going through his when he looked at other women.

I didn't know what to do. Torn between loyalty to my mum and knowing that she'd be so hurt if I told her what I'd seen, I refused to talk to Dad until he cornered me in the reception a couple of weeks later.

'I think you and I need to have a chat,' he said. 'Let's go for a drive, Hils.'

I went because I knew I had to, that sometime or other we needed to find a way to talk about what I'd seen. But after we'd driven in silence and Dad had parked the car, he began to talk about things I was never expecting to hear, a life I'd never known existed. It was then that I heard for the first time about the wife and children he'd had before he met Mum – and the love he'd felt for her which had hit him like nothing else he'd ever known and made him forget everything.

'One day as you get older you'll understand,' Dad said as he stared out of the windscreen.

'Why?' I spat back.

'Because when you're older and you've had a relationship yourself, you'll know they're hard. For now I want to reassure you of how I feel about your mother, Hils. She's the love of my life. The love of my life.'

He told me that he'd been with his first wife for twenty-five years but known things could never be the same again after meeting Mum.

'My first wife was a good woman and I can honestly say that we never had a cross word. But then I met your mother and realized I didn't know what love was.'

So much fell into place as Dad spoke to me about the children he'd had and how much I reminded him of his eldest daughter. There had always been secrets in my family, silences and gaps that had never been filled. I remembered the day when I was about twelve and we'd gone to visit an elderly man in Chester who'd refused to speak to Stuart or me as we sat in his parlour. We'd only stayed about twenty minutes before leaving again. On another occasion, we'd driven to Wales and

I was so excited to be going because I knew we must be meeting someone important if we were driving that far to see them.

But as I sat in the car with Mum and Stuart, I'd watched my dad knock on a door which was opened and then slammed in his face.

'Why didn't they want to speak to Dad?' I asked as we drove away.

No one said a word.

So did it shock me as my father sat in the car and told me about his other family? No. Not much shocked me by that stage, and, as angry as I was with Dad, I felt sad too. Whatever his faults, whatever his shortcomings, he was my father and I loved him. Larger than life, I knew he was the powerhouse who drove our family forward – whatever wrong direction he sometimes took us in. He was the one who'd always made me feel safe and had worked all hours to keep us going. Now he was flesh and blood, a man with faults and failings, and although I wasn't sure I liked seeing them, I knew I could never hate him.

Like all young people, I didn't know when I was a teenager that my father was also the person who'd taught me my most valuable lessons, the ones that would make me the person I am today. That took time to understand. But as the years have passed, I've been able to see more clearly how things were between my parents. My mother, you see, always seemed to resent my father – however much she loved him too. Later she told me that a pregnant woman had turned up on our doorstep one day when I was just a baby and told Mum she was carrying my dad's child. I don't think Minnie ever forgave Arthur and often withdrew from him physically after that – however tied up they were emotionally.

I don't condone what my father did, of course, and I don't know if that woman was carrying his baby or not. But I think Mum's distance meant he went looking for sex elsewhere. It's not an excuse for what he did. But it is a reason. They say love hurts and I think it really did in some ways for Minnie and Arthur.

All I knew as I sat in the car with my father and listened to him talk was that I could never tell my mum about what had happened. Maybe I somehow understood that she didn't want to know as I looked back on all the raging rows they'd had when I was a kid and realized she'd never left for good – however many plates had got hurled or doors slammed.

For better or for worse, my parents stayed together, and whatever their failings, they truly loved each other. No one really knows what happens inside a marriage, do they? What compromises people are prepared to make and how much of the other cheek they'll turn to make things tick along. We're one of just a few species on earth who are expected to be monogamous and it's hard.

I can honestly say I've never betrayed a man I've been with. I've always been too busy working, for all that, and couldn't be doing with the lying either. I'd rather just say, 'I'm not in love with you and I don't want to spend the rest of my life with you but maybe there's someone out there that I can do that with,' and go. But my dad wasn't like that and as I listened to him tell me that Mum was the love of his life, I had no doubt it was the truth.

That day changed something between us, though, because for a while I lost the fierce respect for my father that I'd had since I was a child. In the coming years, he would rebuild it of course, but for now I'd decided that Arthur had lost any right to control me any more.

'I'm fifteen now and you won't let me go anywhere or do anything,' I told Dad. 'After what I've seen, I don't think you've got the right to tell me what to do.'

He looked at me and smiled sadly.

'As you wish, Hils,' Dad said. 'But I'll leave you with a parting thought that I hope you will remember for ever.

'If you can wake up in the morning, look in the mirror and like the person you are, then you've done nothing wrong. When I woke up the morning after you found me with that woman, I didn't like the person I was and I don't want that to ever happen to you.'

I can safely say it was one of the best pieces of advice I've ever been given.

Chapter 6

Today I have houses in London, Miami, Spain and Morocco – as well as the southern wing of a stately home in Leicestershire. But I can honestly say that the summer I spent living in a caravan was one of the best of my life.

We ended up there because Dad had run out of options yet again after leaving a Conservative club in Stockport that he'd stewarded after our stint managing hotels in Manchester. For all I know, there weren't enough Conservatives in Stockport for Dad to make a good bit extra on the side. Either that or he'd fallen out yet again with his bosses. Whatever the reason, we needed somewhere cheap to live and money was so tight that a house was out of the question.

'How about a holiday?' Dad cried. 'I've always fancied Somerset.'

Arthur had come up with 'A Plan' to give us a bit of breathing space plus cheap accommodation, and my mum went along with it because she couldn't wait to get out of Stockport. Be careful what you wish for, though. I'm not sure if a caravan in Bridgwater was exactly what she'd had in mind. Or what the other holidaymakers must have thought of us when we appeared. Amid a sea of shorts and hankies-on-heads, my dad was never out of a proper shirt collar and Mum looked as immaculate as ever. Think of Joan Collins slumming it in a deckchair and you'll get the picture.

Whatever our neighbours thought, though, the Brewsters had a riot – and me in particular. Not that I relaxed of course. Instead I got a night job pulling pints and by day worked on an ice-cream van which toured all the caravan sites in the area. The bloke I worked for was so tight he never gave me even a single free ice cream. But penny-wise is pound-foolish because what he saved in free ice creams, he lost in wages. I'd managed to negotiate a commission on all the ice creams I sold, you see, and was soon shifting them by the ton as the selling skills that had been sparked into life on Pot Bailey's got well and truly honed.

'Can I have a lolly?' a child would ask as they stared up at me with a sixpence in their hand.

'No,' I'd tell them. 'But you *can* have a lovely cornet.'

As I held out a huge ice cream towards them, I'd watch their eyes come out on stalks.

'Do you want a Flake with that too?' I'd ask.

Without even knowing I was doing it, I'd started to upsell by convincing my customers to pay a little bit more than they originally wanted to get extra in return. It wasn't hard because selling ice creams was well and truly child's play and I soon decided to generate more sales by targeting the parents too. Once I'd delivered ice creams into the sticky hands of their waiting children, I'd turn to the adults.

'You're surely not going to stand there and watch your kids eating these without enjoying one too?' I'd ask.

Once again, I took a chance on getting the sale by filling up the ice-cream cone even before they'd decided they wanted it. Then I'd wave it from my van window, and nine times out of ten, they'd buy.

'Would you like a Flake too?'

Sure enough, the ice-cream man soon realized that I was costing him far more than he'd anticipated and put me on to an hourly flat rate. I still did OK though because I did a lot of hours.

Things weren't so easy moneywise for my parents. By the end of the summer, it was obvious they weren't getting back on to a level footing financially, because after leaving the caravan my mum and I ended up staying in a B&B while Stuart and Dad slept in the car because we couldn't afford two rooms.

The thing you have to remember about my dad is that he never panicked, whatever was thrown at him. Our life might have been a rollercoaster but Arthur Channon Brewster never nervously clung on. He just sat in his seat and trusted that gravity – or Fate – would keep him safe. And somehow it always did.

It taught me one of my most valuable business lessons: that you can never lose your nerve, however bleak the future seems. I've got to within a hair's breadth of losing everything more than once, but each time I did, I'd think back to my dad and how he'd always managed to come up with a plan to get us out of whatever hole we were in. Following his lead, I'd keep my head and find a way out.

The other thing the two of us shared was an ability to keep laughing.

'Dad,' I said one day as we walked around Bridgwater in the hunt for yet another B&B.

'Yes, Hils.'

'There's a church down one end of this road where you can pray. Or there's a pub up at the other where you can get a pint. It's a toss-up.'

Guess which one he chose.

I can't be sure if it was that particular pint that gave him the next bright idea but we were soon back in Bolton where Mum, Dad and I moved into a crummy bedsit while Stuart went to stay with Evil Emily. Each night, my parents settled down to sleep on a bed behind a curtain while I stretched out on the sofa. It was obvious things couldn't go on as they were though and I soon learned that Dad had put his name down on the council waiting list for a house.

I've often wondered since how Arthur felt about it all. The Jag and the big house were long gone but Dad had always managed to keep a roof over our heads. Now he couldn't even do that and I'll never know what happened to all the money he made. There's one story though that Mum told me which I've never forgotten. She said that Dad had blown £500 at the casino tables in one night when things were good, which was a huge amount back then. But Arthur didn't even keep a fiver in his pocket for a taxi home when he started to lose, and by the end of the night he had nothing. That was the way he was. Now he didn't have enough for a home at all. The fire in his belly which meant he never did well working for anyone else had finally really burned us.

We were only in the bedsit for a short time because Evil Emily soon appeared, clutching a letter that the council had sent about a house in Blenheim Road. My parents didn't bat an eyelid about what a state it was in when we went to see it. With three bedrooms, a good-sized lounge and another room that Dad later knocked through to create a kitchen-diner, they could see its potential, and I got to choose my bedroom carpet for the first time. A purple plush was soon laid down for me.

That was the beginning and end of the mollycoddling, though, because as soon as we got settled it was made clear that I was going to have to pay my way now. This time there wouldn't be a job with Dad because he'd decided to go back to working for himself fitting central heating full-time. I was sixteen and my parents weren't going to support me any more. It was time for me to earn my keep.

I'd always wanted to be a vet, but knew when I started looking for work that it was never going to happen because I didn't have a single qualification. So instead of spending my working life shoving my hand up cows' behinds, I decided to go to the other end of the scale – by totting myself up and talking posh while answering the phone. I wanted to be a receptionist. I'd been on my feet working hard for years by now after all. It was time to sit down – *and* get paid for it.

The only trouble was that the top brass at my first job weren't quite so convinced. After arriving half asleep on my first day, with wet hair that was beginning to stick up like a scarecrow, I was sacked by lunchtime.

'That's one of the best lessons you'll ever learn in life, Hils,' Dad said when I got home spitting with anger. 'Don't ever work for anyone else.'

I didn't listen because I was determined to be a receptionist and soon got a new job, at a law firm in Mawdsley Street.

I lasted longer there but memories of the Crompton's Monument flooded back when I saw a rat in the huge cellars where all the files were kept and I handed in my notice.

Next stop was an office suppliers called Guest Brothers – none other than the family business, still owned by Evil Emily's posh descendants. They had no idea who I was of course – the granddaughter of a distant and fallen relative – and I never told them. But once again, luck wasn't on my side because some items were stolen from the showroom while I was on duty one lunchtime and my bosses blamed me. I wasn't actually sacked but didn't want to be somewhere that I wasn't trusted.

A few months into my official working life, I just didn't understand what I was doing wrong. I knew I was a good worker but I was going from job to job and couldn't seem to settle at anything. No wonder. After moving around so much as a child, it was hardly a surprise that I struggled to settle down when my parents finally came to rest. But now that they had a house, were both working and didn't need my help any more, I finally realized what I needed to do: spread my wings.

'Bloody hell,' Dad said as he turned towards me. 'Good luck, lass.'

I stared through the windscreen at the Dunoon Hotel. I didn't know what Dad was talking about. The hotel looked nice. But then again we'd crossed the border into Wales and Arthur had always hated the Welsh.

'See you soon,' I trilled as I pulled my suitcase out of the car and slammed the door.

I didn't care what Dad said. Llandudno might as well have

been Las Vegas to me that day. I was on my way and soon met the other girls who were on the journey with me. Wendy, a Mancunian, was ten years older than me but in love with a much younger guy who told me tearfully one night that he was gay. I wondered why he looked sad when he was telling me he was happy. Sophia, a Londoner, came from a big Italian family and cried so much for them every night that I had to set her straight because we were sharing a room.

'I know it's hard,' I told her a few weeks after getting to Llandudno. 'But you've got to stop crying or else I'm going to drown in your tears.'

Lee was a Glaswegian who drank like a fish but never spent a penny on booze when we went out because she always managed to persuade men to buy drinks for her. Meanwhile Simone had a plum in her mouth and came from Oxford so we were never quite sure of what she was doing getting her hands dirty with the likes of us. Then there was Irish Irene and I couldn't understand a word of what she said for the first few weeks at the Dunoon.

'For feck's sake,' she'd shout. 'Feckin' hell. What the feck is this?'

She said it a lot because our working days started early with chambermaiding, carried on through lunchtime with wait-ressing and into the evening with another stint in the restaurant. We hardly noticed the hard graft though because we were laughing so much.

I wasn't a natural waitress. Give me a pint to pull and a punter to put down and I was fine. But waitressing was a different story because however much I looked the part, in my black pinny with a white frill around it, my clumsiness often got the better of me. Thankfully the American tourists

I served tea to each morning were so sleepy they didn't notice all the brew I'd slopped over their trays. Or they were that busy talking at dinner, they didn't care if I spilled soup on the tablecloth.

The chef, who also owned the hotel, did care though. In fact, I soon realized that he was trying to terrorize me out of my job because he took so much against me.

'If you can't get it right then I'm going to sack you,' he'd roar at me from across the hotplate. 'You've got one more week and then you're fired.'

There was no way I was going to let that happen. For the first time in my life I had freedom and I wasn't going to let it go in a hurry – or be sent home with my tail between my legs. Besides, it wasn't just my fault that I got things wrong. The chef didn't help because he was always sending out the wrong dishes to the wrong tables. There was one thing for it: I had to set him straight.

With Irene one step behind me, I marched up to talk to the chef as he spooned food on to plates one night.

'If you gave me the right dishes for the right table then we wouldn't have this problem,' I told him. 'You've just got to get a proper system in place then we'll all know where we were.'

The chef went as purple as the beetroot he was dousing in white sauce.

'What do you mean?' he roared.

'That you couldn't organize a piss-up in a feckin' brewery,' Irene hissed. 'It's not Hilary's feckin' fault.'

The chef didn't stand a chance. Faced with the pair of us, he backed down, got organized and I was soon the best waitress he had.

With my job secure, I could concentrate on having fun and

us girls lived for the precious few hours after we finished on weekend nights. As soon as the restaurant was closed, we ran to our rooms, got changed and were out the door as soon as possible to make sure we made the most of whatever time we had until the hotel was locked at 12.30 a.m.

Moving round the pubs of Llandudno, I felt safety in numbers and soon got so bold that I was more than happy when we found a way around the curfew by nicking the door key, getting another cut and letting ourselves in at whatever time we wanted. Not that there was much to get up to in Llandudno other than nursing half a cider for hours before sharing a bag of chips on the seafront. But as I danced in a nightclub wearing the Ozzie Clark jumpsuit I'd treated myself to before leaving Bolton, I thought all my Christmases had come at once.

My clumsiness did for me in the end though after I dropped a bowl of tomato soup down the front of an American man's suit. The chef's eyes were almost popping out of his head with rage as he told me to make sure the suit was clean by the next day because the American was leaving. I sadly told Irene that I was going to have to spend my night off cleaning up Heinz stains.

'No way!' she exclaimed. 'I'll help you wash the suit and then we'll hang it from the heating pipes before going out. Trust me. It's warmer than the gates of hell itself down there so it'll be dry by the morning. Then all we need to do is press it.'

Now this American was about twenty-five stone so there was a lot of suit to wash. But Irene and I doused it down before wringing it out and hanging it off a pipe. Then we skipped out the hotel door to trip the light fantastic, pleased as Punch that our evening hadn't been ruined.

The smile was wiped off my face the next morning though when I went to get the suit. Because instead of the giant jacket and trousers I was expecting to find hanging off the pipe, I found something that one of Snow White's seven dwarves would have been hard pushed to get into.

'What am I going to do?' I wailed.

'No feckin' clue!' Irene exclaimed. 'You'd never think something could shrink so much, now would you?'

There was nothing else for it. We hurriedly packed up the suit in brown paper and I ran up to reception where I found the American waiting with the chef. Handing the parcel over, I told myself that he wouldn't open it until he was on the other side of the Atlantic and what could he do then?

'So sorry to have troubled you,' I said with my sweetest smile before turning on my heel and walking towards the restaurant.

I didn't get far.

'Hilary Brewster!' the chef roared. 'Come here now!'

Irene and the girls scuttled along behind me as I walked back to reception, where I found the American staring at his tiny suit jacket in disbelief.

'What's this?' the chef screamed.

For once, I was completely lost for words as the other girls started spluttering with laughter behind me.

'Shame we didn't feckin' wash him, hang him off the pipes and shrink 'im as well,' Irene shrieked.

That was it for me and the Dunoon. I burst into laughter, the American looked as if he'd burst a blood vessel and I was packed off back to Bolton.

I had no idea of what I was going to do, of course. All I knew was that I'd had a taste of freedom I would never forget. But when I look back now on what happened next, all I can think is this: how the hell did I get away with it?

Chapter 7

First stop Llandudno. Next stop the world. But how was I going to get there? I had neither a penny nor a single qualification and my career history wasn't exactly unblemished. Whether it was my scruffy hair or the fact that I couldn't keep soup in a bowl, I'd been sacked from almost as many jobs as I'd had when I wasn't working for Dad.

Salvation came as I walked down Great Moor Street in Bolton a few weeks after getting back from Wales. Hanging in a window, I saw a poster advertising for army recruits and knew instantly what I was going to do. Joining the services meant travelling, didn't it? Yes. But green wasn't my colour so I couldn't join the army. Blue was better. I was going to sign up for the Women's Royal Air Force (WRAF) – which used to be the Women's Auxiliary Air Force Service so we still called ourselves Waafs.

After passing the medical and IQ tests, I went home to tell my parents.

'Good for you, girl,' Dad said, because however much he wanted to control my private life, he'd always encouraged me to work. 'If you're following your heart then it will do you good.

'It doesn't matter if you end up cleaning dustbins. If you

have a smile on your face then you know you're doing the right thing. I hope you enjoy it.'

Minnie wasn't quite so happy though.

'TWO YEARS?' she screeched when I told her that I'd had to sign up for a minimum time. 'Two years? I don't want you to go!'

'She'll be fine, Win,' Dad reassured her. 'What does she want to end up stuck here for?'

'But where are you going?'

'Herefordshire.'

'HEREFORDSHIRE?'

'It's not that far, Mum.'

'It's almost Wales!'

'I know. But after I've gone there for my basic training, I could get sent anywhere in the world.'

I wondered if Waafs got sent to places like Paris or Hawaii? They didn't get to actually fly planes but there were women mechanics and engineers, drivers and air traffic controllers who got sent abroad. I didn't care where I went as long as it got me away from Bolton again, and two weeks after turning seventeen in March 1974, my dad dropped me off at the station. When I opened up the lunch he'd packed in a Tupperware box for me, I found a handwritten note.

Hilary darling, I love you dearly. Dad.

I kept that letter for years to come.

To this day, I'm sure that Sergeant Gibson was half man, half woman. Short, squat and with hair cropped closer than a cricket square, she put the fear of God into me with a voice that was louder than most of those Irish road diggers I'd once known.

Above left Me aged two on the beach, in coordinating hat and shorts. Mum always made sure I was well-dressed!

Above Mum always wanted me to be the picture-perfect daughter, and here I am, aged four, looking the part in my pretty dress. I was probably playing in the dirt ten minutes later. This is outside our house in Hulton Lane.

Here I'm aged six, just before Dad went bankrupt and our life was to change so dramatically.

Mum and Dad on their wedding day, with Auntie Peggy on the left and mum's brother, Chris, on the right.

Mum with her sister Peggy, who had glorious red hair and always looked glamorous.

My cousin Janet hand in hand with Gary and Stuart.

The women of my family liked to gather in the Pack Horse in Bolton and set the world to rights over a bottle or two of Mackeson Stout. From left to right: a family friend, Auntie Peggy, my mother and my grandmother Evil Emily.

With my great uncle Harry in Blackpool. I was ten, and by now working in my dad's pub.

Mum and Dad looking happy together on holiday in Majorca. They were completely in love, however many ups and downs their marriage may have had.

My wedding day, with Malcolm and Mum and Dad, in Bolton Parish Church, February 1976. I'm wearing a replica of Princess Anne's dress!

The new Mr and Mrs Sharples cutting the cake and looking so happy. I was a month shy of my nineteenth birthday and too young to realize the marriage was not right for either of us.

By the age of twenty-five I'd left Malcolm and had my own house and a job at Leisure Circle that involved managing hundreds of people. I loved my independence.

Holding Mevlit, who was one week old, in December 1986.

Hussain was always a natural dad, and confident in handling our newborn son.

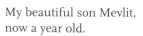

My beautiful son Mevlit, now a year old.

Mevlit aged two, playing outside our house.

Standing with Mum and Len on their wedding day in 1990.

'By the end of this, Brewster, you'll be walking with your shoulders BAAAAAAACK!' she'd scream as I marched across the drill square.

Sergeant Gibson was the officer in charge of our basic training and there was an awful lot of it because the thirty-three of us who'd started on the same day were up at 4 a.m. during our first week in order to be out on the drill square by 4.30. After three hours of marching practice we had break-fast, followed by another two hours of physical activities. In the afternoons we did more sport.

Health and safety legislation didn't really come into it. If I hadn't learned to parachute then I swear I'd have been pushed out of the plane. It was so bloody terrifying that I screamed all the way down until I hit *terra firma* again. After pounding over the assault course all morning, we'd be put into a hut where we'd have to practise getting our gas masks on and off while the real thing was pumped into the air around us.

My fellow-trainees dropped like flies – and not only because they weren't quick enough with their gas masks. Basic training was all about pushing us as far as we could go in order to see who could last the distance, and even though we were allowed an extra half-hour in bed with each week that passed, it was too much for many of the recruits.

RAF Hereford was a training base where long lines of accommodation dormitories, a big NAAFI and canteen jostled for space with officers' messes and aircraft hangars. It wasn't much to look at but I didn't feel homesick at all because there wasn't time to be. While other recruits dropped out of training, I threw myself into it. Physically fit after a lifetime of work and with a stubborn streak inherited from Arthur Channon Brewster, I was determined to prove my superior officers wrong when they made it clear they thought I'd be one of the first to give up.

I can understand why they decided that, because trouble and I were never far from each other. It started soon after I got to the camp and realized that the lads who were also training couldn't stand all the ironing and cleaning we had to do to keep our kit up to scratch. With dozens of pieces in it – from boots and best blues to working blues, hats and gloves – it took hours to make sure it was fit for inspection and I was sure the boys would pay well for help.

The female and male recruits didn't mix at all during training but we got to meet in the NAAFI or canteen and as I chatted to the boys there, I told them about my business plans. Soon my bunk on F block had become the headquarters of a thriving black-market business and a few of my new friends had got involved too.

Most of them wanted extra money to spend when they went off base on a Saturday night. I wasn't allowed to go with them because my parents had refused to give permission for me to go off camp, but I still enjoyed weekend nights in the NAAFI, where we'd drink cider or beer and sometimes have a dance. Most of the other girls were romanced by male recruits – and more than one of my fellow-trainees had to go home after getting pregnant – but I never was. I wasn't looking for all that.

I was more interested in business and soon spotted a gap in my booming market: bulling shoes. It was everyone's worst job because it meant polishing the leather until it came up like a mirror and took hours. After warming the polish with a flame, you had to rub it in, patch by tiny patch, for what felt like for ever until the leather glistened.

But when I discovered that spraying aftershave on the shoes took a fraction of the time and brought them up just as well, business got even better. We increased our trade and no one was any the wiser until the day it started to rain as we stood on the parade ground. Shaking with laughter, the girls and I watched the boys' shoes turn white in the rain. Seconds later, the officers started to roar, the boys' guts were hung up for garters and, as the ringleader of the whole thing, mine were too.

Being punished was called being put on a charge and it was a bit like getting detention at school because you had to work when everyone else was on relaxation time. Think of the worst duties you could do and times them by a hundred. Every back-breaking, mind-numbing chore was mine, and the one I hated most was cleaning the nicks between the toilet tiles because the officers always found the tiny scrap I'd missed so I'd have to do it all again. And again.

I soon made friends with everyone in the guardhouse, where I had to report as part of my punishment. In fact, I charmed them with my rock buns. Because I'd never been one of those kids who had the right ingredients for cooking classes at all the schools I'd been to, instead I'd had to use whatever was in our kitchen cupboards, which was usually flour, eggs and currants, so I'd become a bit of a rock-bun expert. Sitting with the guards, I'd listen to their stories of the Second World War and all they'd done for their country as they ate my cakes.

It was good they liked them because those guards saw a lot of me. I was constantly up on charges for something or other and sometimes even managed to make one punishment lead to another. When I was ordered to paint the black rocks lining the drive into the base white and the white ones black, it just seemed like common sense to swap them over. Little did I know I was being watched. I was put up on yet another charge.

Then came the afternoon when I was sitting on my bed with a few of the girls as we chatted over a fag.

'Ma'am's coming,' a voice suddenly shouted. 'Kit inspection.'

Ma'am was the flight lieutenant above Sergeant Gibson – the woman in charge, the queen bee. Tall, blonde and elegant, she appeared without warning at all hours for inspections.

'What are we going to do with all this?' my best friend Shirley wailed.

We looked at my bed. It was covered in cigarette packets and ashtrays.

'Shove it into my wardrobe,' I replied. 'It's a kit inspection so she won't look in there.'

I laughed as hard as everyone else as we rammed everything into my wardrobe and slammed the doors. Just in the nick of time, I got to the end of my bed and stood ramrod straight as the flight lieutenant marched in looking like Grace Kelly in uniform. Wearing her best blues of a skirt, smart double-breasted jacket, hat, tights and black court shoes, she was followed by Sergeant Gibson, looking as ever as if she'd just chewed a wasp. I held my breath as the pair of them walked up and down the dormitory, peering at kit, picking up buckles and buttons to see if they shone. Then I breathed a sigh of relief as they reached me and looked at everything neat and folded on my bed before moving on to the next girl.

I breathed too soon. Those two didn't need a sniffer dog to smell out trouble.

'I'm going to do a bunk inspection now,' the flight lieutenant said and my legs nearly gave way beneath me because I knew it meant she was going to inspect our beds – and wardrobes too.

There was nothing I could do as Grace Kelly walked back down the dorm, moving from bunk to bunk, opening doors and checking the beds were perfectly made. Standing there knowing that the wrath of God was about to rain down on me, I waited until she reached my bed. Then I held my breath as she opened the wardrobe door.

Out fell half a dozen ashtrays followed by several fag packets. The flight lieutenant's face curled into as close to a grimace as a face that beautiful could get. But it wasn't over. Not by a long shot. Time went into slow motion as I watched a pile of my dirty laundry tumble out of the wardrobe and sail through the air towards my commanding officer. First it knocked off her hat. Then it took out her wig.

Why she wore one I'll never know because the flight lieutenant had perfectly nice short, blond hair. But as her wig landed on the floor and my friends started to giggle, I felt laughter boiling up in me yet again.

'BREWSTER!' Sergeant Gibson roared and I knew that this charge would be the worst yet.

I lost all my privileges for three weeks, but didn't learn my lesson even then, because I was high on the camaraderie of my training, the feeling of such strong friendship that quickly grew between us all. Shirley, me and our friends were in it together and I was having the best time of my life: learning new things, working so hard that I dropped into bed each night to sleep like the dead and finding that I really enjoyed the discipline and teamwork that life in the WRAF forced on me.

I wonder if I responded so well because for the first time

ever in my life I knew exactly where I was. Life with my parents had never been predictable but now I was part of a well-oiled machine. I was part not just of a team but a bigger unit as well, with rules and procedures that had got wars fought and survived bomb blitzes. I responded well to that kind of authority, so well in fact that it makes me wonder today if more kids couldn't do with a spell in the forces. Why shouldn't National Service be brought back? I'm quite sure it would change the face of Britain and the youth of today. It did me no harm at all. In fact, it brought out the best in me – and sparked a tenacity that has been one of the keys to my success in business. Maybe more kids should be given the chance to discover it.

Those officers were clever though, because as much as they guided me, they made sure to teach me a lesson, and their chance came when I overslept on the morning that I was responsible for waking up the rest of the dorm. I'd been dreading this duty because I'm not a morning person, so I'd borrowed at least a dozen alarm clocks to make sure I didn't sleep through. But even all that ringing didn't wake me up and I felt awful when I realized that I'd made everyone over-sleep. I couldn't face owning up.

'I've been ill all night,' I said in a croaky voice. 'I'm so sorry. I must have thrown up that much I was exhausted.'

The officers were rubbing their hands in glee the moment the words were out of my mouth. I'd given them the perfect excuse to send me on an extended stay to the sick bay and was given every arse injection known to man and enema that I could cope with there.

'I'm better now,' I kept insisting to the nurses. 'I really am. I feel fine!'

But they wouldn't listen.

'We must make sure you're fully fit, Brewster,' the medical staff kept telling me as they brandished the thermometer in front of me again and told me to turn over.

For all the trouble I got into, though, I managed to make it to the end of basic training and Mum and Dad came to watch me on the day of my passing-out parade. I could see how proud they were as I marched down the drill square in my best blues and even Sergeant Gibson finally managed to crack a smile.

'I'm PROUD of you, Brewster,' she boomed at me. 'I have made you officer material. It's down to me. I give you ten out of ten for tenacity, Aircraftwoman Brewster.'

Travel and adventure were top of the list now that I'd finished basic training but sadly the closest I got to seeing the world was a room filled with maps in Oxfordshire. When everyone was sent off to different bases to be trained up for jobs, I was told that I was going to RAF Brize Norton to learn air traffic control. We'd been streamed for job training according to how well we'd done in our IQ tests and I'd been told I was eligible to train for some of the hardest, like engineering or accountancy, because I'd done better than most.

Filled with excitement about what my new life would bring, I was brought back down to earth with a bump. Gone were the days of being in it together with all my mates during training. Shirley and I were sent to different bases and I missed her a lot even though we kept in touch through letters. It just wasn't the same and suddenly the camaraderie I'd loved so much was gone.

RAF Brize Norton in Oxfordshire was a fully functioning base where I now had my own room instead of being in a dorm. I hated being on my own and didn't feel nearly so at home with the NCOs or officers as I had with my fellow-trainees. Instead of pounding across the parade ground for hours, I now spent most of my time with my head between the covers of whatever book or manual I was learning that week because there were so many codes to master for air traffic control. I also had to study for O levels in geography, maths, science and English, and although I passed with flying colours, I wasn't happy to be studying every hour God sent.

I had no choice though, and when I wasn't learning codes I was standing for up to ten hours a day staring at a map almost as big as the room it was housed in. In teams of three, we plotted routes for planes because there were no computers to do it for us. Hour after hour all I could hear was the low hum of traffic controllers tracking co-ordinates on the map before giving them to pilots over radios to make sure they kept to their routes.

As irresponsible as I might have been at times, I was under no illusion about how important my job was. Any tiny mistake could have had serious repercussions and I felt my responsibility greatly even though I was only at the bottom of the food chain. It's the way I'm made and to this day one of the biggest things that drives me businesswise is the thought of my employees and the families they have to feed. My company is now so all-consuming that there are days when I really do think about selling up, walking away and living a far quieter life. But I just couldn't let people down like that. Not when there's still so much work to do. Making my business grow and expand is how I will repay all the hard work and loyalty my staff and customers have shown me and my company.

After my spell on air traffic control, I was sent to train in the supply accounts department back in Hereford because my superiors weren't sure yet what job I was best suited to. Supply accounts related to procuring everything that was needed to run a base – from the sheets on the beds to the diesel needed to power vehicles – and once again I had to learn quickly.

I was soon wondering why someone didn't cut through all the bureaucracy. Talk about wasting time filling in forms and going from A to Z and back to B! From the age of seven, I'd learned about maximizing profit and minimizing waste thanks to Arthur's Mild. Now I felt sure there must be an easier and cheaper way of doing things but making my voice heard was impossible. I was buried at the bottom of a long chain of command and no one was going listen to an upstart like me.

Bit by bit the excitement I'd felt about life in the WRAF drained away. Instead of spreading my wings, they were being clipped, and the final straw came when a moratorium was put on female service personnel being posted abroad after a rape in Cyprus. Never mind Hawaii or Paris, I was stuck back in bloody Hereford and struggling with the realization of just how regimented the forces really were. My inquisitive nature meant that if I was going to follow orders, I wanted to know why I was following them. But it didn't go down well in an organization in which people were expected to follow protocol without question.

It would be years before the entrepreneurial spirit that was bursting to the surface even then would find an outlet. For now I just wanted to leave the WRAF and the only way to convince my superior officers to release me from the two-year contract I'd signed up for was by telling them that I was depressed. Let's face it, I'm probably the last person who'd have got depressed back then. But after having interview after interview, all the time insisting that I was ready to fling myself under the next plane that landed on the tarmac, I was finally released from life in the WRAF.

Chapter 8

Some time after James Booth set up his haulage company in Bolton in the early 1900s, the company adopted the slogan 'For cheerful service'. All I can say is that I decided whoever was running the company by the time I joined it as an administration assistant was the most miserable bastard I'd ever met. Even the door to his office was painted in such a glossy black paint that he could keep an eye on what everyone was doing in the reflection.

Looking back, I think I got him wrong. He was just a disciplinarian and I wasn't in the best frame of mind after leaving the WRAF. Unless you've been in the forces, it's hard to explain. But adjusting to life on Civvy Street was far harder than I'd ever thought it would be. As much as I'd looked forward to getting back to normal life after rebelling against a regime of set meals and a constant timetable, I can honestly say that I felt lost without the WRAF for a good while after leaving.

Little did I know when I first started working at James Booth's that I'd end up building an empire in the haulage industry. But I got my first introduction to the world of transport there and decided the lorry drivers who were in and out of the office each day with their tachograph print-outs were real gentlemen. I didn't hang around long enough to find out any different either, because by now Mum was working at the huge Littlewoods distribution centre housed in a converted mill just outside Bolton and I soon moved on to a job there.

With a weekly wage packet, I took the easy option of a cheaper rent back at my parents' council house rather than renting something for myself. Stuart was there too, doing an apprenticeship as a sheet-metal worker, and the four of us rubbed along together because things were much calmer at home now. Dad's central heating business was doing well, which meant life was more financially secure, and his temper had also cooled now that he'd got on a bit.

I'm not sure if it was Mum who suggested Littlewoods or not but however it happened, I got a position in the personnel department there. Why? Because after leaving the WRAF, I'd decided that I was a People Person. What did that mean? That I could find a way to make most people laugh and enjoyed doing it. Personnel management was for me, I decided, and even signed up for a college night course in it because passing my O levels in the WRAF had given me some confidence in my abilities. I paid for it myself and studied hard during my evenings off. By day, I hoped for some on-the-job training from my Littlewoods boss.

Sadly, Mr Russell wasn't much of an inspiration.

'Shirley Hughes and David Thomas are off sick today,' I'd tell him as I walked into his office at ten sharp each Monday morning to report the late arrivals and absences.

'Probably been shagging faaaaaar too much all weekend,' Mr Russell would reply in the poshest voice I'd ever heard.

The next morning I'd tell him that Janet Smith wasn't in because she'd sprained her ankle.

'Pissed last night, I suppose,' he'd bark at me.

God knows what Mr Russell was doing in a personnel department. He wasn't a 'people person' like me. And I soon realized he expected me to oversee the most delicate negotiations that he'd be sure to mess up.

'I want you to meet with Lillian Finan,' he'd say. 'She's got something she wants to discuss. Sort her out, Miss Brewster.'

I swear the image of Lillian Finan standing in front of me looking like she'd been sucking lemons since the day she was born will flash before my eyes in my final seconds. Lillian was the head of the union and hardly an hour went by without her marching into our offices to demand everything from bigger pay rises to shorter working hours and longer toilet breaks.

It was the mid-seventies, you see, and the unions were very powerful back then. Seeing as how I was used to working round the clock and had been taught to believe in a fair day's work for a fair day's pay, I didn't hold much truck with the union's unrealistic demands because even as a teenager I knew that people would be out of jobs in the future if they got their way.

I don't believe in unions much more today because I don't think there should be a need for them. If all employers treated their staff properly then they would know they were working in a place where they were listened to and there wouldn't be a need for intermediaries. In my own business every employee is interviewed once a year about the company, what they like and don't like. They're also asked about the ideas they have on how the business might change, and some amazing ideas come out of it. It's a policy I'm proud of.

Make no mistake: Pall-Ex is commercial and profit-driven. But my human resource is one of the key things that has made my business what it is and I want to look after it. Not every one of my employees has a hotline to me, of course. I insist on the right communication channels, from sales director to deputy managing director to finance director to managing director to me. People have to go through others to get to me because if not I'd never get any work done. That's not to say I won't chat to anyone though. If I catch a forklift driver walking through the Pall-Ex reception, I'll tell him that I don't want muddy bootprints on my black marble floor. Not because I'm any better than him. I just run a tight ship and like to think that my company has a heart because I still have people with me today who were there when Pall-Ex started.

Not every employer takes these responsibilities so seriously though and there are also employees who have no idea how to state their point of view. If you ask me, it's down to our disgraceful education system. Over the last twenty years, we've started to treat children as adults and adults as children because the British are like bloody sheep. The tables have turned and we've lost any idea of who's actually in control. Parents are blamed when their children misbehave and yet they're often not allowed to discipline them properly. Meanwhile there are children who have no idea how to respect authority and don't have a sense of social unity, of us all pulling together. I don't have all the answers but I'm convinced we need a proper education system to give children the where-withal to fight for their rights at work as adults.

Lillian Finan certainly didn't have any such problems. In fact, if I'd been any more shy and retiring then she'd have had me quaking in my boots. In her early fifties, Lillian had coal-black dyed hair and a huge gob. Day after day, she'd stand in front of me and snarl as she crossed her arms over a chest that was always straining out of the seams of a too-tight blouse.

'It's just not good enough and we're not having it,' she'd snap. 'We're going out on strike.'

At first I tried to listen to her because I was keen to be a good people person. But as time passed I heard so much of Lillian's moaning that I ended up thinking just one thing as she stood in front of me listing her complaints: 'Well eff off and go on strike then.'

I couldn't say it though so I'd go in to Mr Russell to see if a compromise could be reached.

'They've said they're going on strike if you don't sort this out,' I'd tell him.

'Miss Brewster!' he'd boom. 'It is your *job* to soothe their egos and *stop* them going on strike, so go back out there now and do it.'

Stuck between Mr Russell, the mill manager and the production director, who all wanted different things, I'd have to massage so many egos that I was exhausted before I'd even begun dealing with Lillian's. But I slowly started to develop a new string to my selling bow, because after shifting pots and fabrics, pints and ice creams as a teenager, I began to see that I'd got it all wrong. Selling, I realized, wasn't actually about selling at all, but getting people to *buy* – and it was at Littlewoods that I learned how to persuade people to buy the most difficult thing of all: a concept.

I didn't have a product to show Lillian, you see. But I learned to use the technique I'd honed as a youngster to convince her and the union to buy into concepts like longer working weeks, overtime without pay and unpaid breaks: by charming them into it. I didn't agree with the changes management wanted to make, to be honest, but did my job well nevertheless. Realizing that I could sell a concept was what was helped me to take my sales skills to another level and convince Lillian not to go on repeated walk-outs. And the more I did it, the better I got.

A leopard can't change its spots completely though, can it? I still had a very low tolerance level for bullshit and after months of being nice to a woman who would have driven Mother Teresa to drink, I'd finally had enough. So in the end I marched into Mr Russell's office determined to make him do some of the talking for once.

'She's totally unreasonable,' I said to him. 'And if you send me back out there then I'm telling you that I'll end up throwing Lillian Finan out the window.'

Our office was on the seventh floor.

'Miss Brewster!' Mr Russell roared. 'What on earth do you mean?'

'I mean that you're going to have to talk to her.'

'*Talk to her?*' he exclaimed. 'That is *your* job, Miss Brewster. And if there is one thing I demand in my department then it's people skills. You are clearly not cut out for this job.'

My mouth opened wider than the Mersey Tunnel when I heard that. But I was more than happy to be moved to run the staff-discount shop because I'd already heard it was the best job in the building. Why? Because it was a basically a licence to chat all day. Other than taking staff orders and payments, dishing out receipts, doing the ledgers and balancing the books against stock, there was nothing much else to do but while away the hours with a gossip and a joke. How on earth I did that job for any more than a month is still a mystery because it wasn't challenging in any way – and I'd always thrived on being thrown in at the deep end, even if I did sink from time to time. All I can think now is that my mind was very much elsewhere: on marriage, to be exact.

Malcolm Sharples was the boy from almost next door, the teenage sweetheart who lived around the corner. I'd met him when I was sixteen after my parents had moved into their council house following our stay in Somerset and I'd started working. Malcolm was going out with one of my Tonge Ward friends called Elaine at the time, and the two of them would invite me and his best mate Paul Greenhalgh to hang out with them sometimes at Malcolm's house, which was near my parents'.

'Sing it out, son!' Dad would roar at poor Paul whenever he came round to pick me up.

Paul had a stutter, you see, and would dutifully try to sing out his words just as my dad had ordered him to. He went on to marry a beautiful girl called Julie and you might know of their son, the actor Paul Nicholls, who was once in *EastEnders*. We were kids though when we met so Paul and I didn't date. We just made up the party with Elaine and Malcolm, and I became good friends with both lads. But by the time I got home from RAF Hereford a few years later, Malcolm and Elaine had split up and he and I started going out together.

It wasn't a big romance, more a question of good friends becoming something else. Malcolm was tall, handsome, well dressed and a lovely guy to boot. I genuinely loved him – and his mum Mary. In fact I've wondered since if she was the thing I loved most of all about my relationship because Mary to me was all that a mum should be. With an immaculate home, she was endlessly kind and even served a proper meal at a proper table each night.

I should have been over the moon to have a boyfriend – particularly one as nice as Malcolm. But I don't think I was. What had happened in Accrington had never left me, you see, and even though I was eighteen by now, I just wasn't interested in romance like other girls my age were. So even though I'd never had a boyfriend, in my heart of hearts I never let myself love Malcolm as he needed to be.

I didn't know that then of course. I was just happy to let the comforting routine of a relationship slip over me like a blanket. Every Wednesday, Malcolm would leave his job as a toolmaker to come and pick me up from Littlewoods and take me back to Mary's for tea. Then on Friday and Saturday nights we'd go to the pubs in Bolton town centre, followed by a curry at the Rajmanzil with our friends Horace and Pauline, Bernie and Lol. Later on we'd all go to watch Malcolm play guitar in his band.

I was soon so caught up with it all that I forgot the ambitions and aspirations I'd had for so long. Why? Because Malcolm and I were ports in a storm for each other: he offered me the kind of stable life I'd always dreamed of, while he was suffering after the death of his dad and needed the same kind of security I think. That's why I did what most Bolton girls did when they met a bloke: decided to settle down. When Malcolm proposed a few months after we started seeing each other, I accepted. I loved him and in my teenage brain it seemed logical that we'd build the kind of life together that I'd never had.

I can't even remember what Malcolm said when he proposed or where it happened. Most girls dream of that moment all their lives, don't they? But wedding fever didn't get me in its grip. It got Mum instead, and she more than made up for my lack of enthusiasm by working all the extra hours she could get. As she saved up every spare penny for the wedding, she'd spend hours discussing the best kind of vol-au-vents to serve at the reception while I wondered what all the fuss was about. The pinnacle of the whole thing was the replica of Princess Anne's wedding dress that we hired from a shop in the town centre. Mum almost fainted when she saw me dressed up, looking not a million miles from how she'd always wanted me to look on Singer's Day when I was a child.

Dad just wasn't nearly so interested. In fact, when I took my parents to meet Mary, he only managed to sit still for a few minutes after she'd wheeled her hostess trolley into the lounge, laden with the best china.

'I'm off to the pub,' he said as he got up. 'Thank you for the tea, Mary.'

Mary looked at me in shock as Dad walked out the door.

'He's gone where?' she said confusedly.

'The pub.'

'Does he always do that?'

'Yes,' I replied.

Deep down I knew what was wrong with Dad. In fact, I can remember looking out of the bus window on the way home from work the day before my wedding in February 1976 and knowing something wasn't right between Malcolm and me. But I pushed the thought away and walked downstairs the next day dressed up like Princess Anne to find Dad waiting for me.

'Do you want a whisky?' he said.

'No.'

Arthur said nothing as he poured himself a drink and knocked it back in one gulp before looking at me.

'You don't have to go through with it, you know, Hils,' he said.

'What are you talking about?'

'All this. The wedding. I'm sorry, love, but Malcolm's not the right man for you. He's a good bloke but you'll never make each other happy. Take that dress off and I'll go and tell him.'

I looked at Dad, refusing to listen to him. Or myself.

'I can't do that,' I said. 'Everyone's waiting for me.'

'Doesn't bother me. I'll tell them.'

I stared at the tiny solitaire ring on my hand and thought of how happy I'd felt on the night of our engagement party. Now all our friends and family were waiting at Bolton Parish Church to see me walk down the aisle. Then the forty of us were going to a nearby hotel for a sit-down meal. We were having a disco and cake. There would be presents and congratulations. Malcolm was waiting for me. Mum. And Mary.

I loved Malcolm. I wanted to have a proper home with him. A home of my own.

'Come on, Dad,' I said. 'Stop talking daft and wish me luck.'

A month shy of my nineteenth birthday, I walked down the aisle on 21 February 1976 to marry Malcolm Sharples. We didn't have a honeymoon. Instead we moved straight into the house we'd bought for £6,750 on Rossall Road, which soon became my pride and joy. A quasi-semi, it was one of a small terrace of four, and the first thing I bought for it was a dining table with a smoked-glass top so that I could serve up dinner each night just like Mary. Some people have rosaries, others have statues of Buddha, but in the years to come dining tables became for me the closest thing I had to religious relics. When the one with the smoked-glass top later got replaced by a beautiful Italian mahogany table, I moved it into every house I lived in and, however battered it got, however many scratches were carved into the wood, for me it meant home. And that was something I had faith in.

After picking up a thing or two during a childhood spent watching Dad do DIY, I was up and down ladders painting walls, hanging doors and glossing woodwork from the moment Malcolm and I got our house keys. Then when all that was done, I turned my attentions to becoming a perfect housewife. On weekend nights while Malcolm was out playing with his band, the new Mrs Hilary Sharples could often be found standing in the kitchen, shoving clothes through a mangle after they'd come out of the twin-tub. In other spare hours, I'd lovingly prepare home-cooked meals and even did my own baking when the bread strikes started.

Unsurprisingly, Malcolm – who at the age of twenty-two was far more interested in playing the guitar than becoming my second-in-DIY-command – didn't share my obsession with home improvements. After Dad showed him how to wallpaper one weekend, I left him to it in the living room and decided he'd done quite well as I gazed at the cream Anaglypta we'd chosen to cover up the old brown wallpaper. The dream fell apart though when I next vacuumed. Pulling the curtains to one side, I realized that Malcolm had only papered either side of them. Two brown tombstones of old wallpaper lay hidden behind the curtains for the rest of the time we were in the house, an enduring reminder of how different we were.

But as much as I refused to let anything ruin my dream

for me, I couldn't stop running from reality any more when Dad phoned on 5 November 1976 to say that he wanted to take me out for a drink. I knew in that moment that something was seriously wrong.

Throughout my time in the WRAF, my mum had kept telling me something wasn't right with Dad.

'What do you mean?' I'd ask her on the phone. 'What's wrong with him?'

'I can't put my finger on it,' she'd say. 'But I know he's just not himself.'

I got more and more worried about it all. But as much as Mum loved to talk about her own health problems, getting information about anyone else's was like extracting teeth, so I never got to the bottom of it. I was relieved though when I got home to find that while Dad looked tired and had lost some weight, he certainly wasn't at death's door. Mum had always had a touch of the drama queen in her when it came to health.

But in the time leading up to November 1976, she'd gone into hospital for a gall-bladder operation and Dad had come over for his tea with Malcolm and me. After making him his favourite – liver, bacon and onions with mash and gravy – I'd watched him go to the bathroom, where he'd been sick, and it had worried me. Then when he rang a few weeks later to ask me to the pub and walked back to our table with a pint plus a large whisky for himself, I knew something serious was going on.

'I'm dying, Hils,' Dad told me.

He always was blunt.

'I've got cancer,' he said.

I couldn't take the words in. They couldn't be true. My dad, ill? He was the strongest man I knew and only sixty-three. It was nothing really. He had years to go. Minnie's hypochondria must have finally got to him.

'Don't be daft!' I said, feeling my heart beating in my chest.

I couldn't let the words sink in even as Dad told me that the doctors had found a shadow on an X-ray he'd had a couple of months before following a bad fall. That's why I didn't ask questions or demand any answers and Dad didn't mention anything more about doctors. Instead there was something far more important he wanted to talk about.

'I want to know that you've left your marriage before I die,' he said as he looked at me. 'Believe me, Hilary, you have to think long and hard about what I'm saying – and about having children with Malcolm.

'You'll never be happy here in Bolton, living the kind of life he wants you to lead. I know you think you're happy but I'm telling you that you never will be.'

I didn't say anything. I just sat with my mind racing as Dad finished his drinks before ordering more. But even though he was well on the way to being rat-arsed by the time he drove me home, I was nevertheless unprepared for what happened when we got there.

Not long before, I'd had a huge argument with Malcolm, which Dad was still fuming about. The trouble had started when I was moving things in the wardrobe one day and had picked up one of Malcolm's cardigans. I couldn't believe it when a mound of cash fell out of one of his pockets. I'd been working every hour of overtime I could get to make our house a home, spending every penny I had on our life together *and* running it for the both of us. But when I asked Malcolm about it, he just couldn't see why I was so furious, and I was still boiling a couple of days later when he spent yet another afternoon twanging on his precious guitar. In a flash, I realized where I could hit him hardest – just as he'd done to me.

'I'm sick of that effing noise,' I screamed as I threw the guitar down the stairs.

Understandably, Malcolm was furious, and as we argued he unintentionally caught my face in such a way that it was bruised. Now Malcolm wasn't a violent man and to be fair I had destroyed the most important thing in the world to him so he was bound to be upset. He hadn't meant to hurt me. But Dad had gone mad when he saw the bruise and after breaking the news about his illness and taking me home from the pub, he marched into our living room like John Wayne preparing for a particularly bad run-in with a Red Indian.

'Take off your glasses,' he said to Malcolm.

Malcolm did as he was told because no one ever disobeyed Arthur when the wind was really up him. The moment the glasses were off, Dad smacked Malcolm in the face.

'If you ever lay another finger on my daughter then I'll kill you!' he roared before turning on his heel and leaving.

My head was spinning with it all by the time Dad left the house. But I still didn't mention what he'd told me about being ill to anyone. You see, I so badly didn't want to hear those words that I pushed them down and tried to forget them, somehow believing they wouldn't be real if I kept silent. A couple of weeks later though I went round to my parents' house for the evening and when Malcolm tooted the car horn outside to let me know he was waiting to pick me up, Mum called me into the kitchen.

'Your dad's got cancer,' she whispered. 'He's not got long to live.'

I couldn't pretend any more now that Mum had said the words out loud. I ran out of the house sobbing and walked around in a thick fog for days as the information slowly sank in. The only other time I've found news so hard to digest is when I later discovered that my son Mevlit was a heroin addict. I understand why now: how can you let yourself feel when your worst nightmare is facing you?

Death really is the greatest taboo, isn't it? One of my biggest regrets is taking part in the charade we all played as Dad was dying and my family gave Oscar-worthy performances in a film that no one else was watching.

Maybe it's hardly surprising we didn't find a way to talk about it when so much else had been left unsaid throughout the years. Of course if that was the way Dad wanted it to be played then I can put my hand on my heart and say that I honoured his wishes. Looking back, though, I can't help feeling it was Mum who refused to talk about what was happening, not Dad. I followed her lead and in many ways wish I hadn't.

In the months that followed the news of Dad's illness, we all kept up the charade that he was going to get well again. In fact, I had to play the scene over and over so many times that sometimes I almost believed it myself. There were days after I'd gone home for a visit, sat and chatted with my parents before kissing them goodbye, that I'd get on to the bus home almost convinced Dad was improving. I'd cling on to any tiny thing: a bit more colour in his cheeks or the glimmer of a twinkle in his eye. Going over every detail again and again, I'd tell myself that Dad was getting better.

There were so many other days though when I just couldn't pretend. Week by week, Dad got thinner, paler and weaker and although he still knocked back whisky and smoked John Player's untipped like they were going out of fashion, I could see just how unwell he was. I'd paint on a smile of course and pretend as if nothing was out of the ordinary. But I wish I'd never played along with the conspiracy like I did because there were moments when I looked at Dad and felt sure that he knew exactly what was happening. How I regret it now. I wish that I'd talked to him, told him just once how much I loved him and all he meant to me.

I never did though – even after Dad went into hospital to be operated on to see if there was anything they could do and I rang the doctor to find out how the surgery had gone.

'I'm afraid your father's illness is too extensive for surgery to be of any use,' he said. 'We simply opened him up and then closed him again.'

I found out then that Dad had stomach cancer and now his whole body was riddled with it. But I never said a word about what I knew to Mum, and she didn't ask so I didn't push it.

Dad went quickly downhill and soon had to stop working so money dried up. I did what I could of course. But I wasn't earning a fortune at Littlewoods and my parents fell so behind on their bills that Mum opened the front door one Saturday afternoon to find a bloke from the TV-rental company standing on the step.

'I've come for the television,' he said. 'Your payments aren't up to date.'

I could see that Dad was livid because he was looking

forward to watching a football match with Stuart that afternoon. But as the rental man walked into the living room and
made for the TV, it was obvious that his mind was whirring.

'Working on a weekend?' Arthur said.

'Yes.'

'Can't be much fun. Why don't you sit down? Have a drink.
Do you want a beer?'

The TV rental man looked at him uncertainly.

'Go on,' said Dad. 'Take the weight off your feet for a minute.
Get the man a beer, can you, Hils? How about a whisky too?'

As I went into the kitchen to get the drinks and Mum started
muttering in a loud whisper about the shame of neighbours
seeing the TV being taken, I knew exactly what Dad was up
to. His plan went like clockwork. Soon all thoughts of taking
the TV had been shelved for the duration of the match and
Dad and the TV rental man were chatting as if they'd known
each other for years. The bloke was so pissed by the time he
left that he staggered out the door with the TV before throwing
it into the back of his van. I'm sure it must have been useless
by the time he got it back to the shop.

By late spring 1977 it was obvious that my parents
couldn't cope any more. Mum was trying to inject Dad with
morphine but it was too much for her and she couldn't
lift him as he needed to be. I was worried she was going to
get ill herself if it carried on and was relieved for them both
when Dad was taken into hospital where he could be cared
for properly.

For the next few weeks, I took three buses after work each
night to go and visit Dad. As the sickly-sweet perfume of
morphine hung in the air around him, I'd sit beside his bed
and chat. But day by day I watched the man who'd always been

larger than life slip further away. Dad had always been a big man but he'd lost so much weight by now that when I went to visit him one day, I actually walked past his bed. I didn't recognize the tiny, frail person lying in it. I thought my father must have been moved to another ward.

'Hils!' I heard a weak voice cry and realized my mistake the instant I turned around.

'I'm sorry!' I said as I smiled brightly. 'I was miles away. Stupid of me, Dad. I'd forget my own head if it wasn't screwed on sometimes.'

As I sat down beside Dad and took his hand, I hoped that he couldn't see my heart breaking.

In the early hours of 9 June 1977, I got a phone call to say that I should come to the hospital immediately. I arrived to find Mum and Stuart sitting at Dad's bedside and knew that we would soon lose him. Dad was drifting in and out of consciousness; the last threads of the indomitable strength that had been my bedrock for as long as I could remember were finally failing him.

His last words were simple.

'Win, Stuart, Hilary,' he said as his eyes focused for a moment on us.

That was the kind of person my dad was: a man who loved all of us more fiercely than we'd ever been loved. And although it would take almost four years until I realized the truth of what he'd told me about my marriage to Malcolm, I would eventually understand that my father had spoken the uncomfortable truth to me for the same reason he'd always done – love. You see, Dad was unlike anyone I'd ever known. Arthur Channon Brewster was quite simply one of a kind.

Chapter 9

'Can you tell me if I'm going the right way to get to Vauxhall please?'

'Vauxhall?'

'Yes.'

'You're miles away, love. Vauxhall's south of the river.'

'South of the river? As in the River Thames?'

'Yes.'

'And where am I now?'

'Norf. Way norf. You got a map?'

Yes. But a fat lot of good it did me for the first few months after moving to London. Even if I was working in logistics, I had no idea where I was most of the time. I had to learn quickly though because the company I was working for in Leeds had decided they needed me in the capital to work a patch that none of their other reps could hack. I was the first woman to be doing the job so there was a lot at stake.

So how did I go from gassing most hours of most days at Littlewoods to being responsible for a budget worth millions? By throwing myself into work in the years after losing Dad. Instead of getting depressed, I got busy, as I channelled all my feelings into work and for the first time I no longer just did a job – I had a career. My horizons shifted for ever when it started.

I'd left Littlewoods not long after Dad's death and went to work for a Manchester-based company called Leisure Circle. My job there was to recruit and train direct salespeople who then went out and sold membership to a book and record club. I wasn't qualified for it, of course. I'd been yakking in the Littlewoods back office for a good while, after all. But I got the job by using my sales skills to sell myself and then it was just a question of selling the dream of the job to the people I was going to employ – salesmen and women hungry enough to generate all their own income in the days of commission-only salaries.

I was good at what I did – very good – and after all those jobs which hadn't worked out, I began to discover that I could motivate and inspire people, and enjoyed studying maps and planning the routes that my teams worked door to door each day to ensure they maximized sales. I thrived on the challenge of hitting targets and the thrill of seeing an increasingly good pay cheque at the end of each month because my people and I had done well. To this day, I'm grateful I had that job because I still believe a stint in direct selling is the best basis for any businessperson. It's tough, competitive and not for everyone. But if you can sell then you can market, and if you can market and sell you can run a business.

Soon my world had started to open up as I not only climbed the sales ladder but made friends and went out after work with colleagues. Seeing couples together, though, made me realize just how far Malcolm and I had drifted apart and, as my confidence and ambition were fired up, I could no longer run away from the fact that I wanted a different life. Dad had been right. Just as I'd always known he had been. But it still took me time to accept that Malcolm and I were better off apart because I genuinely loved him. I just didn't know then that it was more a brother kind of love than that for a husband because I was too young to understand yet what being *in* love was.

Malcolm deserved more than me in so many ways, not least because I had never forgotten that awful night in Accrington and there was a part of me that was always distant with him. It wasn't his fault. Just as it wasn't down to him that we wanted different things. We'd just married too fast and too young to know who we really were. But by the age of twenty-three, I'd grown up enough to finally begin to realize that. Even so, I didn't actually mean to leave Malcolm when I did. It was more of an accidental thing, after I went to watch the first Bolton marathon in 1981 and then met up with friends in the pub. Malcolm wasn't with me as I stood watching the couples together and realized that he and I hadn't had that kind of fun in years. The only thing he seemed really interested in was his music, and so I decided to let him stew in his own juice by temporarily disappearing.

After flouncing back to the flat that Mum had moved into after Dad died, I fully expected Malcolm to turn up begging for me back within hours. But it must have been two days before he knocked on the door and by then I'd realized that my plan had badly backfired. He either hadn't bloody well noticed I'd gone – or he didn't care. What kind of marriage did we have left? I just couldn't stop wondering and didn't open the door when he finally came to get me because I didn't have the answer yet.

I wanted to think, and a few days later I went back to our house, where I told Malcolm that I was leaving for good. He was upset but deep down I think he knew as much as I did that our marriage was over. It might sound hard but I didn't cry or grieve when I finally made the decision to leave him because I knew it was the right thing for us both. Malcolm deserved to be happy and I wasn't the woman who could do that for him.

Just as Malcolm and I hadn't had a big romance, there was no big final falling-out either. In the years after Dad's death, we just grew apart as I changed and Malcolm didn't. He still wanted what he'd always wanted: a comfortable life in Bolton. But even though I'd tried to settle down, the nomadic life that had been bred into me as a child was never going to be easily left behind.

Meanwhile Mum's life was changing too, and I was happy it was because there were times after Dad's death that I'd wondered how she'd ever be able to cope without him. I'd always known that Mum had been cosseted, of course, but had no idea just how lost she'd be without Dad. I filled the gap after he died and was the one who took Mum shopping, ferried her to and from work, sorted out all her bills and was on the end of the phone every minute in case she needed something. I was happy to do it and we became closer than we ever had been.

But I was also pleased when she met a man called Len on a Christmas holiday to Benidorm about eighteen months after Dad's death. Mum was only in her late forties when she was widowed, and still very beautiful. Tiny and as immaculately dressed as ever, she continued to make men want to look after her, and deserved more happiness. Len was perfect. Seventeen years older, he was as attentive to my mum as Dad had always been and she was soon spending far more time at his home in Hertfordshire than in Bolton.

I didn't look for anyone to replace Malcolm, though, as the months after leaving him turned into years. I was happy with my newfound independence and after a couple of years at Mum's flat I bought a little bungalow in a village called Little Lever just outside Bolton. As well as saving the good wage I was earning at Leisure Circle, Malcolm had also bought me out of our house in Rossall Road so I was able to pay cash for it.

It was like a dream come true. Hilary Sharples had her own house at the age of twenty-five and a job which involved managing a hundred people. But there were still moments though when the wheels almost came off my love affair with independence. After getting burgled one night, I ended up sleeping on the sofa for weeks because I was worried the thieves would come back for more. The bungalow felt like Buckingham Palace with just me rattling around inside it after a lifetime spent surrounded by pub customers or my family at the very least.

I felt so lonely that I spent hours talking in my head to Dad because I missed him so much. Poor Dad. I think all my rabbiting must have been what forced him to make an impromptu visit back from the dead. It happened when I was sitting alone on my bed one day and felt someone sit down next to me. Then an arm went around my shoulder. Simple as that.

'It's going to be OK,' Dad's voice said, clear as day. 'You'll get through this.'

He never came back to me again but the strength he gave

me that day was enough to keep me going. You might think I'm talking claptrap but I'm not. I'm absolutely certain Dad was there with me in spirit – even if he wasn't in body.

After climbing the sales ladder, I left Leisure Circle to work for another Manchester-based company called Hunt Noble, where I was put in charge of even larger sales teams. Their job was to sell life insurance to students and trainee nurses and doctors, and I continued to thrive. By now I was managing around 150 people, earning a very good wage and working nationwide, driving all over the country to recruit people and keeping track of their performance. Work really had become my all and nothing got in the way of it. So although there was the odd boyfriend, I wasn't at all tempted to settle down again because I wasn't ready to.

I was far too busy having too much fun because a great friend I'd made at Hunt Noble called Audrey Mulligan, who had represented Northern Ireland in the Miss Great Britain competition, had moved into the bungalow with me. Roaring around in the TR7 I'd had customized with a Union Jack, we went here, there and everywhere. When that fell to bits, we got into my Lada. Everyone made fun of me because of that car, because until then I'd always driven something sporty. But my boss at Hunt Noble insisted he'd only help pay for a new one after the TR7 died if I made a more sensible choice. That's how I came to get a Lada and ended up having the last laugh because it kept going for years. Snow, ice, gales and storms, the Lada just kept on trucking. My boss George was right to insist on getting it. Just as Alf on Pot Bailey's had once done, he also predicted that one day I'd end up a millionaire if I was as good with money as I was with people.

Malcolm and I didn't divorce until there was an unexpected knock at my bungalow door one day and I opened it to find a man outside clutching an envelope.

'I'm here to serve your divorce papers,' he said.

'But what have I done wrong?' I asked.

'Nothing, I don't think.'

After closing the door and opening the envelope, I read through the papers and saw that Malcolm was divorcing me on grounds of desertion. It was fair enough. I'd heard that he'd met someone else and now he obviously wanted to move on. I was grateful that he did because I'd always felt guilty for leaving.

Malcolm and his wife have been together ever since and I'm glad that he went on to be happy. We all make mistakes in life, don't we? But sometimes we're lucky that no one gets lastingly hurt when we do. Not long ago, the press went knocking on Malcolm's door trying to dig up dirt about me but he sent them away. He didn't have a bad word to say about me because that's the kind of man he is. A good one.

So how did I end up in London? Well, at the ripe old age of twenty-six, I spotted an advert for an account manager in the fashion industry and after six years of managing direct-sales teams, I fancied the idea of being suited and booted, mixing with the fashion élite. Little did I know that the closest I'd get to a catwalk was buying a new kitten. Instead of sipping champagne and discussing the latest trends, I was at the rough, tough end of the fashion industry – getting clothes from the factories where they were made into the shops where they were sold.

The job was with a company called Tibbett & Britten, a major clothing transporter which was the first to offer hanging-garment distribution to retailers. Keen to cut out warehousing and pressing costs, companies like Marks & Spencer used Tibbett & Britten's fleet of lorries fitted with load-locking bars to move garments that were still hanging directly to their shops. I basically had to make sure that the right clothes got to the right place at the right time using Tibbett & Britten's lorries.

Using the experience I'd gained from managing sales teams, I spent my first year based in Leeds, working with clients like Austin Reed, Burberry and Windsmoor, and did so well that I was asked to move down to London to run one of Tibbet & Britten's most challenging patches. The capital was a completely different kettle of fish to anywhere else in the country because as well as working with retailers, it also meant liaising with the cut, make and trim manufacturers based in the East End. Rep after rep had left because they couldn't hack it. Now the Tibbett & Britten powers-that-be had decided I might be the one to make it work.

Cut, make and trim manufacturers, or CMTs, were a key area of business for Tibbett & Britten. In those days, there were limits on how much stock retailers could import from other countries and so they used British-based CMTs to make up their garments using the pattern and fabric that the fashion company provided. So a CMT might make up, say, 5,000 navy winter coats for Debenhams or 10,000 summer tops for Marks & Spencer. I would be the link between Tibbet & Britten, the CMTs *and* the retailers they were producing garments for, responsible for moving clothes from the factories to the shops.

Deliveries might seem easy when a man knocks on your door and hands you a box. But believe me when I say they're not as simple as piling a few boxes on to the back of a lorry.

Moving thousands of garments to hundreds of shops involves dozens of factors. Where is the pick-up? How many lorries do you have available on any one day? What are the most efficient routes they can drive? How many hours will it take? How many times will the driver have to stop *en route*, because it costs money each time he does? How full will his lorry be too, because empty space costs?

As well as making sure that the Tibbett & Britten fleet was used to its fullest capacity, I was also going to have to get the garments delivered in the right size ratios, because every piece of clothing is specific to season, cut and even colour. Not many size-16 woman are going to buy a clinging tight white summer dress, for instance, while most size-8s won't be too interested in clothes that are more generously cut because they'll be swamped in them. I had to understand the product and where it was going, decide on what ratio packs the garments were sent out in – how many of each size went to which shop to ensure that the retailer didn't end up with unsold stock. In an increasingly competitive commercial environment, our customers couldn't afford mistakes.

It was a huge challenge and no rep had ever stayed in London for longer than about six months. But it didn't daunt me and I was excited to be closer to where Mum was living now with Len in Hertfordshire. In fact, the only thing that worried me was the thought of leaving the north. I was Bolton-born and -bred. What was I going to make of all those soft southerners?

I told my manager that I'd take the job but wouldn't sell my bungalow and move properly to London until I knew it was for me. He agreed to put me up in a hotel at the cusp of the M1 and M25 while I found my feet, and I moved down to

London prepared to hate it. It took all of a month for the vibrancy of the East End rag trade to win me over – even if it did take a bit longer for me to understand London geography.

The East End was rough and ready and some of the men I had to deal with were not exactly gentlemen. But I thrived on the challenge and realized that working in the East End was my ticket to seeing the world. As I walked into factories, I saw women dressed in brightly coloured saris, others wearing headscarves and men in turbans. Every day was an experience as I collided with cultures I'd never experienced before. Brick Lane, where all the leather garments were made, was full of Jews. Nearby Roman Road was where all the Indian cotton factories were based, while Cambridge Heath Road was full of Turks. Whitechapel was where the whole lot of them collided as curry shops jostled with kebab houses and kosher restaurants.

Living in a motorway hotel wasn't exactly homely, and I didn't know a single person in London so there was no chance of a social life. Instead, I threw all I had into the challenge of my new job and found that the intricacies of logistics stretched my brain to its limit every day. I loved it. It was like being given a huge jigsaw puzzle of pieces each morning and knowing that by the end of the working day I'd have to move enough to get the right fit. No day was ever the same, there was unexpected problem after problem, and the work was far from glamorous. But I loved every minute.

To say I was a woman in a man's world might sound like a cliché but I really was. Call it logistics, transport or just plain old lorry-driving, the world I work in has changed a lot since I started. But when I did, there were no other women doing the same job as me and some of the men I worked with just didn't know what to make of me. As I strode into their dirty, noisy factories wearing a cerise satin shirt and dogtooth-check pencil skirt, they'd stare at me as if I'd landed from Mars. They soon realized that I meant business.

I didn't succumb to the pressure of being one of the boys. I wasn't going to start cracking filthy jokes or hiding myself in drab clothes. I just cannot understand all those women who work in the City and go to work in a black suit every day. I was determined to be me, and if the men I was working with didn't like it then they could lump it. I've never thought that a woman should change in order to be professional. You don't need to throw your weight around or grow a pair of balls (although you might have to show that you have them every now and again). Women have just as much toughness inside them as men, and being a rarity meant I could do things a bit differently. I soon found that wrong-footing people could be the most effective way of persuading them to do things my way.

Leeds had been a cakewalk compared to the East End rag trade, where corners were cut at best and health and safety was completely ignored at worst in order to maximize profit. I couldn't even begin to take all that on though when my job was purely about the logistics of getting the right garments to the right places and it was all I could do to ensure it happened when dealing with some of the men who ran the CMT factories.

'So you'll be ready for the House of Fraser order next week?' I'd ask when I went in to see them.

'No.'

'Why not?'

'Because we won't be.'

'Well then you'll have to be, won't you? The order needs to go and so you need to deliver what we agreed.'

Squaring up to men who thought nothing of running what were little more than sweatshops in many cases was one thing. But there was the odd time when I lost my nerve if I thought that just keeping life and limb together would be too much. Some of the areas I had to visit were far from suitable for a young woman alone and I'll never forget going to a workshop in Long Street, Hackney.

It was a dark winter's night when I parked up. I was there to see a man who worked alone in his workshop, because orders were sometimes made up by several individuals who each produced, say, fifty leather jackets that together made up a delivery.

As I got out of my car, I could see young men eyeing me up as they hung around on the street corner. Walking towards the workshop, I felt more and more nervous with their eyes on me and when I saw the huge industrial lift I was going to have to use to get to the workshop, I knew I wasn't going to get into it alone. But after telling my boss I hadn't been to the appointment, he put me straight.

'Go back and keep it,' he said.

I just had to steel my nerve – and make sure that it was daylight the next time I went back.

I did a fair bit of the wide-eyed-Bolton-lass routine though as I tried to sort out all the problems with the CMT bosses, but if that didn't work, I didn't shout or scream. They say women fling their handbags at dawn but in my experience men do it far more – metaphorically speaking at least. Even then, I was convinced that direct challenge is often the worst way to get a constructive dialogue going and as I watched the men around me hurling expletives at each other, I'd wonder when they'd ever learn that it was a sure-fire way of making any discussion implode. Then when they'd finally calmed down, I'd do what most women do: flatter enough egos to find a solution without wasting time arguing the toss.

Most of the men I worked with soon saw that I was professional – but that didn't put the odd one off a bit of good old-fashioned sexual harassment. Most of the time, I laughed it off. If I was chased around an office at the end of a meeting, I always somehow managed to put whoever was doing the chasing back in their place. But there were times when that kind of thing came from the most unexpected sources and it was then that I was almost outwitted. Almost, but not quite.

Take the ageing Jewish factory owner who insisted we have a business meeting over lunch at a kosher restaurant one day. He must have been eighty if he was a day and I smiled as I helped him out of his car and he admired the black leather skirt and jacket I was wearing with a white shirt and black dickie bow. It was all the rage in the eighties and he was just taking a grandfatherly interest in a well-dressed woman. Half an hour later, I almost choked on my salt-beef sandwich when I felt his hand go up my skirt.

'She's gone now,' he said.

For a moment, I didn't know what to do. Then I realized that the poor man must surely have lost his wife and be in the grip of mind-altering grief. Only that could explain why his hand was trying to slowly creep up my thigh.

'I'm so sorry,' I said, as I tried to shift back in my seat rather than kick him in the shins.

'Things weren't working out between us,' he said as he

looked at me through rheumy eyes, and I realized that he talking about his latest girlfriend.

'You're definitely what I want now, my dear,' he said as his eyes suddenly gleamed. 'I have a five-bedroom flat in St John's Wood that I will give to you if you come home with me after lunch.'

Dirty old bugger. I told him where to stick his flat and made sure I never met him for lunch again.

The worst sexism I experienced though was far closer to home. In fact, it came from my own colleagues. Most of the time I laughed it off it as they questioned my ability to operate in the testosterone-filled world of lorry drivers because the jokes and put-downs rolled like water off a duck's back. But there was one guy at Tibbett & Britten who was nastier than the rest.

'You're quite fuckable really, aren't you?' he'd suddenly say in a room full of colleagues as we sat discussing how to get 1,000 coats from the Windsmoor warehouse in County Durham to their concessions in every major department store.

Usually I'd just ignore him and carry on discussing the business that we were there to sort out. But gradually I realized this wasn't working. In fact, the man seemed so determined to get a rise out of me that I decided to give him one. Just not the one he was expecting.

'Hilary?' he said during a meeting one afternoon with about half a dozen of our Tibbett & Britten colleagues.

'Yes?'

'I want to lick your c*nt.'

I looked at the man without a word. He obviously thought that after all the months of trying to push me to the edge, this was going to finally do it. All he really wanted was for me to start shouting or crying – and 'prove' to everyone that I wasn't up to the job. He had no bloody idea.

As some of the men in the room stared into thin air, others hurriedly left for a pee and a few joined in the laughter, I turned to him.

'Let me get this straight,' I said as I smiled at him sweetly. 'You. Want. To. Lick. My. C*nt?'

I said each word clearly, calmly – and very slowly. The man started to go pale.

'And is that the kind of thing you'd like your wife or daughter to hear you say?' I said in my smoothest tones.

With that he went white as a sheet, the laughter stopped and I never heard a word out of him again. They say attack is the best form of defence. Sometimes you just have to deliver that attack with a killer smile.

Chapter 10

I didn't expect to fall in love, the kind of love I'd never known before and never would again. But the love of my life was the man I first set eyes on four years after my marriage to Malcolm had ended. I'd just turned twenty-eight when I went to a CMT factory on Cambridge Heath Road and a man with jet-black hair and brown eyes walked out as I walked in. He was about my height, stockily built and wearing expensive hand-made shoes.

'I'm here to see Hussain,' I said.

'That is me,' he replied in a thick Turkish accent. 'And you are?'

'Hilary Sharples. From Tibbett & Britten. We have an appointment booked at two p.m.?'

He'd obviously forgotten all about it but I was too busy being hit by a bolt of lightning to care. Hussain led me back into the factory and after having our meeting, I left with my knees still knocking and the hope that I'd see him again sometime. A few hours later, following appointments with other clients, I called in to the office from a phone box to pick up my messages.

'You've got several from one client,' the secretary told me.

'Who's that?'

'Hussain.'

I'd obviously had the same effect on him as he'd had on me. I waited until the next day to ring him.

'I need to see you,' Hussain said, and I knew exactly what it was about.

'Is there a problem with an order?' I replied innocently.

'No. I'd just like to discuss something with you. How about we have lunch?'

We didn't even pretend to talk about work as we sat down in a bar on Bethnal Green Road a couple of days later.

'What would you like to eat?' Hussain asked me.

'A sandwich?'

'Cheese or ham?'

'I don't like ham.'

He smiled at me. I didn't know what on earth he was so pleased about but later discovered that Hussain was Muslim so pork was forbidden by his religion. I liked that he was different. Exotic and unusual, Hussain was unlike anyone I'd ever met, and while Malcolm and I had slipped into a relationship, Hussain spun me head-first into romance. Lunch turned into dinner and then date after date.

Hussain was obviously successful. That much was clear. In places like the Savoy and the revolving restaurant at the top of the Post Office Tower, he nonchalantly dropped £50 tips on the table. I ate vine leaves for the first time with him in a Turkish restaurant in the West End, he took me for Sunday-afternoon tea at the Inn on the Park on Park Lane and drove me to Kent in his red Ferrari where he cooked a barbecue for us on the banks of a lake.

It wasn't Hussain's money I liked, though. I was earning

enough of my own by then. What drew me to him was that he made me feel as if the sun was always shining on me. Attentive and charming, he was always interested in me and my thoughts. We spent hours discussing our lives and work, chatting about anything and everything, and he made me laugh more than any man I'd ever met. It had been four years since Malcolm and I'd been so focused on work that I'd almost forgotten what it was like to get attention from a man. Then Hussain wrapped me up like I was a precious stone and the past in Accrington that I'd never been able to forget was finally left behind. Hussain helped me to do that and I soon fell in love with him: completely, passionately and almost without knowing it.

He told me that he'd grown up in Turkish Cyprus and moved to England when he was seventeen. Then he'd built up a successful business but lost it after falling out with his partner. After that, he'd opened his factory and built it into another thriving concern. Now he lived with his sister, which is why we had to spend all our time alone together at my flat. I didn't mind. I was happy to live in a bubble with Hussain because I'd never had the time to make friends in London and wanted to spend every spare minute with him.

Fourteen years older than me, he was worldly, sophisticated and made me feel safe. Not long after we met, I went on holiday alone to Corfu and a taxi driver who was supposed to be taking me to my hotel instead drove me to a deserted beach where he told me to 'streeeep'. I battered him so hard with my handbag that he soon got the message and then ordered him to drive me to my hotel. By the time I got there, though, I was a bag of nerves and rang Hussain to tell him what had happened. Within hours he'd torn a strip off the hotel manager for failing to take proper care of me and within two days had flown to Corfu to get me. Hussain made me feel more protected than I ever had before. Nothing else mattered when I met him.

Our relationship moved quickly and within months I'd left the place where I was living in Winchmore Hill to rent a flat in Upminster with Hussain. Not that we were there a lot, because both of us were so busy at work. Hussain worked dawn to dusk six days a week at his factory, while I was covering the West End as well now and managing huge accounts like Burberry and Jaeger.

But at the end of each busy day, we'd get home, eat dinner and chat. The more I knew Hussain, the more I loved him. He wasn't one of those men who gave up after they know they've got you. Instead he would constantly surprise me with flowers, and after cooking dinner one night, he laid the table with candles and a bottle of champagne. As I sat down, he poured me a glass and I watched a gold pendant float to the top of the bubbles. It was a hexagon studded with tiny diamonds, rubies and emeralds that Hussain had designed and had made for me. It was just one of many pieces of jewellery he bought me and each one made me feel as if I was the only woman in the world.

After almost a year together, a baby felt like the natural next step because I'd always known I wanted children. Hussain knew I wasn't taking precautions and when he told me that we'd marry one day, I felt sure we would. He loved me for who I was and didn't need me to convert to Islam. We were going to be together for ever and were both overjoyed when I fell pregnant in spring 1986 at the age of twenty-nine.

I didn't tell anyone at work about the baby for as long as

possible, though, because I had more than a sneaking suspicion that my job might get even harder if I did. Luckily I didn't show too much and never actually had to wear maternity clothes. I just put some elastic through the buttons on my skirts and wore baggy tops. It wasn't until I was seven months pregnant that people at work realized and I just kept working as hard as ever – maybe harder in fact. I didn't want anyone to think I was slacking and no one was going to cut me any even if I'd wanted them to. I was going to get just four weeks' maternity leave and would lose my company car while I was off.

Getting up at 6 a.m., I continued to do fifteen-hour days as I drove into the West End to see clients and attend one meeting after another. I felt increasingly tired and got even more exhausted when we bought a two-bedroom house in Grays, Essex, three months before the baby was due. With hardly a stick of furniture between us, I had to sleep in a deck chair until we got a bed delivered, but I didn't care. Because as I sat in that chair watching our tiny portable TV and stroking my belly, I knew that soon my family life with Hussain and our child would start – and I couldn't wait.

On the morning of Wednesday, 10 December 1986 I gave a presentation to House of Fraser before going for a check-up at Orsett Hospital in Grays. After that I was going to go Christmas shopping with Mum because the baby was due on Christmas Day and I wanted to be sure everything was wrapped, ready and waiting for him or her under the tree. Mum and Len only lived about fifteen miles away from Hussain and me now so we saw a lot of each other and I was looking forward to a final waddle round the shops.

But then the doctor told me that I wouldn't be going anywhere because the baby was in distress and I needed to be induced. Panicked and more than a bit scared, I was given drugs to start my labour, but things didn't go to plan. It took almost two days for Mevlit to be born, after a forceps delivery followed by a minor operation for me. Battered, bruised and exhausted as I was, though, all I could think of was Mevlit, who'd been put into an incubator because he was jaundiced. As I looked at him, I thought I'd never be able to love him more than I did in that moment. Like every other mother, I went on to surprise myself in the years to come.

I was terribly upset by the fact that I couldn't breastfeed after developing an infection and still felt poorly by the time I went home. But Hussain stepped in from the moment we crossed the threshold and confidently scooped up Mevlit, making his milk and feeding him. He was such a natural dad that even if I wasn't sure of what to do, he always seemed to know. Like the day he came home to find Mum and me washing Mevlit so carefully you'd have thought he was as delicate as the Turin Shroud.

'Don't be scared of him,' Hussain said with a smile. 'He's a big boy and a big boy needs a proper bath.'

With that, he took Mevlit upstairs and got into the bath with that tiny slip of a baby. I couldn't believe it but Hussain didn't bat an eyelid – and neither did Mevlit. It was as if Hussain had handled children all his life and I was happy to see what a devoted dad he was going to be because I needed all the help I could get, given that I had to go back to work so quickly.

Mevlit was as good as gold for the first four weeks after I did. Then he woke up with a vengeance, and it felt as if I hardly slept for the next two years. But however bad the night had been, I still got up the next morning and, like any working mother, prised my eyelids open with matchsticks to start the day. I tried as much as possible to juggle motherhood with my job. For instance, if I knew I had an appointment with a friendly customer, I'd take Mevlit, because there was always someone who was happy to look after him while I did business with their boss. Or else I'd do four really long days to make sure I had Fridays off to spend with him. At my next appraisal after Mevlit was born, my boss sarcastically commented on how well my short week was working for me.

'I do more business for you in two days than most people do in two weeks,' I told him. 'So if you think I'm going to spend a day looking at the architecture in the West End after getting all my work done then you are very much mistaken.'

He didn't question how I structured my time again. Later on in my career, I experienced the guilt that many working mothers feel. But I can honestly say that I didn't when Mevlit was small because I knew he was well looked after. My mum and Len had agreed to take him each day after I'd realized that I couldn't leave Mevlit at the local nursery where I'd arranged a place for him. Something about it didn't feel right and so Nanna and Gangan had agreed to step in. Mum and Len were retired by now and I knew they were both devoted to Mevlit so I was glad he was with them.

I felt more and more dreadful though after going back to work. In fact, I almost began to wonder how on earth other working mothers coped. Feeling increasingly exhausted, I just didn't understand why I was so drained because I'd never been the kind to tire. I'd worked sixty-plus hours a week for years now. Why was I suddenly finding it so hard? But then one night the police pulled me over on the M25 because I was

driving erratically and the next thing I knew I was in an ambulance going to hospital. I was diagnosed with gestational
diabetes, which hadn't been picked up during my pregnancy,
put on an insulin drip and sent home after twenty-four hours.
Twelve-hour days, a newborn baby and diabetes: no wonder
I'd felt so bloody terrible.

You don't always see the clouds when they gather on the
horizon, do you? And if they're black enough, you will do
almost anything to ignore them. That's what I did when my
relationship with Hussain started to sour. It's only as I've
looked back that I've realized the signs were there all along
of the storm that was to come.

I'd known since before Mevlit was born that Hussain's financial situation wasn't as good as it had appeared to be when I
first met him. I understood though when he told me that he
was having cash-flow problems. Everyone hits bad patches in
business and I was no stranger to men who had money falling
out their pockets one day and none the next. I'd known it all
my life with Dad, after all.

So when Hussain asked me to lend him money, I was happy
to do it. He promised it would all come back to me and I felt
sure it would. Then when he asked me to sell some cabbage
for him on a trip back north, I also agreed. Cabbage is the
garments made up from fabric left over at the end of making
up a retailer's order. With a good pattern cutter, there can be
a lot of cloth left and factory owners were always keen to make
extra profit out of it. It was a perk of the job which everyone
was aware of and I came back with £1,000 in cash for Hussain.

Money continued to be a problem for him, but at least I
was still earning a good wage and able to get another mort-

gage when we sold our house with a £40,000 profit. Mevlit was about five months old when we moved into a three-bedroom home in Linford, Essex, and I was as impatient as ever to get started on home improvements. Within a few months, I'd saved enough to have the kitchen refitted.

On the morning the man arrived to start the work, I talked excitedly to him about exactly where I wanted the hob and how the tiles should be placed before leaving for work. I was so pleased to be home when I got back about six that night. Not only would I be able to see what had happened to my kitchen, I could also hear Hussain with Mevlit upstairs. Hussain had picked him up from Mum's and now I'd get to spend some time with them both. Holding a bag stuffed with clothes for Hussain which I'd bought from the discount shop at Farah menswear after an appointment that day, I walked into the bedroom.

'Hello, my darlings,' I said with a smile as I opened the door and walked towards Mevlit, anxious to give him a cuddle after a long day.

The next thing I knew, Hussain's arms had gone around me and I was being dragged off my feet. One moment I was smiling at my son. The next, his father had thrown me across the room and I'd landed sprawled against the wardrobe. I stared up to see Hussain standing above me with a look of rage on his face.

'You slag,' he screamed. 'You filthy fucking slag.'

I froze as Hussain started to slap me. I couldn't understand or even recognize the man in front of me with a look of such pure hatred on his face. For what seemed like for ever, Hussain screamed every insult under the sun until Mevlit began to cry and his tears seemed to snap Hussain back to reality. He stopped shouting at me almost as quickly as he'd started and picked up Mevlit without another word before leaving the room.

I couldn't believe what had happened. I lay almost dazed against the wardrobe as I stared at the open door, unable to take in what Hussain had done. He'd slapped me, screamed insults that I'd never heard him utter before. I just didn't understand what had made him do it. As I started to cry in shock, I got myself up and walked downstairs, where I waited for Hussain to come down and apologize, tell me what on earth I'd done to make him so angry.

But when I heard him go into our bedroom and shut the door, I knew he wasn't going to come and see me. I told myself that the only way to get any answers was to wait until he had calmed down, so I slept on the sofa. After sleeping fitfully and crying for most of the night, I walked into our bedroom the next morning to get ready for work with red eyes and a face puffy from tears.

'And now I love you more,' Hussain said as he looked at me and with a shudder I felt sure he meant that he was enjoying seeing me suffer.

I didn't say a word because I just didn't know what to say.

For the next few days, Hussain and I managed to avoid each other. He was already gone when I woke up at 5.45 a.m. to get Mevlit ready because I had to be on the road into London early. When I got home at night with Mevlit, I would go to bed alone and feel Hussain get in beside me later.

'I saw you talking to the kitchen guy,' he said when I finally spoke to him about what had happened.

I stared at him, confused. What on earth did he mean?

'You were flirting with him. Chatting him up. I saw it. I know what you were doing.'

I couldn't quite believe what I was hearing.

'I wasn't. I really wasn't. We were just talking about the kitchen.'

'Don't lie. I could see.'

I looked at Hussain, totally confused. I'd never known anything like it. He obviously believed what he was saying, and how can you argue with someone who's so convinced they're right even when you know they're wrong? For a moment, I felt chilled to the bone as I realized that Hussain believed he was right to do what he'd done. Then I forced myself to try and understand. Hussain and I loved each other completely. He'd got it so wrong because he loved me. I was sure he'd never hurt me again.

Chapter 11

I know what you're thinking: why didn't I leave? How on earth did someone like me not realize that night was the start of a slippery slope? I don't know why exactly to this day. All I know for sure is that it marked the beginning of my love for Hussain being twisted into something far darker which left me hardly knowing who I was any more. And if you think that kind of thing only happens to the weakest women, then you're wrong.

The outburst about the kitchen fitter wasn't the beginning and end of something, as I'd tried to tell myself it was. It was just the start. In the months that followed, Hussain became more and more jealous: when I said I'd be home at five from a shopping trip with Mum and got back at ten minutes past, he slapped me before dragging me inside as soon as I got out of the car. When the M25 ground to a halt one night and I arrived home late, he screamed at me until dawn was almost breaking. I never knew what I'd done but time and again he'd shout at me for hours as he told me that I was a whore and a slag who'd crawl in the gutter if I left. All I can say is that when the man you love with all your heart tells you that, you slowly start to believe it if you hear it enough.

It was like being pulled away from every guiding point I'd

ever known as I was sucked down so deep I began to lose myself. And when love is twisted into something else, it's hard to know when to let it go. There's always the hope inside that you will get back to where you were. But bit by bit, you lose trust in yourself and start to feel sure there must be something you can do to stop the man you love so much from hurting you, that if only you love him just a little bit more then he will stop. You become a victim. I did.

I know some people will find it hard to understand. And if you are a woman who can put your hand on your heart and say you've never put up with a boyfriend who doesn't call or turn up when he says he will, then maybe you can't. But I think most women know what it is to love someone who isn't worthy of them and my relationship didn't go from good to bad overnight. It was a gradual process, a slow erosion of all that was good. Like a rock being smoothed to a pebble by the sea, I was gradually worn down until verbal abuse became my normality. I told myself that the Hussain who did these things to me wasn't the man I'd fallen in love with. And while he never apologized or promised not to insult me again, I clung on to the good times when they returned because he was as loving as he always had been when he calmed down. More so, even.

We're told as kids that sticks and stones might break our bones but words will never hurt us. What a load of rubbish. Words do hurt. I know they can crush every bit of life out of you if you're told you're worthless enough times. I don't think I'm alone in being the kind of woman who can succeed professionally and yet make mistakes when it comes to relationships. I could hold my own in a man's world, compete with them and outperform them even. But in my own home, I was as isolated as I had been all those years ago when I was a child living in pubs.

Hussain didn't hit me again for a while after that first incident. That only came later. And even to this day, I can't tell you exactly why I stayed. Can any woman in that kind of relationship ever fully explain it? Maybe I did because what had happened to me in Accrington had left a scar that made me believe I really was worthless – however much I'd proved I wasn't in the outside world. I don't know. All I'm sure of is that none of it mattered when the man I loved seemed to hate me.

My world became increasingly divided between day and night, work and home, because no matter how late I'd been kept up by Hussain screaming abuse, I'd still get up the next day and do my job well. To the outside world, I looked like a woman with it all: a man, a baby and a home. But really I just learned to put on a mask, hide whatever was hurting inside me – and in some ways I think I'm still wearing it today.

All I could think was that my first duty was to my son, and whatever was happening to me didn't affect him because Hussain never started on me until after Mevlit had gone to bed. To me, leaving for good meant depriving my son of the kind of stable family life I'd always wanted and I couldn't bring myself to do it because Mevlit loved his father, and whatever he did to me, I can honestly say that Hussain was a good dad while we all lived under the same roof. Sometimes I left for a night at Mum's but Hussain was clever and knew when I'd had enough. When that happened, he'd go to one of two extremes: either he was so attentive that I'd think he'd finally seen sense, or he'd threaten that I'd never see Mevlit again if I left for good. I knew it was perfectly possible if he took him abroad.

Even so, I still find it hard to understand what kept me there for so long. All I know for sure is that I loved that man the moment I laid eyes on him and the feelings I had were so strong they took years to break. Even when I finally did leave, it took me years to forget Hussain. So before I tell you the rest of my story with him, there is one thing you have to remember: domestic abuse isn't about money or class. It's not about being strong or weak. It's about lies that turn your world upside-down and power games that leave you reeling. The drip, drip, drip of fear that makes the landscape of your life change completely.

Mevlit was about eighteen months old when the phone rang one night as Hussain and I sat watching television together.

'Is that Hilary?' a woman's voice said.

She had a strong Turkish accent.

'Yes.'

'My name is Elif.'

I didn't know who she was.

'How can I help you?'

'I'm Hussain's wife.'

I froze.

'Did you know that he has five children and one of them is only a few months younger than your son?' the woman said.

I didn't understand what I was hearing. Hussain was married? He couldn't be. He came home to me every night, however long his day had been. We lived together with Mevlit. We had a life together. Who was this woman?

'What do you mean?' I said. 'What do you want?'

I didn't wait to hear any more. I didn't want to hear it. I

couldn't hear it. I handed the phone to Hussain, who started talking in rapid Turkish as I walked into the kitchen and poured a whisky. I don't know why I did that because I've always hated the stuff. But then I walked back into the living room on autopilot and threw the whisky in Hussain's face as he put down the phone.

'Is it true?' I shouted.

'Of course not. How could I be married? We have a life together. We have Mevlit. How could I have that with anyone else?'

'But why would anyone lie like that? Why would they say such a thing?'

'I have enemies. It's business. That's what happens in business.'

'Not my kind of business!'

'Maybe not. But I work in a different kind of world. You know that. You have to believe me. This is nothing but someone trying to make trouble for me.'

I looked at Hussain, unsure of what to do. I was hardly able to take it all in.

'Just tell me the truth!' I shouted as rage filled me. 'Why on earth would someone phone up like that and lie?'

'Because they want to cause trouble.'

'But that's ridiculous.'

'Hilary. Listen to me. It's not true.'

For the next few hours, I ranted and raved, pleaded with Hussain to properly explain what had just happened. It didn't make sense. But whatever I said, he just kept insisting that the woman was lying and there was nothing to hide. I wanted to believe him. I really did. And when a man rang the following day to tell me that Hussain was right – they'd had an argument over business and he'd just wanted to make trouble so he'd asked a woman friend to phone me – I clung onto the explanation. But however much I wished my doubts away, there was a voice whispering at the back of my mind that the woman had been telling the truth.

I couldn't shake off my suspicions in the months that followed, because the more I went over everything, the more the pieces seemed to fit as I wondered how much I really knew about Hussain. For a start, his life away from me had always been a closed book because he only mixed in Turkish circles. I knew a bit about that world because of my work, but wasn't truly part of it. Then there was how much time we were apart because the only day we ever really spent together was Sunday, when we'd take a picnic into the woods with Mevlit or go for a pub lunch. We hardly saw each other for the rest of the week and I'd always assumed it was because we were both busy with work. Now I wondered if it was something more. Was Hussain going to see his other family?

I thought back to how easily Hussain had cared for Mevlit as a baby. Back then, I'd assumed he was a natural but now wondered if he'd known what he was doing because he'd done it before. When I'd got home with Mevlit and wondered if I was bottle-feeding him correctly, Mum had laughed as she'd told me that she didn't have a clue because it was nearly thirty years since she'd last done it. Hussain had known though. He'd also been reluctant for me to meet his family when we first got to know each other and although I'd been introduced to his sister Sabiha and brother Ali by now, I'd never really got the chance to get to talk to them properly. Sabiha was the only member of Hussain's family who had invited us over for a meal, and I couldn't talk to her properly because he never left us alone together. I felt as if I was kept away from anyone connected to Hussain and there was nothing I could do to get closer to them.

All these things crowded into my mind the more I thought of what the woman had said in the months that followed the phone call. But whenever I tried to talk about it to Hussain, he would tell me that I was mad. He would shout and scream that I was paranoid, a fool who was imagining things. He even insisted to Mum that I'd misunderstood the phone call because I was drunk the night the woman phoned.

If you've never tried to reason with someone who lies so well and so much that you begin to wonder if you're the one losing their mind, then you won't understand what I'm saying. But if you have then you'll know what it's like to look the person you love in the eye and feel the world almost slip away when they tell you that you've got it all wrong. You end up doubting yourself because it's easier than facing the truth about them.

'Have you seen my gold necklace?' I'd ask Hussain as I hunted for a chain that I knew had been on my dressing table.

'No, Bobos,' he'd say, using the nickname he'd christened me with soon after we met.

'Are you sure?'

'Of course. What would I want with a necklace? It must be there somewhere.'

But after hunting high and low, I could never find what I was looking for. Clothes and money from my purse disappeared too. I just couldn't understand where things kept going and began to wonder if I was imagining things because each time I'd ask Hussain about whatever it was I'd lost, he'd look at me as if I was crazy.

Bit by bit, I felt as if I was spinning out of control. Was I imagining things, just as Hussain told me I was? Why couldn't I just trust him? Maybe he was right. Maybe I was just a bad lot as he said I was. As time passed, I began to doubt myself so much – my sanity even – that if Hussain had said the sky was pink, I'd probably have had a look just to check for myself that it was blue.

Torn between wanting to accept Hussain's denials whenever I asked about his wife, I tried to push my worries down, ignore what might destroy all I had in order to keep my family intact. I did such a good job of ignoring it all in fact that when a friend called Len, who was a quality controller for Debenhams, told me that Hussain was indeed married, it took me months to act on what he'd said.

'I'm sorry, Hilary, but I think there's something you should know,' Len had said when he phoned me one day. 'Hussain is married.'

'Are you sure?'

'Yes. And you have a right to know. My daughter got mixed up with a man like him and nothing good came of it. I wanted to warn you.'

'But how do you know?'

'Because two of his sons work in his factory.'

'What do you mean?'

'Burak and Hasan. They're his sons.'

I knew the two of them in passing because I often popped into Hussain's factory. But it still took me time to pluck up the courage to do anything about what Len had told me because I was so afraid of finally finding out the truth. When I finally did question Hasan, though, he just hung his head as he told me that he wouldn't have Hussain as a father. I didn't know what to do as doors were slammed in my face every time I tried to open one and find out the truth.

'It's like history repeating itself,' Mum would say as I talked it over with her. 'He's just like your father.'

But still I told myself to trust what Hussain had told me and when my doubts became too much and I questioned him again, his abusive behaviour worsened. Occasionally he would answer my questions with his fists. Not always. I can count on two hands the number of times that Hussain actually struck me and sometimes weeks or even months could go by before he'd go for me again physically. But if I screamed at him too loudly as I pleaded with him to stop slinging insults at me in the small hours of the morning, he would start to shake me or push me against a wall as he screamed. If I asked him for the thousandth time to tell me the truth about his marriage, he'd silence me with hours of aggressive verbal abuse as he turned everything on to me, the failure that I was, the whore, the slut.

Was I afraid of him? Yes. At least, bit by bit I started to be. Living with someone so unpredictable is like surviving in a war zone, waiting for the next bomb to drop. When Tibbet & Britten went computerized, I was asked to spend a week in Leeds showing customers how the new system worked and told Hussain about it weeks in advance. He didn't say a word until the night before I was due to leave, when he told me that I couldn't stay overnight. The next day I got up at 4 a.m. and drove to Leeds before driving back home to Essex that night. I did the same for the rest of the week. I hardly knew who I was any more.

*

I was deeply asleep when the phone rang in the middle of one night about six months after the phone call from the woman claiming to be Hussain's wife.

I turned over to see if he was going to answer it. He wasn't lying next to me. I picked up the phone.

'Hello?'

'This is the police. We're trying to contact Hussain.'

'Why?'

'Because his factory is on fire.'

I sat up and looked around me.

'But he's not here. He's not with me.'

'Where is he?'

'I don't know.'

Panic filled me. There were nights when Hussain didn't get home until the early hours because he had a habit of falling asleep after putting on the fire in his office when he worked late.

'He might be in there,' I said hurriedly. 'He might have gone back to the factory to do the wages or something. It's Friday tomorrow. He could be there. Please try and find him. You've got to try and find him.'

There was nothing else I could do as the phone went dead. Mevlit was sleeping and so I just had to sit and wait by the phone. Eventually it rang at about 3.30 a.m.

'Hussain was not in the building,' a voice told me. 'We're sure of that.'

'You are?'

'Yes.'

'And the factory?'

'It's badly damaged.'

I felt sick as I put down the phone. Hussain's business was

already in trouble. What would he do now? And where was he?

The phone finally rang again at about 8 a.m.

'Bobos?' Hussain said.

'Where are you?' I cried. 'Have you heard about the factory?'

'Yes.'

'I've been so worried.'

'I'm sorry. I was standing outside watching it all and couldn't call until now. I've been with fire assessors and the police.'

'You were watching the fire?'

'Yes. I got up early because I had some paperwork to sort out and didn't want to wake you so I left you sleeping. But then I got to the factory and found it on fire.'

In the rush of relief that Hussain was safe, I didn't stop to question his explanation. I was so lost by then that it didn't even occur to me to ask if he'd been with the wife he denied having that night.

As time passed it was as if my life with Hussain had two distinct parts: one in which to the outside world we were moving on to new things together, the other in which we were locked in an ever-decreasing circle of distrust and anger. After leaving Tibbet & Britten, I went to work as a national sales manager for another hanging-garment carrier called Scorpio and made two good friends there. One was Adrian Russell, the ops director, who I got on with like a house on fire, and the other was my boss, Keith Sabey.

'Your phone bill stretches to John O'Groats and back again,' he'd say with a laugh when he phoned to gently tell me off.

'Well, doesn't that prove just how hard I work?' I'd tease him.

Meanwhile, Hussain and I had also moved house again, to a place in Eastwood near Southend-on-Sea, because he'd used the insurance money he'd got after the factory fire to open a restaurant on the seafront there. We moved to be nearer to Mum and Len and I could afford a bigger mortgage thanks to the salary I was earning at Scorpio plus the equity from our other houses.

But even with a fresh start, the spiral continued downwards because by now I knew that Hussain wasn't the businessman I'd thought he was when I first met him – and I was the one who had to carry him. Short of washing the pots, I basically ran his restaurant. After doing a twelve-hour day at Scorpio, I'd often get a phone call about 9.30 p.m. telling me that I was needed. With a heavy heart, I'd get Mevlit out of bed and take him down to the restaurant, where he'd sleep on a bed that Hussain had made up for him while I waitressed. I hated that Mevlit had to do it but I didn't have a choice. After finishing about 1 a.m., I'd take him home and get a few hours' sleep until my day started again at 5.45.

Outside of that, I did Hussain's books, payroll and stock-ordering – and told him that he was losing money hand over fist as I did fag-packet sums which were enough to tell me he was. Whatever I did to help, though, Hussain just couldn't get control of the restaurant finances. I thought he was ploughing his money back into the business because I paid the mortgage and bills at the beginning of every month. It was only later that I learned he'd run up massive debts.

As things spiralled downwards, he became more abusive. He broke the second finger on my left hand by throwing me down the stairs one day, and on a rare night at home with

Mevlit, I was happily arranging some flowers in the living room when Hussain walked in through the patio doors.

'You scared the life out of me,' I said as I looked at him.

He didn't say a word before slapping me in the face.

'I need to know what you're doing, who you're with,' he then screamed. 'You fucking bitch. Dirty slag. Filthy whore.'

There were a few punches too. In fact, Hussain once hit me so hard that he left the imprint of his ring on my right cheek and I had to tell people that I'd walked into a door. Not everyone believed me. A cleaner we had looked at me one day and told me I had to leave. She'd arrived that morning to find yet more smashed glass on the living-room floor, because I often ended up throwing something at Hussain when the screaming got too much. Neighbours even called the police a few times, but I'd always insist that whatever argument we'd been having was over by the time they knocked at the door.

So why couldn't I admit to anyone what was happening – even Mum? Because deep down I think I was ashamed, and did all I could to pretend to the outside world that my life was normal. Besides, no one asked questions and so I didn't give them answers. Len had health problems, Mum had more than enough on her plate and I didn't want to worry them – or have them interfere. Just as I'd learned to do as a child and then as a teenager in Accrington, I knew I had to live this on my own.

I stared down from the bedroom window at the garden outside. Our house in Eastwood was all I'd ever wanted. With four bedrooms, a huge lounge and a garden, it was perfect for a loving family. But I didn't see anyone or pick up the phone. In fact, I hardly dared go out when I wasn't working, for fear of the trouble it might cause. The only place I went was to the park, with Mevlit, to run off some of the energy that filled him now he was three. Usually just watching him rush around was enough to take me out of myself for a while because he was such a cheerful little thing and so full of life. But when I'd recently gone to the park and sat down on a swing, it was dark before I realized that I'd been lost in my thoughts for hours.

Looking out of the window, I saw a man in his garden cutting grass and children playing. Normal family life. What was happening to me? I was hardly sure any more but knew that I couldn't leave. My childhood had been so unpredictable and uncertain. I'd always known that I was loved, but missed out on the kind of consistency other kids had, the friends and memories I'd never known. I wanted something different for Mevlit.

I could cope with the odd bruise anyway. I'd seen violence all my life: in the pubs as a child and all around me growing up, because men often clocked women in the world I came from. I remembered Dad buying Mum a steak to put on a black eye he gave her once – never again; the purple bruises that often shadowed Auntie Lily's face. Maybe I'd just learned somewhere along the way that occasional violence was what happened between men and women. And Hussain was so loving the moment he'd stopped hitting me that I was sure he'd never do it again. It didn't happen often, after all.

I walked towards a pile of clean washing that lay scattered on the bed and started folding it. I wished I could forget all the questions about Hussain because he still refused to talk to me about what I was certain I knew. But I just wanted to hear the words from him, to understand why he had done what he'd done. Maybe his marriage was over in all but name? There must be some explanation for all this. Whatever it was, I just wanted to hear Hussain admit that I was right. I wanted to know why someone who I had once believed loved me with all his heart had told so many lies. I had to know that I wasn't the one going mad. After all the suspicion and uncertainty, I needed to be sure I wasn't imagining things. I wanted proof I wasn't.

All this and more ran through my head as I walked back to the window and looked out for a final time at the life going on around me. I wondered what husbands and wives were doing together – a bit of DIY, or cooking a meal? Were they laughing together, talking about their children and making plans?

Mevlit was playing with his toy cars in the living room when I went downstairs. This was such a beautiful house for him to grow up in: huge patio windows overlooking the garden lined one end of the room, and I'd painted the walls in pale blue, had matching curtains made with a silver trim. I'd even picked out the colours when I'd painted the coving and the ceiling rose. Then I'd taken off every door in the house, rubbed them down and attached panels to make them look Georgian. Down the corridor was the dining room, painted peach and pale green with a gorgeous walnut table in its centre ready for meals full of laughter and love. Upstairs was Mevlit's room, decorated with white wallpaper embossed with navy-blue and red motorbikes. There were matching curtains and a duvet, and a rug with a picture of a motorbike on it because he was mad about them.

This was the house I'd always wanted, the life I'd dreamed of having since I was a child. But as I looked around it now, I knew it had become my prison.

It was in late 1990, more than two years after the phone call from the woman claiming to be Hussain's wife, that I finally went to see his brother Ali.

'I have to know,' I said to him as we sat in the office of his garment factory in north London. 'I want to know if he's married or if he has children.'

Ali put his head into his hands, as if surprised that a woman could be so stupid.

'Of course he's married,' he finally said. 'Of course he has children.'

I felt the ground give way beneath me as he reeled off a list of names.

'Will you come home with me and talk to him please?' I asked, knowing that this time I couldn't let Hussain lie to me again.

I drove Ali back to our house and listened as he spoke to his brother.

'Why are you doing this?' he asked him. 'Why are you denying your children?'

Hussain didn't say a word. He just got up, picked up his car keys and told Ali that he'd drive him back to London. Later I'd find out that he'd married in Cyprus when he was seventeen and his wife lived about twenty miles from us in Essex. But when Hussain walked back into our home after dropping Ali off, there was only one thing I wanted to know.

'Why, Hussain? Why all these lies? For all these years? Why did you do it?'

He looked at me coldly.

'Because I knew that if I told you the truth, you wouldn't stay with me. And if I can't have you then no one else can.'

Chapter 12

I pulled back the curtain and looked down. Hussain's car was parked outside, just as it had been on so many nights since I'd left him, not long after the conversation with Ali. I'd just packed up and gone one day after finding a flat to rent. All I'd taken were the suitcases stuffed with what Mevlit and I needed because I knew Hussain would never leave if I tried to kick him out. If I warned him about what I was planning, I was also afraid that he might carry out his threats to take Mevlit.

I'd tried to keep where I was going a secret when I rented the flat in Leigh-on-Sea. But Hussain had soon found out where we were. He must either have followed me back from an appointment in the East End after a tip-off from one of his cronies, or waited outside Mum's for me to pick up Mevlit. He hadn't knocked on our door though. Instead, he'd just parked outside it at night, sometimes waiting until morning broke, watching me, letting me know he was there.

The grotty flat was so cold that there were nights when I had to cover the windows with tin foil to try and keep some warmth in the rooms. I'd even wrapped Mevlit up in it one night, a trick I'd learned from Dad as a child when we'd wake up in some of the pubs to find frost covering the inside of the windows. It didn't do much good though, and Mevlit often went to stay with Mum because I didn't want him to get ill.

He'd been there when Hussain had come and taken him without a word as he played in the front garden. Mum was inside and had seen Hussain through the window. By the time she got outside, he'd driven away with Mevlit and refused to let me have him back when I phoned frantic with worry. I knew what Hussain wanted: to force me to go back home. He got his wish. After three days without Mevlit, I couldn't stand it any more and returned home.

Hussain was as remorseless as ever, almost triumphant even. But when I phoned Len a few days later, he heard in my voice how desperate I still was.

'We're on our way,' he said. 'We're coming to get you and Mevlit.'

I'd never thought it was possible that I could love someone almost as much as Dad, but Len had grown to mean so much to me over the years. He was full of kindness and love. But as I threw things into a suitcase, Hussain found me.

'What are you doing?'

'Leaving. I can't do this any more. We're going for good this time.'

'You're not going anywhere.'

'I am. And so is Mevlit.'

As I heard Len's car pull up on the drive, I walked downstairs with Mevlit. Opening the front door, I ushered him outside and watched as he ran to Mum, who put him in the car. Then I turned to get our suitcase and saw Hussain behind me.

'You're not going,' he snarled as he grabbed my arm.

'She is,' Len replied as he grabbed the other.

I wrenched myself away from Hussain as I bent down to pick up the suitcase and throw myself out of the door. But when I turned to pull it closed, I saw Hussain behind me again. He was holding an angle-grinder saw which had been lying in the kitchen because the legs of a new fridge needed to be cut down to get it under the worktop. With a rush of fear, I knew that Hussain wasn't going to try and hurt me this time. His rage was aimed at Len. The two of them had never liked each other: Len was Jewish, Hussain a Muslim, and the religions often don't mix. Now Len was helping me to get away and Hussain couldn't stand it.

'Get out the house!' I screamed at Len, and we ran as Hussain walked out after us.

It was his calmness that scared me most. Hussain just laughed as Len and I ran to the car and jumped in before driving away.

'If you don't get out, Hilary, you're going to end up dead,' Mum said as she turned around to look at me.

It was the first time she'd ever told me that she knew what was happening, and she shook her head in disbelief as she spoke.

After that day, she and Len had made sure to never let Mevlit out of their sight and went shopping in faraway towns rather than risk bumping into Hussain. Meanwhile, I was busy with my job at Scorpio while weekends with Mevlit were spent as they always had been: preparing meals for the week, when he'd be with a childminder or Mum, and enjoying every minute with him.

Hussain was constantly in the back of my mind though. Where was he? What was he going to do? I felt as if I was being slowly crushed by it all, so exhausted by work and all the problems at home that the police had stopped me as I drove back from Leeds one night to ask if I'd been drinking.

'No,' I said. 'What was I doing?'

'Driving erratically,' the officer replied. 'We thought you must have been to a Christmas party. Have you got far to go?'

'About fifteen minutes. I'm sorry. There's just so much going on.'

'Well, wait here and I'll get a car to escort you.'

After following me home, the policeman parked my car.

'Now make sure you get some proper sleep,' he said.

But I didn't in that cold, lonely flat. I felt so unsure about what I was doing. How could I care for Mevlit in a place like this? And what was I going to do about money now that Hussain had emptied our bank account? He'd cleared it of every penny by 11 a.m. on the day after I left with Len, Mum and Mevlit. I had nothing, not even my month's wages, and had had to borrow from Mum. What about our house – all the money I'd saved to put into it and the mortgage payments I'd honoured? If I didn't go back, I'd have nothing.

At least Christmas was coming soon and Mum had invited us to stay. I'd have to decide what to do when the new year came, though, because we couldn't stay with her and Len for ever. In the mean time, I'd forget it all and just make sure that Mevlit had a lovely time. So on the last Saturday before Christmas I took him to visit Santa's grotto at Lakeside with Mum. But as I pulled into the car park, I saw a light flashing on the huge carphone I'd just had installed for work.

'I've got a message,' I told Mum as I bent towards the phone. 'I better listen to it.'

I picked up the receiver and heard a voice start to speak.

'This is a message for Hilary Sharples,' it said. 'This is Rayleigh Police Station. We need to talk to you. Can you please come in to see us before five p.m. today?'

Completely at a loss as to why the police would want anything from me, I took Mevlit to see Father Christmas before dropping him off with Mum at her flat and driving to the station alone. As everyone else in the world hurried home to put on the tree lights and feed their Christmas cake a last tot of brandy, a police officer – who I'll call PC Plod because he was that stupid – told me that my partner Hussain had made an allegation of child abuse against Len. I stared at PC Plod in disbelief. It was an absolute pack of lies.

But even as I tried explaining to him that the whole thing was ridiculous and Mevlit was about to spend a happy Christmas with the Gangan and Nanna he adored, I was told he would either have to go home to Hussain while the allegations were being investigated or be taken into care by social services.

'Are you joking?' I asked. 'This is ridiculous.'

Intent on enjoying his moment of festive cheer, PC Plod wasn't having any of it. As I pleaded and remonstrated with him, he just wouldn't listen.

'There's no way I'm sending my son home to his father with all this going on,' I kept saying. 'And hell will freeze over before my child is taken into care.'

With that, Mevlit walked into the police station with Mum and Len, took one look at me and made a flying leap into my arms.

'Mummy!' he shouted.

'Can't you see he's absolutely fine?' I pleaded. 'Just let him stay with me.'

PC Plod, though, just wasn't budging. My blood boiled as I looked at him and knew he'd already convicted an eighty-one-year-old man of being a paedophile without even a scrap of evidence. Luckily, his boss – who'd overheard everything – had a brain.

'We have to act in the child's interest,' she said as she looked at Mevlit. 'But it's clear that he's well looked after, so if you agree not to go back to your stepfather's address then he can stay with you.'

'Yes. I'll do anything. But can you clear this up as soon as possible?'

'We'll do our best.'

As I gathered Mevlit up and headed towards the door, I heard PC Plod's boss tearing him off a strip. What an unfeeling bastard.

I hit rock bottom that Christmas. After calling my boss Keith Sabey and waffling on about some problems at home, he'd arranged for Mevlit and me to go to a hotel without asking too many questions. Then Mum and Len were both admitted to hospital with heart problems because of the shock of what Hussain had done. As I ran from one side of the hospital to the other, I could hardly believe that he had sunk so low. Or myself either.

Hussain could do what he liked to me. I was so numb to it by now that I almost didn't care any more. But it was another thing when it started to affect Mevlit, Mum and Len. As January got under way, I stayed at Mum and Len's until they came back from hospital before moving back to my freezing flat with Mevlit. There were visits from social workers – who could see that he was happy and well cared for – and he also had to undergo a medical examination, which found no evidence of abuse. It was clear that Len had done nothing wrong and we were told that no charges were going to be brought. But it still sickened me that any father could do such a thing to his four-year-old child, and I felt full of hatred for Hussain.

Towards the end of January, I set off from home at about 5 p.m. because I was going to stay overnight just outside Dewsbury for a business meeting the next day. When my carphone rang, I answered it on speakerphone.

'Hello?'

It was Hussain and in a flash I knew what I was going to do. Grabbing the mini-tape recorder I always carried with me to dictate notes and letters on to as I drove, I switched it on.

'Bobos?' Hussain's voice said.

It was the first time I'd spoken to him since he'd made his allegation of abuse.

'How could you do it?' I exploded. 'How could you subject your own son to social workers and doctors? He's a baby, Hussain. What is wrong with you? You've gone too far this time.'

'Because of that old bastard Len,' I heard Hussain's voice spit over the loudspeaker. 'And if I'm not having you then no one fucking else is.'

I took the tape to the police, who said that they couldn't press charges because they didn't have any evidence to prove that Hussain hadn't believed what he'd said at the time he said it. At least I had the satisfaction of seeing PC Plod squirm, though. He knew how wrong he'd got it.

Try not to throw this book in a corner and scream when I say that I went back to Hussain not long after this. It was partly that I felt lost without him, because when you've been ground down that much, you start to wonder if you can cope alone. Mostly, though, it was a question of money.

I remember a night in our flat when Mevlit cried because he was so hungry, and as I looked at him I knew I couldn't hurt my son, even if it meant I couldn't save myself.

'I think you're more tired than hungry, my darling,' I said to him as he cried. 'Why don't I tuck you up and make you a chucky egg and soldiers?'

Mevlit loved boiled eggs and the toast that went with them because I always let him make faces in the soldiers. Still sobbing, he agreed to lie down until the egg was ready and I clattered around the kitchen as I put on a pan of water to boil, knowing as I did that I didn't have enough to even buy a box of eggs because there wasn't a penny in my purse.

It was completely empty because Mum had started on me when I'd gone to pick up Mevlit a few hours before.

'I need some money for his food, Hilary,' she'd said as soon as I walked through the door. 'We can't keep him all the time, you know.'

She'd had a bad day with Mevlit and I wasn't in any better of a mood because I'd been up at 4 a.m. to drive to Bradford and back. Anger flared up inside me as Mum shouted.

'Well have the lot then,' I'd screamed back as I picked up my purse and emptied it on to the table. 'You're welcome to it.'

With that, I'd picked up Mevlit and stormed out of the house. It was only when we got back to the flat that he told me he hadn't had any dinner and I realized that I didn't have a penny to buy some eggs. I just prayed he'd go to sleep and forget his hunger, which luckily he did. But between trying to care for him as a single parent with a very demanding job and my money worries, I didn't know what I was going to do.

I couldn't dump myself back on Mum and Len in their tiny flat, or keep asking them to have Mevlit so much. But the flat I'd rented was almost uninhabitable and all the money I had was tied up in the equity I'd built up by buying and selling houses. Now it was all invested in the home I'd made so beautiful. The UK was in a deep recession and I was also pretty sure I was going to lose my job at Scorpio, because I'd been told by a good friend that the company was going down the tubes.

What choice did I have? Go back to Hussain or watch my child cry with hunger? Even so, I knew when I returned home with Mevlit that we were either going to have to give up the house in Eastwood or it was going to be repossessed, because I couldn't afford the mortgage payments any more. Interest rates had rocketed and Hussain had never helped me with the bills other than the odd £100 here and there. So after going back I decided to hand the keys back in to the building society – one step short of having our home repossessed – because then they would have to give me some of the money I had in the house if they sold it.

Hussain, though, hardly seemed to care that I was back. In fact, the only time he really spoke to me was when he started screaming abuse and I realized that what he'd said about Len would apply to every other man: even if Hussain didn't want me any more, he didn't want anyone else to have me either. We were trapped in an ever-decreasing circle.

His aggression worsened when we moved into a rented house after he lost the restaurant (about six months after I went home) because his rent arrears and debts had got too much. I wondered how much lower we could go. We had lost our house and now Hussain's business had gone too. I was the one keeping things going and so I did what I'd done for years: clung on to working as hard as I could and caring for Mevlit.

When I was approached by the leading logistics provider TNT about becoming a national sales manager, I jumped at the job. In addition to managing about sixty staff made up of sales reps, logistical analysts, account managers, operations managers and marketers, I would be in charge of getting a £13 million upturn in their hanging-garment business. Working for them plus my previous track record at Tibbet & Britten would allow me to walk into almost any logistics job in the future.

But even though I was back on a good wage with an established company that I knew I could stay with for years, I still didn't leave Hussain. After Mevlit started school, we moved from the place we'd rented to a house in Chafford Hundred, where the arguments just got worse. Like an addict who keeps going back for a fix of what might one day kill them, I couldn't see a way out.

It must have gone on like that for a year or so until a night came which changed everything because it made me realize the most important thing: I couldn't pretend any more that Mevlit wasn't aware of what went on between Hussain and me. It happened as we were arguing after I heard Hussain on the phone telling someone in Turkish that he loved them.

'Are you crazy?' he screamed at me when I asked him about it. 'I was talking to a man.'

'But I know what I heard, Hussain. I've been with you long

enough to understand "I love you". I heard you with my own ears. What's going on?'

'You're crazy, you know? You're a fucking bitch, aren't you? What the fuck's it got to do with you anyway?'

Standing above me as I sat on the sofa, he carried on screaming insults at me until I looked up to see Mevlit crying at the door.

'Mummy!' he cried and Hussain stepped away from me as I got up to go and soothe him.

I couldn't stop thinking about Mevlit after that night. Could I really let him grow up seeing how things were between Hussain and me? Was that what I truly wanted for my son? It was one thing for me to be pushed around and screamed at, but another for a boy to see his mother treated like that. I felt so tired of it all, exhausted. But I still wasn't sure that I could find the strength to leave. It was all I could do to perform at TNT and keep things as calm as possible at home.

I didn't believe Hussain for a second when he told me in late 1991 that he was going to northern Cyprus to investigate setting up a business to export tractors out there. After over-hearing that phone call, I was sure he was going to see another woman, and he made a couple more trips over the next few months. Years later I found out that my suspicions were right. Hussain had got married for a second time because his Muslim faith allowed him to have more than one wife. He was preparing for a new life without me.

I didn't know that back then, but even so my worries about Mevlit slowly sparked something inside me as I thought about what kind of life I wanted for him and what I'd do if I left for good. For a start, I knew I'd have to leave the area to get away from Hussain. But where would we go? All the money I'd put into our houses – and the equity we'd earned from them – had gone, and although I was on a good wage, Hussain had done a good job of spending it. After all my years of hard work, I still had nothing more than my next month's salary.

The more I thought about it, though, the more I knew I didn't want Mevlit to grow up seeing first-hand the poison running between his father and mother. Of course, knowing you must leave and actually going through with it are two very different things. But then I learned an important lesson: that breaking the silence can plant a seed inside which gives you the strength to leave. It happened after I broke down at work in front of a rep who worked for me called Alison Brewin Smith and finally told someone about what was happening. Alison listened sympathetically and told me that I had to get away.

'You could rent a house somewhere new and get a transfer with work,' she said.

I still wasn't sure, but Alison didn't let me off the hook so easily. She soon started looking in local papers for houses close to the TNT headquarters in Atherstone near Leiceister.

'It makes sense to move there,' she told me. 'You'll be closer to work and there are some lovely places to rent.'

It took her about three months to find the right house, but when Alison called to say she'd found a three-bedroom former show home in Leicester, I went to see it and knew instantly that I wanted to build a new life there. After speaking to my bosses, TNT agreed to pay my moving costs and I got a call from an operations manager called Bob Smith.

'Alison has told me what's going on,' he said. 'And no one else needs to know. Just name the date and I'll send some guys down with a lorry big enough for all your things. You women always have so much.'

It was a Sunday afternoon in the summer of 1992 when I walked out into our garden to talk to Hussain. I'd just been to drop off Mevlit at Mum's for the night and knew that we'd be gone by the following morning. I wasn't scared as I walked towards Hussain as he cut tomatoes. The previous week, he'd brandished a knife at me as we argued in the kitchen and I feared then that if I did not leave he would either end up killing me – or I'd kill him in desperation. The threads of what was keeping us together had to be finally cut once and for all.

'I'm leaving with Mevlit tomorrow,' I said.

Hussain didn't say a word as he looked at me and I walked calmly back into the house. He could do what he liked. I didn't care any more. Come tomorrow morning, I would be gone. Hussain didn't touch me though. I think he'd known what was coming for a while because it was as if the fire between us had been slowly burning out for a while now and things had been quieter for a couple of months. So when the TNT lorry pulled up outside the door the next morning and I got into my car, he just stood silently as the movers took every single piece of furniture out of the house.

I was lucky. I honestly believe that for some women there really is no way out, particularly if there are children involved. It's never as easy as simply leaving an abusive partner. It's about finding strength somewhere when it's all been drained out of you; courage after so long spent living in fear; and having the financial resources to leave. Luckily for me, I had a good salary and somehow found the other two buried deep inside me. But I didn't feel triumphant after putting

Mevlit into my car and setting off for Leicester. There was no rousing music playing in my head as the final credits rolled on the film of my life with Hussain. I felt utterly deadened.

Chapter 13

I warned you from the start that this wasn't a story full of Hollywood moments. Funny ones, yes. Inspiring ones, maybe. Daft ones, definitely. But Hollywood ones? No. You see, I didn't leave Hussain and realize with relief what kind of man I'd finally escaped. I was still with him in my head and heart for years after walking out the door because I missed him as I grieved for the fantasy of what we'd lost, the stable family life I'd always wanted. Questioning where I'd gone wrong and what I might have done to change things, it took a long time for me to realize that I'd done the right thing by leaving. Even longer for me to admit to myself that I'd been in an abusive relationship.

After moving to Leicester, I concentrated on work and home like a robot. Between an all-consuming job at TNT and trying to be two parents in one for Mevlit, there was a lot to do. At work I was constantly on the go, with meetings, strategy-planning, managing my team and driving hundreds of miles a week. At home I was cooking, cleaning, ironing, shopping, entertaining, disciplining and loving my child. I didn't have time for a social life or any interests other than my job and Mevlit.

I'd told Hussain where we were going because I wasn't going to stop him from seeing Mevlit. But for the first couple of months he didn't come and actually see us. Instead I'd see his car parked across the green opposite our new house at weekends, or he'd phone Mevlit and tell him that he was living off tomatoes from the garden. He'd look at me in confusion, as if wondering why I'd made Daddy so sad. All I could do was try and make Mevlit's new life as happy as possible. He started at a new school, went to judo classes on a Friday night and we got a dog called Charlie – a cross between a corgi and a Labrador – who we both adored.

We only actually saw Hussain a couple of times and on one of those he arrived with a £100 remote-control car that wasn't suitable for a five-year-old. I made him swap it for a cheaper one and used the rest of the money to do a supermarket shop because Hussain never gave me a penny for Mevlit. I was on a good wage but money was still tight because I'd hired a live-in nanny to care for Mevlit while I worked. Nasreen, who had run away from her abusive family, was living in a refuge run by our next-door neighbour when we met and I grew very fond of her. But between her salary, the rent and bills, plus the money I owed after standing as guarantor for some of Hussain's debts, there wasn't much spare. Later too, credit agencies would find me and ask for repayments on loans I hadn't even known that Hussain had taken out in my name.

The only other contact we had was when I had a phone call from a lawyer telling me to bring Mevlit to London for a visit to see his father.

'I've got one message for your client,' I told him as Hussain's threats to spirit Mevlit away rang in my ears. 'Tell him he needs a psychologist, not a solicitor. I'm not going to drop my child off alone with him. In this life or the next.'

All this and more is why the next two and a half years while I worked at TNT weren't about me picking apart the prison I'd been living in. I just got on with getting through each day. Work and Mevlit. Work and Mevlit. The only time I really allowed myself to grieve about what had happened was when I took Mevlit on a cheap holiday to the sun. After taking him out for dinner before putting him to bed one night, I felt so alone as I sat in our crummy holiday apartment. I howled and howled as everything flooded out of me.

Other than that night, though, I let life wash over me, almost numb to it all. Looking back, I've realized that one important thing did happen during that time: I grasped how badly some businesses were run, and it made me start to think seriously about setting up on my own. And when I did, I had no idea that the girl who'd got kicked out of her first official job by lunchtime was going to become a multi-millionaire.

First things first: TNT is under different ownership today than it was when I worked for it in the mid-1990s, with a very different ethos. Thank God, because it was the worst bloody company I ever worked for. Not that it didn't make money. TNT was a leader in logistics, and the retail division I worked for was unusual because it was struggling when I joined it. It had been set up purely to service contracts with BhS and Next for their hanging-garment distribution, but now they were both talking about terminating their relationship with TNT. That's why I was charged with replacing £13 million in lost revenue – and did it within a couple of years, after striking deals with Jaeger, Burberry, Frank Usher, Austin Reed and

House of Fraser to use TNT to transport their clothes. I didn't undercut on price because that's never been the way I've worked. Instead I offered better service.

The trouble with TNT was how they got their profits: by chewing people up and spitting them out. Things were rotten behind the scenes and despite all the sales I'd brought in and the subsequent rise in profits, my division started to lose money again because the operations managers above me failed to respond to my sales projections and put enough staff and vehicle resource in place to manage the growth. We had vehicles stacked with garments but no drivers, or clothes waiting to be put on lorries that weren't there.

When a new management team was brought in above me, I swear I wouldn't have batted an eyelid if men in black coats and limos had turned up to spirit people away because they were that ruthless. I completely disagreed with their approach, because even then I believed that looking after your human resource was key to the success of any business. But the powers-that-be at TNT didn't see employees as people, just numbers on a sheet, and if the number crunchers noticed that one of my team was down on sales, I knew that I was expected to sack them.

Everyone has peaks and troughs, though. Salespeople just cannot keep up consistently high results week in, week out, because they're people – not robots. Then as now, I believed that man management was about finding out what made people tick, because it's not always targets and money. Some people need to be patted on the back, others want the security that comes with being micro-managed. Or there are those who want to work hard all week until early Friday afternoon, when they slip off home a few hours early. Most of these are women, anxious to get the weekend supermarket shop done or to get on to the motorway in time to pick up their kids from school. But if people produced results and worked well for me all week then I wasn't going to demotivate them by clock-watching.

The management didn't agree, and I was told to sack two women after it was discovered that they left early on Fridays. Women always got the rough end of the stick back then at TNT: never promoted as readily, paid less and disciplined more easily. It's true that women have a harder time in the workplace than men, but then again they have a harder life in general, don't they?

If you're a wife and mother who doesn't work outside the home then you already have three jobs: as a daughter who generally looks after her parents, a mother who looks after her children and a wife who looks after her husband and home. If you work too, then you have four jobs. How many men have polished shoes, packed lunchboxes, put homework into bags, made breakfast, cleared it up, hoovered and driven kids to school before a 9 a.m. meeting? Not many. I've lost count of the times I've walked into boardrooms and looked at the men around the table with their ironed shirts, clean homes, cared-for children and dinner on the table and wondered what they did with all their spare time.

As a single parent, there was never any lenience shown towards me: if there was a meeting at Bradford at eight on a Monday morning I just had to be there, child or no child. I accepted it – that was my job – and when I'm asked why there aren't more women in boardrooms, the answer is simple: many of them don't want to make the sacrifices that I had to. I didn't have a social life. I wasn't interested in men.

I cared for my child, made a home for us and worked. That was it.

But my experiences as a single parent meant that I wanted to give the people in my team some flexibility. When I wasn't trusted to do so, my job at TNT felt more and more untenable and I didn't make any friends when I refused to play ball with the working culture. When one colleague made it clear that I had to make sure he shagged a female account manager on my team, I told him to eff off.

'You've just signed your resignation,' he snarled.

Bit by bit, I had enough of it all. I was long enough in the tooth by now to know that working in a man's world was always going to be tough for a woman, and I could cope with that. But I couldn't stand the blatant unfairness of life at TNT because it meant that I couldn't do my job properly.

'I'll put things right,' my boss insisted when I resigned and told him that I was going to sue for constructive dismissal.

Bollocks he would.

After leaving TNT, I needed money to see me through until I found another job, and reluctantly went to the local DSS office, where I was told I'd be visited by someone to assess whether I qualified for benefits. When the bloke arrived, he told me he'd make sure I'd be able to sign on in return for some 'favours'. I wasn't that desperate. But after realizing that the only job I'd be able to find was yet another position driving the length and breadth of the country, I knew I couldn't do the fifteen-hour days or overnight stays any more. I wanted to be at home more with Mevlit and see him day to day, so I decided to become a freelance logistics consultant. Within a couple of weeks, three companies I'd contacted had all agreed to use me. At least I was earning again, and while it was hard work, because I knew my services would be dispensed with if I didn't continuously perform, it meant food on the table.

But as I got to work again, I became more and more convinced that I wanted to start my own business. Because the more I looked back on my working life, the more inspired I was to think that I could do it. The entrepreneurial spirit I'd had ever since I was a kid would help me create a company; the lessons I'd learned from Dad and Hussain about how to run a business – and how not to – would help me build it; and the realization that no salaried job was safe would give me the determination to provide stability for myself and Mevlit whatever obstacles were put in my way. If I started my own business, I would do things differently. I'd learned so much at TNT about bad practice and knew that I wanted employees to be given chances and the opportunity to be promoted from within. All these things would combine to make my business a success.

While I researched ideas, though, I would earn my bread and butter as a freelance consultant and with no fixed income needed to cut down my living costs, so I moved back down to Essex to be closer to Mum and Len. As ever, they were more than happy to help with childcare and I'd missed them while we'd been in Leicester. But I also felt guilty about the upheaval it would mean for Mevlit, because aged just seven he'd already been to two schools and would now have to start at a third when we moved again.

It wouldn't be ideal for any child, but Mevlit had always struggled with reading and writing. I'd known from the time he went to school that he made little progress with them and whenever Mum or I sat down with him to look at a book, he just couldn't seem to recognize the words. But while I thought the problems would be sorted out at school, they'd just got worse, and I was also increasingly aware that Mevlit resented my work. If I made calls when I was at home, he'd play up to get my attention or start colouring Charlie's fur with a marker pen. I felt very guilty about it. Mevlit just wanted the normal family life that every child craves, after all. But with his dad gone, I had to keep paying the bills.

I've never met a man who feels guilty about leaving his kids to go to work in the way that a woman does. It goes back to evolution, doesn't it? The man is the provider and the woman is the nurturer. I don't think men ever worry about a home and children in the same way as women do, and it's hard when you're a mother who works – and particularly so if you're a single working mother.

Deep inside me was the memory of those bailiffs who'd come to empty our home when I was about Mevlit's age. I didn't want that for him. I wanted to provide well for him *and* have a career that fulfilled my ambition. If that makes me selfish, then so be it. Thousands of men have both, don't they?

I worried a lot about Mevlit's problems at school though, and wanted desperately to find a solution to them. As my consultancy work got under way, I even took him to see a child psychologist, who told me to give up work and be a full-time mother. How could I do that? I wanted a better life for my son than I'd had. Plus, I couldn't change what I was: a hard worker who gave her all to her job.

I was torn between my career and my child. Like most women, I did the best I could.

*

It was a wet and grey February afternoon and I was standing in the office of a haulier's in South Wales.

'So what is your fleet compilation and what does your O licence allow you to run?' I asked the haulier. 'Can you tell me how you'd operate new business alongside your current commitments?'

I was meeting him because I was consulting for a retailer who wanted me to find hauliers to transport garments to their shops. It was the kind of work I'd been doing ever since leaving TNT the year before, because sadly the first business idea I'd worked on, with Adrian Russell and Keith Sabey, my old Scorpio friends, hadn't panned out. They'd started their own logistics company called Rapide after leaving Scorpio and one of the jobs I'd helped them consult on was advising a company called Palletways which provided palletized freight services to hauliers – in essence moving smaller consignments of goods that weren't large enough to fill a whole lorry.

A pallet is basically a huge wooden base measuring four foot by four that a forklift truck can move on and off lorries. Palletways was a hub-and-spoke operation, which meant that hauliers paid a fee to join the scheme and deliver all their goods on pallets to its central depot – the hub – where their consignments were loaded on to lorries owned by other members who delivered it for them anywhere in the UK – the spokes. Hauliers were basically swapping their goods and delivering them for each other.

The model had first been developed in the 1970s by Frederick Smith, who started FedEx in America after realizing that the traditional point to point way of moving freight wasn't going to keep up with an ever-changing society. It then came to the UK and revolutionized things. Until then a haulier in

Manchester who had a few boxes to go to Truro might have to wait up to ten days to fill his lorry with consignments from other customers destined for Truro before making the journey. Once the lorry had got to Cornwall, it either had to come back empty – which was a waste of manpower and resources – or the driver had to wait for the lorry to be filled again with a backload – which once again wasted time.

The new system meant that Mr Manchester didn't have to wait to fill his lorry with freight destined for Truro any more. He could just fill it up with goods to be delivered anywhere in the UK and drive it to the hub. There, it was picked up by other member hauliers who delivered it for him – while Mr Manchester loaded their consignments on to his lorry. Once the hauliers got the freight back to their own depots, it was put on to delivery vehicles. Suddenly they could offer overnight delivery, instead of asking customers to wait for days for their goods to reach their destination.

Palletways' warehouse lay empty for most of the day though until the trucks delivered freight into it at night, and the bosses there wanted to know if there was a way to better use this space. It's called sweating your assets – and basically means making the most of them. A lorry isn't paying its way if its wheels aren't turning twenty-four hours a day. A warehouse that's empty for half of the day is not being used to its fullest capacity. It's a waste of resources.

The idea that Adrian, Keith and I had come up with was to set up our own business distributing clothes for retailers – the kind of thing I'd been doing ever since working at Tibbet & Britten – using Palletways' warehouse space. But the more we'd researched it, the more we'd realized that the numbers just didn't stack up. There would never be enough profit, because stopping a vehicle costs money and the revenue we'd make per delivery wouldn't be enough.

It left me with a problem. I'd spent my whole logistics career working in the hanging-garment sector. If I couldn't develop a profitable business idea in that area then what was I going to do?

I stared out at the yard in south Wales. It was filled with lorries sitting empty under a grey sky as they waited to be filled. Never mind Palletways' empty warehouse hours. This was just as much of a waste of rolling stock and capital investment. It made no sense. Why weren't these lorries being used to their fullest capacity? The asset sweated to make the haulier the most money possible?

But many hauliers like this one didn't want to become members of a hub-and-spoke operation because the industry was a bit like the Wild West. Trust between hauliers was low, because people couldn't always be sure their goods would be delivered efficiently and haulage companies often went bust too. If they went bankrupt as members of a hub-and-spoke operation then the hauliers who'd delivered their goods for them would not get paid, so many people didn't want to get involved in such schemes.

There was also a fair bit of protectionism at work. If a haulier was using his vehicles more efficiently then he wouldn't need so many lorries – or drivers. He also wouldn't need the traffic operators who rang around his customers to get the lorries filled. The world of transport was a boys' club and they wanted things to stay the same as they'd always been.

And it was then, as I looked at those lorries, that I had the thought that would change my life. Remember the time when I decided to become an entrepreneur as I sat on the lino with a freezing arse? Now I looked out at that yard and wondered if I could deliver more than hanging garments. Could I create a business that did things so differently that hauliers like this one would be prepared to sign up to it? Setting up a hanging-garment distribution network was a complicated process because it involved finding hauliers who owned specialist articulated lorries. The beauty of a pallet network was that any haulier with standard forty-foot vehicles could use it. And right now, I was staring at empty lorries which would be able to put freight into my network.

It was almost too simple. Then again, it would involve skills not just related to logistics but sales, marketing and financing too. I didn't feel afraid though as I looked across the yard and contemplated doing something that no woman had ever done before me. In fact, the moment I had the idea, I felt utterly convinced I could make a success of it.

Chapter 14

The bank manager looked at me.

'I'm afraid I can't give you a loan,' he said, and my heart sank.

'Why not?'

'Because I don't think this business will work.'

'But have you read my business plan?'

'Yes. I don't think it will work.'

It was the summer of 1996 and I was sitting in the HSBC in Rayleigh, Essex. I'd come to ask for a loan of £20,000 to help set up the company I was going to call Pall-Ex after my accountant had registered its VAT and trademark.

For the previous year, I'd lived, breathed and slept my idea to create a palletized freight network. A woman possessed had nothing on me after my eureka moment in the haulier's office, because I knew that if I was going to set up this company then it wasn't just the figures that would have to stack up, but the business model too.

I'd have to cost my product right so that, as well as making my own profit, the hauliers who joined the network would increase their margins too. By attracting the very best hauliers in the country as the founder members of my network, I'd ensure that the company succeeded – and to do that I had to fully conceptualize my business in order to sell it to them. Remember Lillian Finan and the Littlewoods union? This was basically the same thing. I didn't have a tangible product to sell – just the *idea* of a freight network that would do things differently to anyone else.

In the months that followed my trip to Wales, I'd developed idea after idea which had crystallized into my business model. Firstly I was going to offer unprecedented flexibility to my members, because until now hauliers had had to pay for a whole pallet capable of carrying a tonne of goods even if they didn't have enough freight to fill it. I was going to offer them the option of a half- or quarter-pallet. By offering more flexible pallet sizes, my haulier members would be able to attract customers with smaller loads to deliver and increasing transportation costs to drive down – and I'd get their business through my hub.

Pall-Ex was also going to be structured unlike any other hub-and-spoke network. To combat the bad practices and mistrust in the industry, I was going to make my business efficient and accountable. There would be a 'member service agreement' listing every aspect of a haulier's responsibilities as a Pall-Ex member; contracts with each one to formalize our work together; and an insolvency trust fund, which each member would pay into, ensuring that bills got paid if a haulier member went bust – thus reducing the risk for everyone involved.

There would also be set inter-member delivery rates, because the country would be banded depending on how far lorries drove to deliver goods. I would make my money by charging each Pall-Ex member a transshipment cost, which would cover their use of the hub, administrating the transport and logistics of the loads from one vehicle to another, the IT and payment systems and management of the insolvency trust fund.

I'd written my business plan in two weeks and predicted that Pall-Ex would be delivering 1,000 pallets a night by the end of year one, 2,000 by the end of year two and 3,000 by the end of year three. Now I needed about £80,000: enough to rent the hub, three forklift trucks and a Portakabin that I'd use as an office, and to pay wages and my living costs until I could take an income.

So far I'd managed to get together about £60,000, by saving the money TNT had paid me when they'd settled my suit for constructive dismissal before it went to tribunal, and selling some shares I'd bought at Tibbet & Britten before the company floated on the stock market. There was also a significant chunk of money I'd saved since leaving Hussain, because if there was one thing I'd learned with him, it was just how easy it was for the rainy days to come. Then there was some equity I'd got back after the building society had sold the house that I'd handed the keys back in on when I was with Hussain. Now I just needed a £20,000 loan.

'I think this business will be a success,' I said to the bank manager. 'I have seventeen years' experience in the world of logistics, I know my industry well and my business plan is good.'

He looked at me.

'I'm just not sure. To be honest I think you should go home and look after your child.'

'Pardon me?'

'You're a woman trying to do business in a man's world *and* a single parent. I'm afraid that I'm not going to give you a loan. Or an overdraft.'

I stared at the bank manager in disbelief. Was he joking?

'But the fact that I'm a single parent gives me all the more reason to make this work and put a roof over my child's head.'

'Well, I wish you luck.'

Figures ran through my head. I could sell my car, which must be worth at least £10,000. Then there was all the jewellery that Hussain had given me. Surely I could scrape together the rest of what I needed if I sold pretty much everything I had?

'Thank you for your time,' I said and walked out the door.

I wasn't going to plead for help from that misogynistic bastard.

There were 10,666 hauliers registered with the Road Haulage Association in the UK in 1996. I'd calculated that I needed thirty of them to sign up as Pall-Ex founder members in order for the network to deliver to all of the UK's 126 postcodes. After that meeting with the bank manager, I determined to sign them up within three months so that Pall-Ex could start trading by the end of September. I had a business plan which detailed every aspect of how the company would work day to day, a bank account, a VAT number, and had sold everything I could to raise cash – including an antique coal scuttle that Mum had given me that fetched £1,250.

Now I had to convince people to become Pall-Ex members and that was when the hard work really started. For months now I'd been taking down names and numbers of hauliers as I drove around the country doing my consultancy work. I wanted each of my founder members to pay £1,000 to join my network, but knew I wouldn't cash the cheques until the company had been trading a month. I had to be sure that Pall-Ex was going to work before I took their money. But even so, I still needed to sign up founder members to form the operating basis of my network and encourage others to buy into my concept and make it a reality.

It wasn't rocket science. After buying the Road Haulage Association directory and Yellow Pages on computer disk, I scanned though name after name and started contacting people. I'd even stop at traffic lights and write down the company details printed on the sides of lorries stopped beside me.

'My name is Hilary Sharples and I'm setting up a hub-and-spoke pallet network,' I'd say, and often the line would go dead before the words were even out of my mouth.

Or a haulier would agree to see me and then start to laugh when I got in front of him.

'What do you know about driving a truck, love?'

'Not much,' I'd tell him. 'But I know more about business than you do. Look at those lorries parked idle outside. They shouldn't be. They're rolling stock: they should be rolling, working night and day.'

When he heard about my business plan, the haulier would normally start to listen. Except the ones that were blind, stupid and deaf, and I knew they wouldn't be in business much longer so I didn't want them as Pall-Ex members.

I must have phoned hundreds of companies and driven thousands and thousands of miles over the next few months as I worked day and night. I just had to convince a few hauliers to talk to me, because if they did I was sure I could sell them Pall-Ex – and then others would come to me because the industry was so incestuous that everyone talked. I couldn't approach just anyone, though. My business was going to be built on reputation and I needed to know that every haulier who became a part of Pall-Ex was financially stable. If they couldn't produce an operating licence (which would prove they had cash in the bank to maintain their vehicles, because they wouldn't be granted one without it) then I would refuse them membership. I wasn't going to damage my business by sacrificing quality. I just had to hold my nerve until I got the right member for the right area.

Within a couple of weeks, a Cardiff-based haulage company called Logicline that I'd worked with in the past had contacted me. They'd heard about what I was doing and wanted to offer UK next-day delivery. After talking them through the numbers, they agreed to sign up. What convinced them to take a chance on a woman with no tangible product? The fact that I knew my business plan didn't have a chink in it. It gave me an unshakeable passion and conviction for what I was doing. With that, I couldn't fail to succeed.

I'd had a long day. A really long day. After getting up at 4 to drive to a 9 a.m. meeting in Manchester with Failsworth Haulage – who I'd signed up – I'd gone to Liverpool to see A&M Transport, who'd knocked me back. Then I'd driven across the M62 and up the A1 to see Elddis Transport in County Durham and Moody Logistics in Newcastle. I'd signed up Moody's but Elddis hadn't bitten.

The day had been OK but not as successful as it could have been, and so I was in no mood for bullshit when I walked into my final meeting of the day at Stalkers Transport in Cumbria at 7 p.m. From there I was going to drive up to stay in Edinburgh overnight for more appointments the next day.

Walking into the offices wearing a smart black skirt and blouse, I asked to see Hughie Stalker but was told he wasn't there. His brother Gerry would talk to me instead, and I went into a room full of traffic operators, most of whom looked like they'd eaten a few too many Yorkie bars. Gerry was sitting in the middle, chain-smoking, wearing jeans and a checked shirt, as drivers walked in and out of the room after finishing their shifts.

I sat down wearily but forced myself to focus. However long my days were, I had to make the most of each meeting and Stalkers would be a great haulier to become part of the network. But as I started talking, I could see that Gerry just wasn't in the mood to listen. In fact, he laughed at most of what I had to say.

'It's just not economical for you to be running vehicles across the whole country,' I said. 'If you join Pall-Ex then you can reduce your vehicle fleet and capital expenditure and increase your sales and revenue. You will make a lot of money.'

'Aye, pet,' Gerry replied with a laugh, as the other blokes in the room sniggered with him. 'But can you drive a truck?'

'No. But by the looks of it I could run your business better than you are.'

'But I don't want to run less lorries, pet. I like my lorries.'

'Even if running too many of them doesn't make you money?'

It was like that for the next half-hour because everything I said, Gerry roared with laughter and in the end I'd had enough.

'If you can't listen to me about a venture that will make

your company money then I'm not hanging around,' I said. 'I haven't got time to talk to such an ignorant twat.'

I stormed out with the sound of Gerry's laughter still ringing in my ears and thought that was the end of it. But the next day I realized that I might have got him wrong when I got a call from Hughie as I drove home to Essex from Scotland.

'I'm sorry I wasn't there to see you,' he said, and I wondered if Gerry had seen more sense in what I'd said than he'd let on. 'Can you come in to see me on your way down?'

Even if Gerry had given me a good report, I wasn't going to give in too easily.

'No,' I replied. 'I've been away overnight and I have to get back to my son.'

'How about Monday then?'

'I can't see you. I've got to visit my hub site in Leicestershire.'

'Well why don't I meet you there?'

Now that was a bit more serious. We arranged to meet on Monday.

I'd found the hub in a village called Wymeswold, midway between Nottingham and Leicester. I was going against the grain by choosing to locate in the East Midlands, because every other logistics provider was based in the West Midlands. But just looking at a map had told me that the East Midlands was the true geographical centre of the country, and I also felt sure the area would be given a huge boost by expansion at East Midlands Airport, which would mean that more freight forwarders – people who have loads to move but no lorries of their own – would be looking for hauliers who'd need to use my hub. Besides, space in the West Midlands was at a premium and I could get a better price per foot in the East

Midlands. It needed to be as cheap as possible because there wasn't a penny to spare.

The hub didn't have to be fancy. Just somewhere large enough for lorries to move in and out of to deliver freight. And what was the cheapest space I could get? A disused aircraft hangar. I'd found what I was looking for in Wymeswold and when the owner told me it had planning permission for business use, I said I'd rent it.

After going to the site on Monday, I drove to the village pub to meet Hughie and knew immediately that he meant business. He listened closely to what I had to say before asking about me, and I understood why. There were so many bad practices in the haulage industry that the best relationships were based on personal trust and respect. I told Hughie about Mevlit and our life together and he told me about the first grandchild that his daughter was expecting.

'My wife Mabel can't wait,' he told me. 'But I'm wondering if he or she will take over our life?'

'Probably!' I said, and laughed as I told him about how much time Mum and Len spent looking after Mevlit.

'So shall we go and see this hub of yours then?' Hughie asked as we finished our drinks.

Standing in the middle of a field looking at a tin hut that had seen better days since being built in World War Two, Hughie started to laugh.

'How are you going to get a phone in here?' he asked. 'And electricity too?'

I turned to him and smiled.

'Where there's a will there's a way, Hughie.'

He held out his hand to shake mine.

'That's the spirit, Hilary,' he said. 'I'm in and I'll never let you down.'

He was as good as his word. Hughie and I still do business together today.

If Pall-Ex was going to go live on 1 September 1996 then I had to get the hub up and running quickly. To help me, I took on a friend called Andy de Vere, who I'd worked with at TNT. Patient, hard-working and tenacious, I knew he'd be an asset, and while I continued to drive the length and breadth of the country, he was on a mobile setting up meetings and sourcing new leads in the hunt for founder members. Meanwhile, I waited for the BT engineers to come and inspect the site. And waited. And waited.

They eventually turned up after the August bank holiday and then told me they couldn't fit lines because they had to cross a piece of land belonging to the man who ran a go-karting track next to my site. To do that, they'd have to serve Queen's Notice on the land – which would take weeks. I'd never be up and trading by the end of September as I'd planned – and budgeted – to be.

By now I was paying rent, had employed three forklift drivers who needed wages and was running out of money fast. But I had no choice other than to wait for BT to place the lines because Pall-Ex couldn't operate without a phone line. I was truly down to my last brass farthing when Pall-Ex first started trading on 29 November 1996, because I still hadn't cashed the joining fees that my twenty-nine founder members had paid. Thirty lorries rolled into the hub on the first night that Pall-Ex traded and 117 pallets were moved, which earned me £2.85 each. It added up to £333.45 but I knew I'd lose money by the time I'd paid the forklift drivers, my night hub manager and Andy – who took only what I could give him, bless his heart.

I don't remember sleeping much during those first few months of trading. Actually, make that the first few years! During the day I was running the business – liaising with hauliers, looking for new ones to recruit, doing invoices and admin plus sorting out the scores of tiny problems that every day brought. It could be anything from dealing with the black bags of belongings that one angry wife of a lorry driver dumped on my office floor as she told me that she'd had enough of his womanizing, to getting tough with members in order to show them that I wouldn't allow them to contravene our agreement in any way.

For instance, I'd made all my hauliers sign a contract agreeing to pay hub fees every seven days to ensure that I had money in the bank within a week of trading – and kept it there. So every Monday night without fail, I got the invoices on to the lorries, sent them back to their depots and waited for the cheques to come back the next week. But when one member let me down, I told her that I wasn't going to offload her lorry when it rolled into the hub.

'Sorry, Jean,' I said. 'No cheque, no freight.'

I soon got my cheque. But when another haulier from the north-east bounced a cheque on me twice, I warned him that I'd expel him if he did it again. He did and I was as good as my word. He called me a c*nt but I didn't care. He was out of Pall-Ex for good because I had to honour my commitments to my members, which meant I'd be strict when needed. I had to laugh though when a transport magazine printed a cartoon of me in thigh-length boots with a whip in my hand

and hauliers cowering at my feet. It was captioned *The hub mistress*. But as I've said, I was a woman so I could do things differently to how they'd ever been done before.

The nights were just as full as the days. By 7 p.m. I was back in the tin hut, checking the freight in off lorries and doing consignment notes for where it was being moved on to. It was only at about 3.30 a.m., when the lorries had all finally gone for the night, that I'd go home to sleep. Three and a half hours later I'd get Mevlit up, give him breakfast and take him to school. Then I'd work until 3 p.m., go and pick him up from school, take him home and stay with him until the childminder arrived at 5 p.m. before going back to work. Most nights I'd pop back to say good-night to him before returning to the hub. It was relentless.

A month after we started trading, I looked in my purse and realized that I had eleven pence in it. After paying the Christmas wages, I didn't even have enough for that month's hub rent. To say that the delay caused by the BT fiasco had severely dented my cash flow would be an understatement. But I'd known from the moment I'd started Pall-Ex that I was going to do some things differently to Dad – however much I'd learned from him – and his habit of sailing close to the wind was one thing I wasn't going to repeat. I was going to honour promises, never make ones I couldn't keep and always be direct.

Picking up the phone on December 23, I called my landlord and asked him to come and see me.

'I can't pay you,' I said. 'But I promise that I will as soon as I can.'

He scowled at me like the Grinch itself.

'If you don't trust me and allow me time to pay you then I'm going to have to close,' I said.

My landlord looked at me sitting in my office with black shadows under my eyes.

'If I hadn't come down here and seen you then I wouldn't have believed what you had to say,' he said with a sigh. 'But now I have, I will.'

Thank goodness that Mum and Len had arrived earlier that day with a turkey and a new bike for Mevlit. Without them, it would have been a very miserable Christmas indeed.

Chapter 15

Hard work pays dividends. Pall-Ex grew from the day it started trading and after having Christmas Day off, I spent the rest of the holiday rejigging my business plan because I knew that I'd soon need money to spend on branding and marketing.

A new bank manager called Peter Bond had agreed to visit me on site in early January. After my accountant Bill and I met to go over the figures one final time the night before the meeting, we nipped to the pub for a drink. Shame I then emptied the ashtray into a bin full of paper and started a fire in my Portakabin! Thankfully Peter didn't let my charred office put him off and had enough vision to give me a £20,000 overdraft.

I didn't use it in the end, though, because pallets started to come through the door the moment the new year began and my cash flow soon started to move again. One of the things I'm most proud of about the company I built is that we didn't have a bank loan until much later, when we underwent a massive expansion. Today we're one of the few companies who are allowed to direct-debit our invoice costs – it's usually only utility companies who can do that.

We can because I built a strong credit rating from the day

Pall-Ex began by being a stickler for costs. OK then, make that tight. But I'm not going to apologize for it. You don't make a profit by chance. You make money by strategizing, being creative and always, always remembering your bottom line. In my mind, every penny I spent was measured by how many pallets I'd have to move to earn that money, and I was determined not to overspend.

So rather than buying new ink cartridges for the photocopier, I injected ink into them myself with a syringe. Instead of paying to get water on to the site, I shared chemical loos with the lorry drivers and soon learned excellent bladder control after realizing that they couldn't aim at a lav from a foot away. If members came for a meeting I'd make their sandwiches, and I didn't have a cleaner for my Portakabin office. Instead I did the vacuuming and polishing myself and bought such old, cheap furniture that I talked one prospective member off his chair. Literally. The bloody thing collapsed as I spoke to him, but I didn't stop trying to sell him Pall-Ex even as he hit the floor.

Make no mistake, I wasn't chasing money or wealth, because I didn't set up my own business to be rich. I started it because I had a dream of building a company that did things with excellence – and had a strong balance sheet. So I ran my business like I ran my home as a single parent, and accounted for every penny. For the first three years, all I paid myself was what I needed for rent and food. The only luxuries I allowed were the money I spent on sending Mevlit for specialist dyslexic teaching twice a week in Loughborough – because I'd finally discovered the source of his problems at school – and a Chinese takeaway the two of us shared every Friday night.

As 1997 started, I kept on recruiting new members alone

because Andy was far too good to stay with my tin-hut empire. Month by month, I saw a steady upturn in the number of pallets we were moving each night and Pall-Ex was going so well that I probably should have realized there'd be a cock-up somewhere along the way. I had no idea it was coming, though. Or that it would almost spell the end of all I'd built when it did.

By spring 1997, I was confident enough to leave Pall-Ex for a week in the hands of three people I trusted: a woman called Glenys Hargreaves, who'd joined me to help with network recruitment, my accountant Bill Crawford and my night manager. After buying a £99 holiday for Mevlit and me, we went off to Turkey. But on the second day, I got a phone call from Bill, who told me that the local council was threatening to place a stop order on the hub – and order it to cease trading.

I'd been assured that planning permission for business use of the site was in place, but it wasn't, and I'd been too wet behind the ears to ask to actually see it. You live and learn, and like many new entrepreneurs I'd made a mistake. Trouble was, it could cost me everything. The local residents, sick of articulated trucks trundling past their windows all night, were demanding that the council closed us down. I wasn't surprised they were making a fuss if the right planning consent wasn't in place but there was no way I could let them stop me trading. It would mean the end of Pall-Ex.

I couldn't afford new flights but Mum managed to persuade the travel company to take Mevlit and me home two days later by telling them that I'd forgotten the insulin I'd been put on to when my diabetes had flared up again. I'd controlled it through diet for a long time after having Mevlit, but the stress caused by leaving Hussain and working so hard had kick-started the illness again and I now injected myself three or four times a day and had piled on more than three stone in weight.

I arrived back from Turkey in the early hours of a Sunday morning and by 8 a.m. had started hitting the phones to call every single councillor and MP I could get hold of. I didn't care if they were having a lie-in or their roast lunch. There was no way they were going to shut me down.

You see, then as today, the Pall-Ex motto was 'Failure is not an option'. I'd come up with it as I looked at Mevlit sleeping one night and known that my business had to succeed because I'd put every penny I had into it. I'd lose everything if it didn't work, and while I might be able to dust myself off if that happened, there was no way I was going to put Mevlit through what had happened to me as a child.

I couldn't breathe a word about what was happening to anyone, though, because if members discovered the hub was under threat they might decide to leave the network. So when I found out that the stop order was due to be discussed at the next local council meeting, I knew it was my only chance to make those bureaucrats see sense. After spending every spare minute lobbying anyone I could think of, I got to the meeting early enough to get a seat at the front, only to be told that I couldn't speak when an item about a certain aircraft hangar in Wymeswold came up for discussion.

'I thought we lived in a democracy,' I said as I stood up, not taking a blind bit of notice of what I'd been told. 'I want to speak on behalf of the people I employ, my son whose liveli-hood you're taking away, and myself whose business you're threatening.'

As the councillors huffed and puffed, I just kept talking. They couldn't get a word in edgeways as I pleaded my case and told them that they couldn't shut me down.

'If we listen to this then we might as well roll on our backs with our legs in the air and have our tummies tickled!' one Conservative councillor complained.

Thankfully I didn't have to do that. His tummy would have taken hours to tickle. But I did manage to persuade the council to give me a stay of execution for a few months. Now I just had to find a new hub.

When my old friend Keith Sabey discovered that I was looking for a new site, I told him it was because Pall-Ex was outgrowing our current one. It was almost true. On his way back home, Keith saw a TO LET sign in Gotham, Nottinghamshire, and called me. British Gypsum's former distribution centre was up for rent because it was no longer in use. It was perfect.

Only trouble was that getting to talk to any of the British Gypsum powers-that-be was like trying to get down the Yellow Brick Road, past the velvet curtain and face to face with the Wizard of Oz. After discovering that the person I needed to talk to about renting the distribution centre was a man called Dr Noel Worley, I was on the phone to him on the hour, day after day.

Could I get through to him though? Could I 'eck. He was out, he was busy, he'd return my call, he was in a meeting. In the end, I'd had enough. Time was ticking away. If Dr Worley wasn't going to agree to speak to me then I'd have to make him. Arriving at the British Gypsum offices just up the road from Gotham at seven one morning, I waited until reception opened.

'Is Dr Noel Worley here?' I asked the moment it did.

'Do you have an appointment?'

'No.'

'I'll see if he's free.'

If I tell you that I sat in that reception until the end of the day without a thing to eat or drink or a trip to the loo then you'll know how much I wanted to see Dr Worley. When I tell you that I didn't have a fag either, you'll realize just how desperate I was. By the time I walked into his office, I was ready to beg.

Luckily I didn't need to, because Dr Worley was happy to listen. Only trouble was, he was going to have to go high up the ladder to get the right permissions to rent me the site and the whole thing took weeks as it dragged through the wheels of British Gypsum. But finding somewhere that between sixty and a hundred lorries could get into – and out of – each night wasn't easy so I had to wait. All I could do was keep working to build Pall-Ex, knowing I might lose everything but unable to tell a soul.

I've said before that you have to learn to deal with problems in business instead of getting daunted by them. But those months of worry stretched me to the limit and the final straw almost came when the British Gypsum bosses agreed to rent me the distribution centre – before telling me that I had to give them a £60,000 rent bond. It was money I didn't have. Neither would a bank lend it to me because my balance sheet wasn't worth tuppence.

But then Glenys, who'd become a close friend since starting to work for me, offered to lend me the money and threw me a lifeline that I still treasure today. We agreed that I would pay it back with interest, and diggers rolled on to the Gotham site at the eleventh hour to dig a track to the hub. The building's main doors were also extended to allow the lorries to drive through.

When I took Bill to see the site for the first time, he turned to me in shock.

'You must be mad,' he exclaimed. 'You'll be bankrupt in a month.'

I would say, 'Bloody accountants,' but Bill had been a gem after starting to work part-time with me about two months after setting up and was understandably concerned. What I've forgotten to mention, you see, is that the Gotham hub was 78,000 square foot – nearly 50,000 more than we'd been filling in Wymeswold. Add in the fact that my business wasn't going to turn a profit in its first yearly accounts after my set-up costs had been factored in – which meant my company wasn't actually worth anything yet – and you might understand why Bill was worried.

'I'll fill it with new business within six months,' I told him.

I knew I'd prove Bill wrong – if for no other reason than I couldn't find anywhere else to house the hub. I was committed to staying in the area that would offer business opportunities at the right price per square foot, and this hub was it.

You can't build a business alone, though. I've never been someone who shies away from delegation and by the time we left Wymeswold my old friend Adrian Russell had joined Pall-Ex as my operations director, leaving me free to concentrate on new-member recruitment and liaison with existing ones. As we neared the end of our first year, we'd expanded from twenty-nine members to forty-two and I knew we could find so many more.

Adrian came in to take over the day-to-day running of the

hub because a business has to deliver on its promises and Pall-Ex's reputation was dependent on what's called the trunking matrix. It's the times the lorries come in and out of the hub, and had to go like clockwork every day of the trading year. Back then, lorries were tipped and turned – meaning that they were stopped, unloaded and reloaded before going back out on the road – in under ten minutes (today it's four).

If one lorry came in late then the whole trunking matrix was thrown out of sync and deliveries wouldn't be made on time. It would also mean that I'd have to pay people overtime and I was determined to sweat my assets and wasn't going to increase my wage bill. That's why I couldn't let the trunking matrix be affected and so I did what I had to do to make sure my members were reminded every now and again that my balls were just as big as theirs. I might be a woman but the hauliers who worked with me had to know that I'd never shy away from confrontation if necessary. I would do what I needed to do. I wasn't afraid.

There's always one, though, isn't there? When a haulier from Norfolk kept sending late trunks, I wondered if he was trying to take the piss – or just being unprofessional.

'If you do it again, I will take the keys from your driver and he can walk back to your depot,' I told him.

When the driver next arrived late, I did what I'd threatened to do. He shouted and screamed at me before stomping off into the night. Then at 3 a.m his boss rang.

'What the fuck do you think you're doing?' he roared.

I was in no mood to beat around the bush at that time of the morning.

'I warned you that I'd do this,' I shouted back. 'So stop

being a selfish bastard and sending in late trunks. Just get your house in order, operate your business as it should be operated and don't mess with mine.'

Logistics might be a world of hairy lorry drivers but it's still a bit like a family because everything is so interdependent. One late trunk meant everyone was late, which meant deliveries might be missed or drivers would have to leave without freight – and that would affect my reputation. There was also tachograph legislation to consider, because drivers had to strictly adhere to how many hours they were at the wheel and at what speed. By now we were moving 1,000 pallets a night, just as I'd predicted in my original business plan – we went on to hit every annual target I'd set – and that's why the trunking matrix was so vital. All my worries were solved though when Adrian came on board, because I could hand the headache over to him. An old hand at logistics, the best man manager you'll ever meet and my dearest friend then as now, Adrian was and is my most trusted lieutenant.

I knew Adrian would be able to cope – unlike one night manager I'd had, who'd locked himself in my office one evening when too many lorries had started rolling in. I'd had to push up my sleeves, go out into the hub and crack the whip at the drivers to sort out the mess. But as confident as I felt about Adrian, I still shaved the odd few hundred off the number of pallets we were expecting each night, just to be on the safe side. I didn't want to run the risk of making him panic about the scale of the task he had to complete – and the resources he had to do it with – because I ran a tight ship from day one. And so I downplayed the figures ever so slightly as I breezily reassured him that each night would be a walk in the park.

On 5 November 1997 lorries started rolling in through the doors at Gotham for the first night of trading. With Adrian, five forklift drivers, a night manager, Bill, Glenys and a part-time day operation administrator called Lianne Crozier, who liaised with the membership and is still with us today – as much of a treasure as she was back then – my company was on the cusp of a huge upward curve.

In the early hours of the following morning, Mum took one look at me and called the doctor. I'd succumbed to a bad case of shingles and was in dreadful pain after all those months of steering Pall-Ex through such troubled waters alone. The doctor said I was stressed and advised me to rest. There was no way I could do that. Like I said, failure wasn't an option.

Chapter 16

I think of Pall-Ex as a child: it was an embryo on the first night it traded and then it was delivered; in those first few months I nurtured and cared for it like a baby twenty-four hours a day, sleeping when it did before waking again with it the next day. Then Pall-Ex started toddling as I took it through the difficult stages of dealing with the threatened closure, moving to Gotham and employing new staff as volume increased. And as it grew, like any mother I looked after every aspect of its development – from innovating health and safety codes to helping write my own IT system – because I knew one of my greatest assets would be my intellectual property entrenched in Pall-Ex's members' service agreement and IT system.

Most women underestimate just how much growing a business applies to what they learn as mothers: time management, working to a budget, people skills and the patience of a saint. All those things and more went into Pall-Ex and I had Mevlit to thank for teaching them to me.

But while I got on with overcoming the many challenges that Pall-Ex presented, I found it far harder to deal with my own son's. As Mevlit got older, the education system just didn't seem interested – or able – to properly deal with his dyslexia and I was worried sick. He was falling further and further behind, his self-esteem in tatters, and it hit me like a brick when I asked him what he'd like one Christmas and he told me that all he wanted was to be normal.

Mevlit didn't have a dad because Hussain had disappeared after visiting us in Leicester, and while he didn't ask about his father, like many single parents I sometimes wondered if I could be all that he needed. I also worked far more than most mothers did and we'd moved a lot – from Essex to Leicester and back to Essex when I'd left Hussain, gone to TNT and then started my consultancy work. From there we went to Rothley in Leicestershire when I opened the Wymeswold hub and moved again to Shepshed the following year when Pall-Ex went to Gotham. Mevlit's childhood was certainly nowhere near as nomadic as mine had been, but he'd known more than his fair share of upheaval.

To me the answer was simple: if I sent Mevlit to a specialist boarding school then he would not only get the best chance of an opportunity to deal properly with his dyslexia, but also stability. I was busy working during the week, so this way he could concentrate on his schooling and then we would have weekends together. I had a fight on my hands to get him a place, though, and I spent every spare minute during my first year at Gotham writing letters to anyone I could think of.

I even sent one to David Blunkett, who'd just been made Education Secretary after Labour's landslide election win. His boss Tony Blair might have promised 'Education, education, education' but Mr Blunkett didn't even write back to me. No one seemed to want to listen, and Mevlit's story sadly isn't unusual. Dyslexic children often fall through the net at mainstream schools where resources are at a premium – maybe even more so back then. If you want to get them the specialist schooling they need then you have to battle tooth and nail to get it. In the end, I had to take the local education authority to a tribunal for educational neglect. When I did, I won Mevlit a place at a specialist school in Staffordshire. He started there in September 1998 and I cried for days after dropping him off for the first time. I felt lost because I'd always loved him a bit too much.

But I told myself that this would be what Mevlit needed to sort out both his education and his behavioural problems. Kids like Mevlit, you see, are often labelled 'dumb' from the time they go to school. Left behind or, worse, bullied, it takes its toll. Mevlit was no different, and as he'd grown I'd struggled to deal with him at times. He seemed so angry and I was sure that doing better at school would improve things.

The teaching at his new school certainly helped him deal with his dyslexia and he made good progress. But Mevlit's behaviour continued to be a problem as one year turned into two. In fact, after he turned thirteen, I sometimes felt as if my son had gone to bed as Mevlit and woken up as Kevin the Teenager. When I asked him to finish his homework before I took him back to school one Sunday, he smashed his fist into the dining table so hard he broke it. When I tried to speak to him, he'd hang his head and refuse to look at me. He never said a word about how he felt and I had no idea how to get him to tell me.

What can you do with a boy who towers over you and doesn't listen to anything you say? Mevlit had shot up and I couldn't pack him off to his bedroom any more. Neither did he have a father to put him in his place with one look, as I'd had.

Those hauliers were easy to get back into line compared to him.

Len's death at the age of eighty-six after two strokes also hit Mevlit hard. He was the one ever-present male he'd had in his life and all of us were knocked for six when Len died because, like Dad before him, he'd been a rudder for us all. Mum was as lost as she had been when she was widowed the first time and soon moved in with us because I knew she needed looking after.

But if World War Three had broken out all those years before between Dad and me at the Tonge Ward Labour Club, then this was World War Four. Mum, who'd spent years looking after her little Mevie, now clashed constantly with him because she didn't like the fact that he'd started to answer her back. On Mevlit's weekends home from school or during the holidays, the pair of them fought constantly – with me as piggy in the middle – and between the loss of Len, the battles I had to referee between Mum and Mevlit and the stress of setting up and growing Pall-Ex, I felt stretched so thin that I thought I might break.

In fact, I even started noticing large clumps of hair blocking the plughole when I showered and soon realized that I'd developed bald patches on my head, some the size of fifty-pence pieces – one even bigger. The doctor told me it was alopecia brought on by stress, and I felt terrible because I'd always prided myself on being well turned out. I did what I could to cover up the bald spots with a special powder and later had laser treatment, which improved things a bit. But even today I still have to have hair weaved into my own at the front of my head and on my crown because some patches have never recovered.

I was advised to try and relax. But how could I when I looked at Mevlit and worried that he was going off the rails? Maybe I'd made mistakes that I'd never be able to put right? It had been more than six years now since I'd left Hussain and at last I'd realized what kind of relationship we'd had. But as much as I struggled to recognize that I'd been there, I now began to worry that it had affected Mevlit more than I knew. People talk about the terrible twos but they're nothing compared to a teenage boy who won't listen to a word you say.

Looking back, I wonder now if I should have done more than I did for Mevlit. Maybe I should have learned to teach him myself instead of sending him to boarding school? Or spent less time carving myself up between Pall-Ex and looking after him and Mum? I don't know. I just did what I thought would make Mevlit happy by helping him to read and write like other kids. To give him what he wanted: normality. Little did I know that it hurt him more than I could ever imagine. I've learned since then that Mevlit felt as if the one constant person in his life had abandoned him. It is something I'll always bitterly regret.

If you're going to develop a business then you have to think creatively all the time, because businesses either grow or die. I knew I would have to continuously innovate to keep growing Pall-Ex, and after moving to Gotham, I landed the first of three important pick-and-pack contracts to fill some of the extra space we had. Retailers paid me to house their stock in the hub before it was delivered out when it was needed via the Pall-Ex members.

I also started a daytime trunking matrix and began to sign up hub accounts – contracts we got with large third-party logistics operators who oversaw the supply chain for retailers and manufacturers. To do this, they subcontracted out the delivery of everything from parcels to pallets using companies like mine. Pall-Ex was the shop window of the hub accounts and my members delivered out the goods. The first hub account I landed was for Mim's Pottery and in the years to come I would also secure huge contracts with the likes of Black & Decker, Crown Paints, Farrow & Ball, Roca, Unilever and Colgate Palmolive.

These hub accounts generated revenue not only for my members, but for Pall-Ex too. It also meant that my financial risk was significantly decreased because until then I had always been waiting to be paid by haulier members for using Pall-Ex's services. Now I was generating my own income from hub accounts and could use the debt owed to me by members for Pall-Ex services to offset the money due to them for their collection and delivery services on hub accounts. The strategy generated growth, decreased my financial risk and earned both my members and myself money. It was a win-win situation.

The main driver of our profit growths though was simple: volume. But it wasn't just about recruiting more members. I also decreased the size of the areas they covered, which might not sound logical but is. You see, some of my founder members were covering up to seven postcodes when we started and I knew that by doing less mileage they would have more time to pick up freight and deliver it. It wasn't cost-effective for a haulier to deliver at either end of a large area and I lost count of the number of times I stared at the map hanging on my office wall as I longed to rub out a postcode that was proving to be a particular problem.

That's why I spent every spare minute I had during those

early years using that map to strategize about who to recruit for which area. Most evenings when the phone had finally stopped ringing, I'd go in there, make a cup of tea and light a cigarette before leaning back in my chair and losing myself for hours as plans whizzed around my mind.

'What on earth are you doing?' people would ask as they walked in to see my eyes still fixed on the map at around 3 a.m.

They probably thought I was just staring into space but that map was the single most important key to my vision. You see, it enabled me to make sure that every decision I made was strategic, and competitors who've since tried to emulate Pall-Ex have often come a cropper by not doing their research properly. They've just taken on hauliers to cover areas without considering if they're the best fit. They've failed to hold their nerve and think strategically.

That's where I was different. By matching the right haulier to the right postcode, I maximized their revenue – and commanded higher joining fees for Pall-Ex. For instance, Preston would pay me a good joining fee because it's an industrial area full of factories which needed goods transporting. But Lancaster was mostly greenfield so not much of anything went on there, which meant I had to team it with a higher-density area like Blackpool.

There was no Google to help me back then and so I did all this the hard way – by getting books, encyclopaedias and computer CDs to help me study demographics, local industry and the freight each postcode would generate. Then, when I had a clear picture of what would need to be delivered into an area and transported back out of it, I could make decisions that would make my members money.

Take Hughie Stalker. He was already running trucks up and down to Scotland, so giving him the Dumfries and Galloway postcode meant that it wouldn't cost him a lot to stop a vehicle and deliver there, whereas a smaller haulier might have been bankrupted if he'd had to hire lorries to cover the area. Logistics is about right time, right place, right resources. It was my golden rule. Very unusually, hardly any of the hauliers who've joined Pall-Ex have gone bust. It was all about making it viable for them to join so that their business came to me, because that meant bunts on my bottom line.

My focus quickly produced results. In 1997 we moved 158,000 pallets, and a year later we'd more than doubled that to 334,000. By the end of 1999, it was more than 558,000. In 2000 we weren't far short of 800,000 and Pall-Ex had more than its first million banked in saved profits. Our growth was phenomenal and three years after starting Pall-Ex I was able to pay cash for a five-bedroom house in Nottingham. I'll never forget turning the key for the first time knowing that after all that had happened with Hussain, no one would ever be able to take my home because every brick belonged to me.

I'd worked bloody hard for that house but never lost sight of how lucky I was. Think of the men who worked down pits fifty years ago and never saw the light of day, just to make sure there was bread and jam on the table for their family. You don't always get financially well rewarded however hard you work or talented you are. My houses – and the ones I've bought since – are my only true indulgences, because as far as I'm concerned turnover is vanity, profit is sanity and cash is reality. I've rewarded myself but always made sure to keep the lion's share of Pall-Ex's growing reserves in the bank –

knowing even back then that I had big plans for the business that would one day need a lot of money to realize.

The kind of strategic logic I used to grow Pall-Ex can be applied to any business: you have to maximize revenue and minimize downtime and costs. A retailer who has too much stock will fail and a restaurant with a huge menu is far more likely to fold. Holding a lot of stock means financial investment is sitting unutilized and you're also paying for the physical space to store it. You have to sweat assets and do your research.

People today do logistics degrees to learn what I did back then with that map. I just used my common sense. Those hours spent staring helped me build Pall-Ex right from the start, hold my nerve and resist the urge to make short-cuts that would create weaknesses in my business that might one day blow open.

I've been asked a lot since then why I've never floated Pall-Ex on the Stock Exchange and there's one reason: I have a vision for my business that I don't want to see destroyed by shareholders. I created Pall-Ex and understand its culture – as do both my board of directors and employees. I strongly believe that this kind of empathy shared by everyone involved in the company is irreplaceable because it helps create not only a profitable business but a place where people are happy to work – I hope. Men in the City just wouldn't care in the way that we do, and it's been proven to me many times when I've seen businesses ruined by men in suits.

I'm not a dictator, though. If I have a bad idea then I'm told it is. I know my business is in safe hands today thanks to a board of directors I trust. But I'm convinced that remaining the sole shareholder of Pall-Ex has been one of the keys to its success. The buck stops with me. And until someone comes along who can understand the mentality of my business – and has the money to buy it – Pall-Ex will always remain mine. It was like that all those years ago as I drove Pall-Ex forward because, while Adrian looked after the operational side of the business and I had other employees who contributed greatly, I was the one with a unique emotional investment in the company I'd put everything into.

It meant that I continued to work harder than I ever had done before. Many of the men who started networks to compete with mine died prematurely. Thankfully I didn't – even though I covered more than 2,000 miles a week in my car as I went to meet existing members and recruit new ones. I worked dawn till dusk and even managed to find a few hours in between. Most days, I'd work until 4 a.m. and get just three or four hours' sleep a night.

'Do you know what's going on in the world?' Mum would ask in despair as she mentioned something she'd read in the news.

To be honest, I didn't. My business was everything.

One of the key things I learned during that time was how to take the compassion out of a commercial decision when I needed to – and then put the compassion back in when I'd made it. People say you've got to be ruthless to succeed in business, but I personally think it's a load of rubbish. First and foremost you have to be commercial, secondly compassionate, and thirdly empathetic with your business, your people, your product and customers. And if that means you have to make difficult choices for the sake of your business then you have to be prepared to do it. I've removed people who didn't have the passion to change as my business did and also closed down links with hauliers who I knew could threaten the whole of the Pall-Ex network.

Several years after opening Gotham, I drove to north Wales one dark November night to see a Pall-Ex haulier who was near enough a founder member. He was a man who'd become a friend as well as a colleague but we knew his business was in trouble because our member service agreement meant we closely vetted each haulier's financials. If we knew they were in the danger zone, we insisted on seeing monthly management accounts, because if a member put freight into the Pall-Ex network and went bust then he was a threat to others. The trust fund they'd all paid into would have to pay his debts and there would be a weak link in the delivery chain.

Sadly I knew as I went in to see this haulier that I couldn't afford to let him go bust using the Pall-Ex brand. After spending several sleepless nights knowing that I'd soon have to bow to the inevitable, I arrived in north Wales at about 6 p.m. with Martin Field, the financial director I took on in 2000.

The haulier was as welcoming as always when he saw me. His was a family business, clogs to clogs in three generations.

'I know we're having trouble, Hilary,' he said. 'But we're going to change, make sure we improve our margins and sort this out.'

I looked at him.

'It just isn't going to happen, love,' I said. 'We've done the figures, the cash flow and profit forecast. We can't make it work. And if we can't, then you can't either. You've got to be realistic.'

'But I'm going to remortgage my house and put cash into the business that way,' the haulier told me, and this was the last thing I wanted because I couldn't have him losing his home as well as his business.

'It isn't going to work,' I said. 'You're in the abyss and there's not even a glimmer of light. I can't allow you to trade within Pall-Ex. It would be negligent to let you carry on – for your sake as well as the network's.

'If you carry on trading you will be trading illegally because you will be an insolvent limited company and I can't let you do that.

'I'm sorry but I'm going to have pull the plug on you.'

'When?'

'As of now. There is no freight coming to you tonight. We are disenfranchising you as of this minute.'

The man looked at me before starting to cry and I knew that now I'd broken the bad news, I had to do what I could to soften it.

'I'm going to do all I can to help,' I said. 'Let's get the receivers in immediately, get an exact picture of the debtors and creditors, see what there is coming in and what's to pay, and hopefully make a few bob for you with what's left so that you can take it home to your wife.'

I closed down the business that night but did what I could to make sure that the haulier had enough money to pay off his debts by putting him in touch with Pall-Ex members who wanted to buy his vehicles and finding his daughter a job in another local haulage depot.

That's the thing about empathy: you have to know your business, know your market and know when enough is enough. However hard that is.

Chapter 17

'Bloody badgers,' I thought to myself. 'I can't believe they almost did for me.'

I was sitting in my office but it wasn't in a corner of a warehouse in Gotham any more. In fact royalty itself had officially opened Pall-Ex's brand-new £12 million hub earlier that day in March 2003.

'You must be very proud,' Princess Anne had said as she toured the building before officially opening it.

I had met her after setting up a penny-a-pallet donation scheme soon after starting Pall-Ex. For every pallet we moved, money was given to a Third World logistics charity called Transaid and Princess Anne was its patron. Now she'd come to open Pall-Ex's state-of-the-art, purpose-built hub and it had been a great day full of congratulations and laughter. Less than six years after moving our first pallets, my members and I had turned Pall-Ex into the UK's number one network. It wasn't a miracle. Those just happen. This was down to sheer hard graft.

The idea of building my own hub had been with me ever since I'd begun Pall-Ex. Sharing loos with lorry drivers and watching rats scurry past me in the Wymeswold hub had been enough to convince me that one day I'd have purpose-built premises – with gentlemen's *and* ladies' loos. But the idea had only started to become a reality in December 1999, after I'd been approached by a parcel operator who needed a network like Pall-Ex and offered £12 million to buy mine. It was a good offer for a company that was still only three years old and didn't own a single tangible asset, because the hub was rented and all the rolling stock used in the network belonged to members. Personally too, £12 million was still a lot of money even though I was earning a comfortable salary by then, driving a Mercedes and able to afford a holiday each year.

But I didn't think I wanted to sell. You see, then as now, I dreamed of building Pall-Ex into Europe's number one network and felt as if I'd be letting my members down if I sold up so soon after beginning the company. I'd made promises, and who knew what might happen to Pall-Ex in the hands of a new owner? I'd formed not just business relationships but strong personal ones too and didn't think I could just cash in and leave them behind.

If I didn't sell, though, I was going to have to take my business to a whole new level. Pall-Ex had grown more quickly than I'd ever imagined and while I loved the challenge, such rapid success creates its own problems. Take the simple fact of employing more people: if you're the one in charge and put employees in to manage sections of your business, it means that things only reach you when they're problems so large you have to solve them. There are moments when you feel as if all you are doing is fire-fighting.

'I need an answer,' the man who'd made me the offer said when he phoned just before I left for a cruise with Mevlit.

I told him I'd give him one when I got back and set off on

the ship to the Caribbean. But as I lay on my sunbed, I couldn't stop thinking about what I should do. If I was going to turn down such a good offer then I knew I would have to dream even bigger, and to do that I was going to have to find a new hub. We'd outgrow Gotham if business continued to grow as it had, and I had every intention it would.

After befriending an elderly couple over the buffet table, I started to tell them a little about my life and the choice I had to make: sell my business or build a new hub on land I didn't have.

'I might be able to help there,' the elderly man told me.

I looked at him, convinced that he must have had one too many pina coladas.

'My daughter owns land in exactly the spot you're looking for,' he said.

'Where?'

'Ellistown, two miles off the M1 in Leicestershire.'

If the clouds had opened and a heavenly chorus started playing at that moment, I wouldn't have been surprised. Hard work, tenacity and vision had got me so far. Now Fate was lending me a helping hand and I knew what I was going to do.

If only the rest of the process had been as easy. There were times when I was sure that building a Great bloody Pyramid would have been easier than a 267,000-square-foot hub with forty-two lorry-loading bays that covered another 100,000 feet of space and 40,000 feet of office accommodation. From liaising with local residents – and buying them all new double glazing – to the long business of getting planning permission and a gruelling ten-month building project (overseen internally by my finance director Martin after we realized that outsourcing the work would blow our budget out of the water), the process had been all-consuming. Given all that, it was ironic that a piffling badger had almost finished us off.

The wildlife problems had started when we'd had to bring an ecologist in to find out if there were great crested newts on site because they're protected by law. There were some newts. But were they great crested newts? The whole process seemed endless and we were all on tenterhooks as we waited for the ecologists' report.

'There aren't any great crested newts,' Martin told me on the phone one day and I breathed a sigh of relief. 'But there *is* a badger sett and we've got to rehome them.'

Poor Martin. I thought he was about to spontaneously combust.

It cost me thousands in the end to sort out all those badgers and non-existent great crested newts. But at least once it was done, we could all rest easy that we'd done our bit for wildlife conservation and get on with building the hub in peace. By the time we'd finished, I'd taken Pall-Ex from a tin hut to a state-of-the-art building. From the fleet of environmentally friendly forklift trucks powered by compressed natural gas to the non-drive-through hub, an industry health-and-safety first, we would be forging new ground in every area. Scores of trees had also been planted across the site, two natural ponds reclaimed and specialist landscapers employed to minimize noise and light pollution.

But as I sat at my new desk on that first night and stared at the meeting table across the other side of the room, the comfortable chairs in another corner and the thick rose-red carpet covering the floor, I just wanted to be back in my cosy office in Gotham. You see, for the first time since starting

Pall-Ex, I felt almost out of my depth. After all the planning and excitement, the hard work and problem-solving, the sheer scale of where I'd got to almost surprised me now that I'd stopped for long enough to look around. I'd still been cleaning my own office in Gotham. Today Princess Anne had sat in my new one. But there was no one to talk to about how I felt, because the people I loved most in the world were at logger-heads.

Mum and Mevlit weren't the problem any more. Things had calmed down since I'd bought and renovated a bungalow for Mum. She'd soon decided she didn't like it though and so I'd sold the bungalow and bought her a flat instead. At last she seemed settled there – even if she was on the phone to me at 3 a.m every now and again claiming that she'd fallen out of bed.

'I need you to help me back in,' she'd say in a tiny voice, and I'd pull on some clothes before driving over to help her.

Once she was back in bed, Minnie would lie back on the pillows and sigh as she looked up at me.

'I'm glad you're here,' she'd say. 'Now make me a bacon butty and a cup of tea, would you, love?'

She could be a devil in disguise at times, that one. But at least she and Mevlit were getting on better now, so well in fact that they'd united against someone else: my new fiancé. I'd met Ed Devey several years before, after employing his mother Brenda to look after Mevlit during the school holidays and Mum after a hip replacement. Eight years younger than me, Ed was a painter and decorator who I'd known only in passing until last year, when I'd gone to the farmhouse I'd bought in a beautiful village called Moraira on the Costa Blanca.

Ed was also in Spain, to do some work on a restaurant his brother Dean was opening near to my house, and the two of them had stayed when me, Brenda, Mum and Mevlit went on holiday to Moraira. It was then that I'd got to know Ed better and our relationship had started. Easy to talk to and funny with it, I was happy to have met him after so many years alone and as drawn to his close family unit as I had been all those years ago with Malcolm and Mary.

Mum and Mevlit weren't nearly so pleased though because, after having me to themselves for so long, they didn't like change.

'If Ed's coming then I'm not coming,' Mum had said when I'd invited her to the hub-opening.

'Please, Mum. It would mean so much to me to have you there.'

'No. I've told you, Hilary. If he's there then I won't be.'

Mevlit was even more set against my relationship with Ed. In fact, it had sparked a whole new turn for the worse in him and things had got so bad that he'd been expelled from school for fighting before his GCSE mock exams a few months before. After all the work both he and his teachers had done to deal with his dyslexia, he'd thrown his education away just before reaching the final hurdle when he was more than capable of passing his exams.

'Why?' I'd asked as I sat him down in the conservatory of Berry Hills Farm.

It was a beautiful Georgian farmhouse that I'd bought in December 2002. Set in thirty-two acres of land, it was in a village called Ibstock.

But as I talked to Mevlit, he shut down as ever and didn't say a word.

'I'm worried,' I told him. 'Really, really worried. We have to sort this out. You can't just give up on your education.'

But he wouldn't listen, and the best I could get out of him was an agreement to do a three-month brick-laying course. Mevlit insisted though that he didn't want to be at home if Ed was there and so my good friend Glenys had agreed to let him stay with her in an effort to keep the peace. By now Glenys was Pall-Ex's network development director and at least I knew someone I trusted would be keeping an eye on Mevlit. Maybe it was what we all needed to find a way to get on better.

I knew it was a big change for Mevlit to have someone else in my life. But after six and a half years focusing on building Pall-Ex and caring for him, I wanted something for myself – and someone who might look after *me* a little. I'd spent my life working and looking after people – my parents, Len, Mevlit and of course Pall-Ex and my employees. I hadn't been on so much as a date in the decade since leaving Hussain because I'd lost so much confidence in myself after our relationship; I also didn't want to mix business with pleasure, which made life hard because the only men I met were through work.

Now I was ready to have a relationship but hated being torn between it and my mother and son, which is why I felt more alone than ever as I sat in my office. Ed didn't like Mum and Mevlit any more than they liked him, and there were times now when I felt as if I was going to be torn into three pieces as I was caught between the three of them, trying to keep the peace and failing most of the time. I'd hoped that Mevlit's brick-laying course and living with Glenys might be what he needed. But it wasn't to be. He'd left her house after an argument and the first I knew of it was when a new friend of his from Derby had phoned me to say that he was living with her and her boyfriend. The two of them were a couple of years older than Mevlit and had met him through a schoolfriend. Let's call them David and Karen.

'We're happy to have him here but we'll need money to keep him,' she said.

'Let me come and see him,' I said, and got in the car to go and see for myself where Mevlit was.

I cannot describe how I felt when I arrived to find him in a filthy terraced house. I just couldn't understand what he was doing there. Mevlit had been brought up in homes that were always clean and tidy. Now he was living in a place where a baby's cries and the smell of its nappy filled the air. There was clutter everywhere.

'You've got to come home,' I said after persuading him to sit with me in the car. 'Why on earth do you want to be here?'

'Because I like it.'

'Do you really? Just come home, Mevlit. We'll work things out with Ed. The two of you have got to find a way to get along. Can't we try? I can't leave you here.'

'I'm not coming.'

'But why? We need to get you on to a course or something. You can't just leave school and live with friends.'

'I can and I will. I'm staying.'

We must have sat in that car for an hour as I pleaded with Mevlit to come home, but nothing I said made a difference and short of dragging him by the scruff of the neck – which I couldn't do however much I wanted to – there was nothing else but to let him stay where he wanted to be for the time being.

'OK then,' I said eventually with a sigh. 'I'll give David and

Karen some housekeeping for you. But this can't go on for ever. We've got to find a way to sort it out, a way for you and Ed to get along.'

Once again, Mevlit didn't say anything as he got out of the car and I felt lost as I watched him walk back inside that house. He seemed at war with the world and hated everyone in it. Including himself and me.

Nine weeks after the hub opened, I married Ed in a little church on Lake Orta in Italy on a beautiful June day. He'd organized everything in secret and told me just days before we were due to leave. The two of us said our vows in front of two witnesses from the travel company we'd booked through and no one knew we were getting married until I phoned Adrian on the day itself to tell him the news. Wearing a long cream skirt and a bustier top, I exchanged vows with Ed and couldn't quite believe that I'd eloped at the age of forty-six.

We'd told everyone that we were going on holiday but after honeymooning at Lake Maggiore I went home to face the music with Mum and Mevlit. I was sorry about how they felt but didn't think it was right for me to live the rest of my life for them: Mum had been married three times so she should understand why I wanted a husband and companion, and Mevlit was growing too. He'd soon be an adult with his own life, however difficult his teenage years were proving to be.

'You've got married?' Mum said when I rang to tell her that I was now Mrs Ed Devey. 'I'll say one thing, Hilary: you might have a good head for business, but you've got a terrible taste in men.'

Back then, I didn't understand what Mum was saying. I was in love with Ed. We were going to have a happy future together.

I might have got things wrong with Hussain but this time it was different.

All too soon, though, I'd realize that I'd made yet another mistake. Although my marriage to Ed limped on for another five years, we were probably only together under the same roof for about a year because he came and went so much.

Whenever we argued, he'd disappear – often back to his mum's – and I never knew when I'd see him again. It was like a rollercoaster we couldn't get off, because each time he came back things would be fine for a few days until we started to argue again, usually about Mevlit or money. Like many women, I blamed myself most of the time, wanting to understand what mistakes I was making even as I tried to be a good wife. After all that had happened with Hussain, I desperately wanted my marriage to work. But once again, the tenacity which stood me in such good stead businesswise was my downfall when it came to a relationship that I couldn't bring myself to end even though it was never truly happy. They say love is blind. All I can say is that it's sometimes bloody stupid too.

Why? Because I don't think there are many men who can cope with a woman like me – someone so decisive and, let's face it, financially successful. Pall-Ex had made me a wealthy woman and I didn't know that money can change relationships until I had it. Take it from me: a healthy bank balance certainly brings you options, but if you think it will also bring you emotional security and friends, love and happiness, then think again.

That's the thing these days, though: people think you've got it all if you're financially comfortable. Don't get me wrong, I'm not moaning. I own some beautiful homes and will never again have to lie awake worrying about the gas bill. But I do lie awake worrying about my businesses and the people who rely on me for their income. I'm still the same person I always was. There are Primark towels in my bathroom and I spend most of my time in my pyjamas because I'm pretty boring really.

But some people think that if you've got money you've got it made, and I've found it hard when my bank balance has made me question if there was anything real in some of my relationships. Add in the fact that the world I lived in was very different to the one Ed knew – full of work, functions and constant change – and I think he found it hard to adapt to. But as the old adage goes, if you can't say something good about someone then don't say anything at all. That's what I'll do with Ed. Just remember that throughout all that was to come in the years ahead – the worst time of my life – I was dealing with a marriage that was up, down but never truly happy.

I was vulnerable when I met Ed because business success doesn't translate to feeling you've done well at life. I've always worn my heart on my sleeve and trusted too easily. We are what we are though and I'm no different to most women: I want to share my life and have someone to put their arms around me at the end of a bad day, someone I can totally trust. That's human nature, isn't it?

Mum was right though when I told her about my marriage to Ed: I might be good at business but I'm bloody bad at picking blokes.

Chapter 18

Telling you more about the time when I felt as if I was watching my own son die is going to be one of the hardest things I've ever done. It's difficult for Mevlit too because his heroin addiction is behind him now and he worries that all people will ever see is his past. But if anyone reading this learns something that helps them understand what's happening in their child's life – either before or after they discover they're an addict – then it will be worth it.

The only way I can describe the journey I had to discovering Mevlit's addiction was like descending into an abyss. When I finally found out the truth, I felt I'd be lost there for ever because all I wanted, like any parent, was for my child to be safe, happy and well for as much of the time as it was possible for him to be. To know he was in such extreme pain – and to believe for a long time that he was the one inflicting it on himself, before I started to understand he was ill and even then still struggling to fully accept it – was almost unbearable.

But I think that many parents of addicts are just like me: it takes time to realize your child has entered a world you never even knew existed – and have no idea how to deal with when you do. I didn't even drink alcohol until my late twenties because I'd been put off it during my childhood. I certainly didn't know anything about illegal drugs. I'd never seen one, let alone taken one. I'd just read all those horror stories in newspapers and breathed a sigh of relief when I closed the pages that they'd never be part of my life.

That's why it took me so long to see the signs of Mevlit's abuse. There were always clues, but I didn't pick up on them because I didn't know what they were. I thought I just had a teenage son who was going through a few difficult years. I didn't dream he might be an addict.

You've also got to remember that I'm not at all streetwise. Savvy in business? Yes. Able to hold my own in a world many women would find overwhelming? Certainly. But my life had been so full of work since my childhood that I'd been sheltered by it in many ways, so preoccupied with my career and son that being a mother and businesswoman was all I knew. Drugs were like another planet to me. One I never thought I'd visit.

'Do you realize how serious this is, Mevlit? Do you have any idea just how much trouble you could be in?'

Mevlit said nothing as he sat in the car beside me.

'Will you listen to me? Will you tell me what is going on? Do you have anything to do with what the police want to talk to you about?'

He sat silently, refusing to speak to me, just as he usually did these days.

'Did you do it, Mevlit? Did you burgle the flat?'

'No.'

Mevlit would soon turn eighteen and I didn't recognize him

or the life he was leading. He still hadn't found a job and however many times I'd pleaded with him to find work, he refused. All he seemed to want to do was hang around with friends, and I couldn't see why he wanted to live his life this way. He had always seen me work, knew that you got nothing in life without putting the effort in, but didn't seem to care.

Now the police wanted to talk to Mevlit and I couldn't help but wonder if he *had* got himself into trouble, however much he insisted that he hadn't. In the eighteen months since the hub had opened, things with Mevlit had gone from bad to worse. I was trying to keep hold of what felt like the threads of our relationship because he was moody and withdrawn one minute, angry and abusive the next. Friends said he was just going through a difficult patch like so many teenagers do. But I struggled to understand how my loving, affectionate little boy had become such an angry young man.

The only thing Mevlit seemed really interested in was the allowance I gave him each week, and it annoyed me more and more because as much as I didn't want to give up on him, I didn't want to bank roll him for ever either. He'd grown up in a home where there was a work ethic and now seemed hell-bent on never lifting a finger. I just didn't understand it.

But I could never get very far when I tried to talk to him about it because Mevlit wouldn't come anywhere near me – or Ed – most of the time. He only came home when I went to pick him up and took him back to Berry Hills Farm myself and when we got there he and Ed usually started shouting within hours of being in the same house. If I could have banged their bloody heads together I would have.

For a few weeks I'd thought things were looking up, when Mevlit had asked me if I could help him out with the rent on a small flat in Derby in late 2004. He'd finally moved out of David and Karen's house after they'd told him they were having a second baby, and it seemed like a step in the right direction. The flat wasn't much – just a large room with a kitchen and bathroom off it – but I'd kitted Mevlit out with a stereo and a bed, a television and a fridge, and hoped that running his own home might teach him that people have to work hard to create a life.

'What's this?' he'd said on one of the rare occasions when he let me visit and showed me a letter that had come through the door.

'A water bill, Mevlit.'

'A *water* bill?'

'Yes.'

'You have to pay for water?'

'Of course you do.'

Learning to look after himself though hadn't really turned out how I'd hoped it would. Mevlit had continued to spend most of his time with David and Karen even when he moved out, and I didn't have a clue what the three of them did in that dingy house together all the time. I'd also got worried that Mevlit was now starting to look almost skinny. He had always been a big lad and although he kept insisting that he was eating properly, I wasn't sure. I didn't like to see him so slim.

Right now, though, his weight seemed like the least of my worries as I drove him to a police station.

'Some detectives want to speak to him,' Mevlit's landlord had told me when he'd rung.

'What about?'

'I'm not sure.'

'Well, give them my number and ask them to call me.'

I could hardly believe my ears when an officer told me that the police had some questions for Mevlit about a burglary. A TV and stereo had been stolen from one of the other flats in the building but it didn't make sense. Mevlit knew right from wrong and wouldn't need to steal because I gave him enough money to live on. Even so, I'd known for a long time that he always somehow managed to fall in with the wrong crowd – from the teenagers he'd gone to school with to the ones he met when he was at home – which is why I turned to him for a final time as we walked towards the steps leading into Derby Police Station.

'Look me in the eyes, Mevlit, and tell me one thing: did you do this?'

When his eyes met mine for the briefest moment, I knew what he was about to say.

'Tell me the truth, Mevlit.'

'Yes.'

I didn't know whether to batter him or cry as anger and fear rushed through me.

'But *why*? Why on earth would you do something like that?'

'My mates talked me into it.'

'What on earth do you mean? How can *anyone* talk you into breaking the law?'

'The guy deserved it. He'd stolen some of my stuff so I took some of his.'

'Don't be so bloody ridiculous! Do you realize how serious this could be? You're seventeen. You can't just do what your friends tell you and break the law. This isn't school any more. You could go to prison, Mevlit. Do you understand?'

He hung his head as I looked at him. But as angry as I was,

I knew he had to have some kind of help when he went in to face the consequences of what he'd done. With a heavy heart, I called my Pall-Ex company lawyer and explained what had happened. He told me he'd find a criminal solicitor to come down and accompany Mevlit into the station.

Panic rushed through me as we sat waiting for him to arrive. What on earth had made Mevlit do this? Being rude to his mother and a bit workshy was one thing, but burglary? Mevlit wouldn't say another word to me though as we waited and all I could do when the solicitor arrived was watch my son go into a police station as I wondered what would become of him. I hoped the police might give Mevlit a rap on the knuckles because he hadn't been in trouble before. If he had a scare then I'd make sure he didn't do anything like it again.

Two hours later he came out of the station and the solicitor told me that Mevlit hadn't been charged. The police wanted to make further enquiries and he would need to go back to see them in a couple of weeks.

'I advised Mevlit not to comment during the interview,' the lawyer said. 'It's up to the police to gather evidence that a crime has been committed and until they do that he cannot be charged.'

Two weeks later I drove back to Derby to pick up Mevlit and take him back to the police station. As ever, I had to go and get him at David and Karen's house.

'Come on, Mevlit,' I said as I walked into the lounge.

He didn't move.

'Let's go, Mevlit. Let's get this over with.'

He dragged himself off the sofa before looking at me with a surly expression.

'I'm fucking sick of this,' he snarled as he got his coat.

Without a second thought, I raised my hand and slapped Mevlit across the cheek as all the frustration that had been filling me for so long rose up inside me. It was the first time I'd hit him, other than one slap on the legs when he was young. But if he thought he could get away with swearing at me then he had another thing coming because after nearly two years of problems with him, I'd had enough.

'That's seventeen years too late, my lad,' I roared. 'Now get in that car.'

He did as he was told – before jumping out as I stopped at a junction on the way to the police station and running down an alleyway.

'Get the fuck off me,' Mevlit screamed after I'd abandoned the car and hared after him.

I didn't understand where all this was coming from. It was as if Mevlit didn't even care about the lines he'd been taught couldn't be crossed, and anger filled me. By the time we got to the station, it had disappeared though. Instead, all I felt was fear as I watched Mevlit and the solicitor walk into the station for a second time and wondered what would become of my son if he got charged with a crime at such a young age. I'd been wrong to hit him. Underneath the angry teenager, there was still a child who had struggled at school and felt the absence of his dad.

'He isn't going to be charged,' the solicitor said when he brought Mevlit back to the car about an hour later. 'The police didn't have enough evidence so this won't be going any further.'

I didn't understand. Mevlit himself had told me that he'd taken the TV and stereo.

'He didn't comment during interviews and the police didn't have enough to charge him,' the solicitor said. 'They didn't do their job well enough and I did mine. That will be the end of it.'

For a moment, I felt relieved. But as we drove away from the police station, I looked at Mevlit and realized he looked almost pleased with himself. It was as if he was laughing at what he'd got away with – and wasn't in the least ashamed as well he should be.

'Give me your keys,' I said as I pulled up the car beside some park railings.

'What do you mean?'

'Your flat keys, Mevlit.'

'Why?'

'You'll see.'

He handed them to me and I got out of the car, walked to the railings and threw the keys over them into a pond on the other side.

'What did you do that for?' Mevlit asked angrily as I got back into the car.

'Because enough is enough. You're coming home with me.'

Mevlit lasted less than a month at Pall-Ex when I sent him to work in the hub. What I didn't know back then was that the warehousemen were soon making bets on whether he'd work a full week because he was forever off sick. It didn't escape my attention though when he threw a scanner worth £3,000 in a fit of anger and it smashed on the floor. I had no choice but to sack him and soon realized that I'd been wrong to think that having Mevlit back at home might improve things.

In the months after he came home again, things just got worse and worse. It was like living with a stranger, and while

I tried telling myself that this was what many mothers of teenage sons went through, it didn't help me to feel any less worried. But nothing I said had an impact as Mevlit became more and more like two different people: anxious and argumentative one minute, reclusive and monosyllabic the next. Whenever he was at home, he'd spend hours lying in the bath or sitting in his room alone before falling asleep. On the odd occasion he said he was going out, I'd feel happy that he was doing what other lads of his age did. But then he'd come home an hour later and disappear up to his room again, so I knew things weren't getting any better. Mevlit seemed so solitary, almost secretive, and even when his friends did come to the house, they were either so scruffy and ill-mannered that I wasn't sure I wanted them in my home or so pleasant they didn't seem genuine. I didn't trust the lot of them.

Meanwhile, Mevlit and Ed continued to row as first one and then the other left Berry Hills Farm in a fit of anger. As busy as ever running Pall-Ex, it was all I could do to juggle the balls – and keep them up in the air. But after a few months with Mevlit at home, I became more and more convinced that there was something seriously wrong – and the more I thought about it, the more I knew what it was. There was the weight loss and secrecy – and the fact that I'd noticed Mevlit often disappeared to be sick after I'd cooked. He must have an eating disorder. What else could explain his behaviour?

I decided to make a doctor's appointment for him and insisted that he came with me.

'Why are you making me do this?' Mevlit had screamed as we pulled up in the car park. 'You're such a fucking bitch, you know that? I'm fine. Just leave me alone and stop sticking your nose in.'

'Mevlit, please. There's something not right. I think you're ill. We need to find out what it is.'

'Don't pretend to be interested in me! All you care about is your business. It's the only thing that matters to you.'

'You know that isn't true. I've worked hard to make us a life.'

'No you didn't, you stupid cow. You worked to give you one. You and your precious Pall-Ex.'

I'd kept my cool for long enough to watch in disbelief as Mevlit got out of the car and ran off into the distance, leaving me sitting in the car. How was I going to get him to see the doctor? I'd been trying to tell myself this was teenage troubles for nearly three years now but I knew it was something else. So I did the only thing I could: made Mevlit another doctor's appointment and insisted on taking him for a second time. But while he went into the surgery this time, he stormed back out of it about half an hour later.

'I can't wait any longer,' he shouted. 'I've been in there ages.'

'But you've got to wait. You've got an appointment.'

'I can't.'

'Why not?'

'I just can't. Get off my back, will you? They're going to make me another appointment so just leave it.'

'And you'll keep it this time?'

'Yes. Now let's go. Stop interfering. Just leave me alone.'

There was nothing else I could do and that's the thing about a teenager in trouble. You're as frantic with worry about them as you were when they were small but they're too old for you to pick up and make better. When an envelope arrived from the doctor's surgery a few days later, I opened it without a thought for Mevlit's privacy. So many barriers had been broken down during the time that he was at home – from swearing obscenities at me to smashing holes in doors and forcing me to duck when he threw things in rage – that I didn't think twice about opening his letter. Unless I found out when his next appointment was, there was no way he'd keep it.

The letter wasn't about that at all though. Instead, I read with horror that Mevlit had been struck off the doctor's list for being abusive.

'What did you do?' I asked him when I confronted him that night.

'Nothing.'

'But you must have done. The doctor wouldn't just bar you from his surgery for no reason.'

'I don't know. I didn't do anything.'

There were moments now when his lies were so transparent, I was at a complete loss about what to say. This was one of them, but I was learning that it was no good trying to challenge Mevlit. I had to be cleverer than that.

'Well then, we'll just have to find you another doctor, won't we?'

I soon got Mevlit on to a list at another surgery and made him several appointments but he simply refused to see a doctor. It was the same with the dentist, after I noticed that his teeth were becoming discoloured and wanted him to be checked. I'd always been fanatical about his teeth – just as my parents had been about mine – and I didn't understand why Mevlit's were suddenly brown and dirty-looking. It was as if he didn't care about himself at all any more.

'Have you had a shower?' I'd ask him when he finally came downstairs and a strange smell – almost sickly sweet – hung around him.

'Of course I fucking have,' he'd snap.

It was his aggression which worried me most. More than a year on from his arrest, there were more and more days when Mevlit seemed jittery and on edge, as if waiting for a knock at the door which never came, and his requests for money were getting increasingly persistent. I wanted to know why he was getting through so much but if we argued about it – which we constantly did – Mevlit would draw himself up to his full height and scream abuse at me. At moments like those, I glimpsed his father in him and it scared me. It was as if my own son was becoming a stranger, and I had no idea how to bring him back to me.

I put down my mobile on the nightstand by my bed and looked at the clock. It was 3 a.m. and Mevlit still wasn't home. I worried about him constantly when he disappeared like this and couldn't sleep until I heard footsteps and the click of his bedroom door which told me he was home. It was ridiculous really. He'd turned nineteen in December 2005 but I worried about him now more than I ever had when he was a child.

I'd phoned him again and again tonight to find out where he was, wanting to know that he was fine before I went to sleep. But he hadn't answered a single call and I knew I'd never settle until I got hold of him. With a sigh, I got out of bed and pulled on a raincoat over my pyjamas. There was one place he was more likely to be than any other and that was at David and Karen's. The three of them – and two young children – were still together day and night.

I knew Mevlit would be angry when I turned up to find him. He'd scream and shout, hurl abuse at me and tell me I was good for nothing. But I didn't care. All I wanted to know was that he was safe as I drove along pitch-black roads from Berry Hills Farm to the house in Derby where I was sure he'd be. If that meant going to pick him up at this time then I would do it.

But when I got to David and Karen's, they told me that Mevlit wasn't there and I wondered what to do as I got into my car. Would he ever pick up his phone and let me know where he was? Where was I going to find him? When Karen walked outside, I opened the car window to speak to her.

'I can give you an address,' she said.

'What do you mean?

'I know where he is.'

'With friends?'

She didn't reply as I tapped the address she gave me into my sat nav and set off. About ten minutes later, I pulled up my car outside a terraced house in a run-down street. What on earth was Mevlit doing here? Getting out, I heard a low roar coming from inside the house – voices and rowdiness, effing and blinding. If there was a party going on, it didn't sound like a good-spirited one. I wondered what I was going to do when I went into the house. Mevlit would go crazy when he saw me.

Then I looked up at a first-floor window and realized that he already knew I was there. Mevlit was standing looking down at me but pulled the curtain the moment I saw him. That was it. I didn't care if he was nineteen or twenty-nine. He could be bloody fifty-nine. He was my son and he was coming home.

Striding up to the front door, I banged as hard as I could. But no one answered as I stood in the street shivering in my pyjamas. Bending down, I lifted up the letterbox flap and peered through it. I could see a tiny sitting room. It was brightly lit and full of people sitting around. Smoke hung in the air and I could see youngsters holding what looked like tiny pipes.

'I know my son is in there,' I shouted. 'Mevlit Brewster. I want him outside now.'

No one even turned to look at me. It was as if I hadn't even spoken.

'I've got my mobile phone in my hand,' I screamed. 'And you've got ten seconds to get my son out here before I start dialling nine nine nine.

'Ten . . . nine . . . eight . . .'

I must have got to about three before the door opened and Mevlit was pushed out on to the street. I looked at him in shock. He seemed disorientated, almost hyper. His eyes were glazed and he sneered as he looked at me.

'Get in the car,' I hissed at him as I grabbed his arm.

'Get the fuck off me, you bitch,' he snarled.

I knew I wouldn't get anywhere with him so I didn't say any more as he got into the car. But a cold feeling washed over me as I looked at Mevlit. He wasn't drunk. I'd learned to recognize people who'd had a few too many when I was just a child. I knew the look in their eyes and the stagger in their step. This was something different.

And it was then, as we drove home in silence, that a thought came into my mind which scared me. Was it drugs? Was that was this was all about? But what? Marijuana? I'd heard about people getting stoned, kids who experimented with things they'd been told all their life to stay away from.

Nothing more was said until next day, when I went into Mevlit's bedroom and sat down beside him on his bed.

'I want to talk to you about last night.'

Mum had found happiness again with Len, her second husband, photographed at Leigh-on-Sea in 1992.

A single woman again, smiling for the camera on a cruise on the *Oriana*, 1999.

Mevlit at thirteen. I sometimes felt my son had gone to bed as Mevlit and woke up as Kevin the Teenager.

The family at Mum's eightieth birthday party. I'm standing next to Ed Devey. Then seated from left to right are my brother Gary and my sister-in-law Barbara, Mum, my brother Stuart and his partner Angela.

In the hub and at the main depot at Pall-Ex. The responsibility I felt to Pall-Ex and the people who relied on me was the only thing that kept me going as I watched my son battle drug addiction.

In my office at Pall-Ex, being filmed for *The Business Inspector* which was aired on Channel 5 in March 2010.

Receiving an honorary doctorate from the University of Leicester in July 2010. Standing behind me are my MD Adrian Russell, my PA Deena, my financial director Martin Field and Robert Benoist.

I have a lot of admiration for Princess Anne and was honored that she attended a charity dinner I gave at Rangemore Hall in October 2010.

With the Duke of Kent, at a royal evening in aid of the Stroke Association at Rangemore, in November 2011. And, below, with my friend Rick Parfitt.

With my fellow Dragons in 2011. From left to right, Duncan Bannantyne, me, Theo Paphitis, Deborah Meaden and Peter Jones. When I complained about having to sit in the most uncomfortable chairs known to man, I was told they are iconic!

It took hours to get me to look stern enough in this *Dragon's Den* photo.

Having fun at the National Television Awards in January 2012, with Dermot O'Leary.

Relaxing at home with my beloved Yorkshire terriers, Mixie and Dixie – the loves of my life!

'What about it?' he spat.

'I'm worried.'

'Not this again. Leave me alone, Mum.'

I took a deep breath as I looked at him and knew I had to ask the question that I hadn't been able to get out of my mind.

'Are you taking drugs, Mevlit?'

He stared at me as if I'd gone mad.

'Don't be so stupid. I'd never do that. What do you think I am?'

He looked so appalled that I felt almost guilty asking the question but knew I had to.

'Are you telling me the truth, Mevlit? Please be honest. I know something is wrong. I know there is a problem. I want to know what it is and then we can sort it out together. Please, Mevlit. Just tell me.'

He leaned towards me, drawing himself closer and closer until his face was a blur in front of me. I wanted to see into his eyes, to find out if there was anything in them that might tell me the truth. I had to know. But Mevlit was so close to me that I couldn't see straight.

'What do you think I am, Mum?' I heard him say softly. 'Of course I'm telling the truth. I'd never do drugs.'

With that, he got up and walked out. Soon I heard the front door slam and knew that Mevlit would be getting into his car to go somewhere I couldn't find him. I felt completely lost. But more than that, I was afraid.

'Just give me some money, Mum.'

'No, Mevlit. I gave you a hundred pounds three days ago and you have to learn to make it last.'

'Please, Mum.'

'No.'

'You've got to.'

'No, Mevlit. Are you listening to me?'

'Yes I fucking am. Just give me some money.'

'Don't, Mevlit. Please don't.'

'But you can't leave me here without money. Don't you understand? You've got to give me some money. Just let me have fifty pounds. Anything. I need money.'

'Will you stop Mevlit? I've had enough of this.'

'You can't leave me.'

'I've got to. My meeting starts at eight-thirty tomorrow morning. If I don't drive down to London tonight then I'll never get there in time.'

'But Mum . . .'

'Mevlit. I am not going to give you any more money. Do you hear?'

His face was white as he looked at me. He seemed almost afraid.

'Look,' I said. 'Why don't you ring one of your friends? I'll go and pick them up and bring them back here.

'I'll half cook you some steaks so you just have to warm them up, put some jacket potatoes in the oven and make a salad. There are a couple of cans of lager in the fridge. You can have those.'

'Are you fucking joking?'

'No.'

'You're such a stupid bitch.'

'Mevlit . . .'

'Why can't you give me some money? You're so tight. Look at all you've got and you won't give your own son money.'

'Mevlit, please . . .'

'Fuck off. Give me some money. Please give me some money.'

'No, Mevlit. I've bailed you out again and again. I'm not going to give you any more.'

'Don't you see? You've got to give it to me.'

'I don't have to do anything.'

He walked towards me and thrust his face in mine.

'Give me some fucking money,' he screamed.

'No,' I yelled back at him, sick and tired of his rudeness and aggression, at my wits' end about what was becoming of him.

Mevlit turned around as he started to pace up and down the kitchen.

'So you're just going to leave me, are you? Fuck off like you always do.'

'Mevlit. It's an important meeting. I said I'd be there. I can't let them all down.'

'Like you let down your son?'

'Don't start that again.'

'Why not? It's the truth, isn't it? You're a shit mother. The worst mother. You never loved me and now you won't even give me what I need.'

'I will, Mevlit. Just not more money. No more money.'

'You don't give a fuck, do you?' he screamed as he walked towards me again. 'Just give me some money.'

'No.'

'Well fuck off then. I don't care if I never see you again. Tight bitch.'

He stormed out of the room as I bent down to pick up my overnight bag with a shaking hand. It was like this so often now. The arguments we had, the viciousness of his insults, the foul things he said to me and the hurt I felt when I heard them.

'Bye, Mevlit,' I called as I walked out of the door, wondering for the millionth time if I was right to be as hard as I was, knowing I had to be.

I got into the car and pulled down the drive. But as I got to the road, I looked in the rear-view mirror one last time and saw Mevlit sitting in the conservatory with his head in his hands. I knew as I started driving that he'd start calling now, as he always did. Over and over, he'd ring until he got hold of me and then the abuse would start again.

Within minutes I'd pulled on to the M1 at Junction 22. Driving down the motorway, my thoughts were full of Mevlit. I felt angry and hopeless, worried and fearful, as I did most of the time these days. My phone rang again and again as I drove, calls coming in from Mevlit one after the other as he tried to get hold of me. Green. Green. Green. The phone flashing continuously and the sound of its ring filling my car. By the time I reached Watford Gap Services, three junctions down the M1, I knew I had to do something. I pulled in to the car park and looked at my phone. Mevlit must have rung a hundred times. I picked up the phone and started listening.

'Please, Mum,' I heard him sob into to my answerphone. 'Just give me money. I need money.'

Message after message was the same: Mevlit pleading with me, more desperate than I'd ever heard him. He sounded tormented, almost disorientated.

'I need money, Mum,' he cried. 'Help me, Mum.'

Suddenly I felt afraid. There was something in Mevlit's voice that I'd never heard before. Utter desperation. A raw terror. For the first time I felt afraid that he might do something to harm himself. Pulling the car back on to the motorway, I drove until the next exit and turned around for home.

Mevlit was still sitting in the conservatory at the side of the house when I pulled up on the drive. He was hunched over, curled up like a wounded animal, and his head lifted as he heard the sound of my car. As he got up and disappeared from view, I knew that he'd soon walk out of the house and start to beg me again.

For those final few seconds before my life changed for ever, I tried to push away the thought that was in my mind, the fear which had been building inside me for weeks now since I'd switched on a late-night film as I tried to sleep. It was one of those true-life ones, called *Chasing the Dragon*, and I'd watched it almost without thinking. But then I'd seen something that I couldn't forget. The film was about a woman who became addicted to heroin and for some reason I wasn't quite sure of, she'd taken it in the bath. As I'd watched her lying in the water with eyes that were glazed and a body slack from the morphine coursing through it, I'd thought of Mevlit. The bath. He was forever in his. He spent hour after hour lying in the water, so long that I often worried he'd fall asleep and hurt himself.

The mind is a strange thing though. Even after seeing that film, I'd tried to push my thoughts away, stop myself from thinking about something that was too awful to comprehend. It couldn't be. It just couldn't.

But however much I'd tried to push them away, images of that woman lying in the bath hadn't stopped rolling around my head. I saw them again now as I waited for Mevlit to come out of the house. The baths. The hours he spent in the bath. It couldn't be. It just couldn't.

The moods and need for money. The recent trip to hospital after I'd found Mevlit rolling around in agony as he'd complained that his stomach was agony. I'd taken him to the local hospital and he'd been discharged after one night. I'd been told he might have a grumbling appendix but no one had been clear about what was wrong. It couldn't be. It just couldn't.

Mevlit came outside and walked down the drive towards my car. His face was pale and sweating. There were shadows underneath his eyes. He was skinny and unshaven, his skin covered in spots. I wound down the window and looked up at him.

'I need money, Mum, I need money,' he said. 'I need it now. Give it to me, Mum. Give it to me. Please.'

In that moment I knew what to say. In fact, the question came out of me almost before I had a chance to realize I was asking it.

'It's drugs, isn't it?' I said.

The words didn't feel like part of me. How could they be? This was my son. The baby I'd washed and changed, the little boy I'd taught to swim and cooked for, the teenager I'd worried about and tried to protect as best I could. But now all the worry, arguments and suspicion, the lies and deceit, came together as I confronted Mevlit with the one question I never thought I'd ask.

'Tell me. Is it drugs?'

'Yes.'

'Is it heroin?'

'Yes.'

My world collapsed as Mevlit said that word and I didn't

know how I'd ever rebuild it again as I looked at him. I couldn't move. I felt almost confused as I thought to myself that we should go into the house to talk and knew I couldn't bear to. It was our home, the place that should be safe for both of us, and now I knew it wasn't. Something else was in the house with us, something that was stealing my son from me bit by bit.

'Get in the car, Mevlit,' I said.

He was shaking and crying as he got in beside me.

'Calm down,' I told him gently. 'Please calm down. We'll sort this out, Mevlit. I promise you that we will. We'll find a way.'

He sobbed even harder as I started to cry too, unable to take it in, almost wishing that I had never asked the question.

'Please, Mum. Please just give me money.'

I looked at him, trying to find words I thought might never come. But as I did, I suddenly saw what I hadn't before. During everything that had happened over the past few years, I'd seen Mevlit's eyes sometimes empty, sometimes angry. But now I saw for the first time that they were full of pain. My child was in pain. And I was the one person who could help him.

'How much do you need?' I asked.

'A hundred.'

Chapter 19

'I was hoping you might be able to help me. I've just found out that my son is a heroin addict.'

'Certainly, Mrs . . .?'

'Devey.'

'Of course, Mrs Devey. We could admit him on Wednesday. Can we have your credit card details, please?'

I was so naïve when I first found out that Mevlit was an addict in April 2006. I thought rehab centres were places full of people in white coats, like a hospital aimed at addicts. Not true. I thought that addiction, like many other illnesses, could be treated quickly. Not true. Most importantly, I didn't realize that whoever says they can help an addict get clean always has the ultimate get-out clause: if the addict doesn't want to stop then they won't. It's true, of course, but for all the people doing really good work, there are those who aren't – and no one can ever point the finger at them because there's always the addict to blame.

In the days after Mevlit told me he was addicted to heroin, I walked around in a fog. I just couldn't take it in. I could not believe what I now knew to be the truth. My son, a heroin addict? But however confused I was, another part of me was practical. So many things fell into place as I read everything that I could find on the internet about addiction: his teeth, which morphine had discoloured; the stomach pains which were the first pangs of withdrawal; the mood swings as his body was taken over by the drugs and then craved it again within hours. The thing that scared me most though was reading the statistics, some of which told me that the average life span of a person after becoming addicted to heroin was just ten years.

I quickly learned that Mevlit needed the drugs and was in agony if he didn't have them. An addict will do anything to get a fix and so I continued to give him money to buy drugs while I decided what to do. I'm not sure if anyone who's never walked in my shoes could understand that. But all I'll say is that once I'd started to scratch at the fringes of his addiction, I knew I couldn't live with myself if he burgled a house or mugged an old woman to get his next fix.

That's the thing about addiction: you have two choices. Let the person you love go, knowing they might sink even further, perhaps realize your darkest fears when they're found dead somewhere; or do what you think might save them. It's an almost impossible decision to make when it's your own son or daughter. I hadn't asked Mevlit too many questions about how he had started to take heroin and he had not given me any answers because he was in no fit state to. But now I began to suspect that he had been taking drugs for a long time, and while some parents will kick their child to the kerb for the sake of tough love, I just couldn't bring myself to. Until I found a way to help him, I would do what I had to even though it sickened me.

The fear which filled me each time Mevlit left the house or

I heard the phone ring was like nothing I'd ever known. It was as if every minute of every day was spent on a knife edge, waiting for the knock on the door from the police to tell me that he'd been arrested, or the call to say that he had died – even though it felt to me in some ways as if he already had. Finding out that my child was an addict felt like being bereaved. The son I thought I'd raised had gone and in his place was someone I didn't know. Grief filled me, and in some ways it still does. I don't think I'll ever fully understand how we came to where we did.

I knew I had to get Mevlit help. But where? I didn't have a clue what to do and so I did the only thing I could think of: sat on the internet for hour after hour Googling anything and everything that came into a mind numb with shock. The biggest question in my mind was 'Why?' Why would a teenager who'd been loved and looked after want to put such poison into their body? Why would they run the risk of killing themselves even before their adult life had really started? Slowly I learned that addiction is an illness and those in its grip don't feel love or pain, remorse or sorrow. All they can think of is their next fix, the lies they will tell to get it, the objects they will steal to fund it, without a thought for the people who love them. An addict will find heroin in the Sahara if they can. It's as simple as that.

It is the bleakest place that any parent can go to with their child. When you think you can't go any lower, you realize that you can. When you convince yourself there is nothing more your child can do to shock you, they do. When you tell yourself that you know all there is to know, there are secrets waiting to be uncovered.

*

'Your son is a low-life junkie, Mrs Devey,' the drug counsellor intoned at me down the phone. 'And you are nothing but a drug enabler.'

'What do you mean?'

'That you've helped him get drugs.'

'But what else could I do?'

'Refuse to support his addiction.'

'Well of course I don't support it. But I didn't know what else to do. He needed help.'

'Not the kind you gave him.'

I'd called the counsellor every day since Mevlit had gone into a rehab unit in Bedfordshire, ten days after telling me about his addiction, and it was clear the counsellor was getting sick of me. The day I'd taken Mevlit there, I'd gone back to the hub and done a photo shoot with the diet guru Rosemary Conley for a charity project that we were both supporting. I'd carried on working and going to meetings too, as unable to renege on my work commitments as I ever had been. Inside I was wondering how on earth I was going to find the strength to straddle the two lives I now inhabited. But I'd learned long before how to mask my feelings and I did it again now.

I'd found the rehab centre on the internet and was sure it was what Mevlit needed to kick his habit. I'd heard of these places and surely it would be the solution. I'd found him treatment, he'd undergo it and our life could go back to normal. Wasn't that how things like this worked?

After going through the painful process of withdrawal, Mevlit would have counselling, and I naïvely believed it would make him well again. All he needed to do was understand that he would kill himself if he carried on abusing drugs.

There's only one word for how my mind was working during those early days and it's denial.

'What do you mean?' I asked the counsellor, almost unable to take his words in.

'I mean that Mevlit has taken every conceivable drug there is. Your son is addicted to crack cocaine and heroin, he injects heroin and . . .'

I didn't hear another word. Crack cocaine? I didn't even understand what that was. Injecting? I'd clung on to the idea that Mevlit was smoking heroin just like the woman I'd seen in the film, because for some reason I was convinced that it would be easier for him to kick the habit. It took me time to realize that it wouldn't, and that it was possible to hide needle marks by injecting in the groin or foot.

'. . . so you see that it's up to Mevlit to stop taking drugs,' I heard the counsellor say. 'If he wants to then he will. If he doesn't he won't.'

It was like that for the next month, until I got a phone call to say that Mevlit had been kicked out of the rehab centre after selling a television I'd taken down for him. He'd been caught passing money out of a window of the house to a dealer. I was devastated but now wonder, who could blame him? Put addicts into recovery houses on residential streets and drug dealers soon find out where they are. Then all they need to do is hang around long enough to get sales from people they know are desperate for a fix.

It was pointless sending Mevlit to a place like that, but back then I didn't realize – just as I didn't know when I visited him one weekend and took him to a service station for food, because he was too paranoid and jittery to sit in a normal restaurant, that he'd be able to buy drugs when he went to the loo. I don't know where the money came from to this day.

That's the thing about addiction though: the secrecy and lies are like nothing you'd ever be able to imagine until you're forced to. And all the time you're trying to help someone recover, there are dealers in places you'd never expect to find them, the gaps and cracks you wouldn't even notice, just waiting to scuttle out and sell to someone whose desperation they recognize. Mevlit didn't have friends. He knew people who took drugs with him or sold them to him. He didn't have any kind of life apart from waiting for his next fix. And the people who'd help him get it were everywhere.

Dealers hang around street corners and parks, they sell drugs from behind the counters of corner shops or do home delivery for the people they know will pay up. It's a five-star service carried out in the dingiest and most unexpected places by people who make money from slowly murdering addicts. If I had my way, they'd be hung.

But I still had so much to learn when I got Mevlit into a second rehab in Bedfordshire – refusing to believe that this was a problem I couldn't solve.

'I'll do it, Mum, I really will,' Mevlit had told me as he'd looked me in the eye.

I'd yet to learn just how many lies my child would tell in order to hide his addiction. I told myself that the shock of getting kicked out of his first rehab would surely be the wake-up call Mevlit needed to change.

'Do you mind doing me a supermarket shop?' he'd asked when I next went to visit him.

Once again he'd been put into a house full of alcoholics and drug users who lived together as they tried to kick their habits, and I breathed a silent sigh of relief when he asked for food. Surely it meant he was getting better? Mevlit was skin and bone by now because he'd lost several stone in weight and I took his appetite as a sure sign that the treatment was working. Days later, I got a phone call to say that he'd run away from the unit. What I didn't know until later was that he'd sold all the food I'd bought in order to get heroin.

As I drove down to search for Mevlit, I got a call from Karen.

'He's on a train to Derby,' she told me.

'He is?'

'Yes. He wants to stay with us.'

'But he's OK?'

'Yes. He's fine. He just couldn't stand the place. He says he's had enough of all that.'

'He does?'

'Yes.'

'You're sure?'

'Yes.'

Strange as it sounds, some addled part of my brain wanted to believe so much that Mevlit might be well again that I did. He had had some treatment. Karen had told me that she'd make sure he didn't use drugs again.

'You'll make sure he's OK?' I asked her.

'Of course, Hilary,' she said. 'He just needs some time, you know? He can't face coming home yet.'

But when Mevlit did a couple of weeks later, I couldn't pretend any more that he wasn't as addicted as he ever had been. I knew the signs now: hours spent in the bathroom, aggressive and moody behaviour, the glazed look that I some-times saw in his eyes – eyes that had once been full of light and were now empty.

I saw other things, too, for the first time now that I had read all I could about addiction: the 'nod' that heroin addicts give when they're high, slipping in and out of a haze; the 'rattle' they feel when their body shakes as their craving becomes too much and they are racked with pain until the next fix. Now his secret was out, Mevlit didn't try to hide these things from me any more.

Never underestimate how desperate a parent can be to find a cure for their child. As I tried to find a new way to help Mevlit, all the time existing in a marriage that was falling apart and running Pall-Ex, I clutched at any straw I could find. I even sent him to a clinic that claimed to have discovered a scientific method of treating heroin addicts called reverse ionization. He went there only a few weeks after coming back from the rehab units and I convinced myself that this would be what he needed. The centre claimed to be able to cure any addict. They had statements signed by those in recovery, words in black and white which told me about the miracle that cured addiction.

Believe me when I say that places like that clinic prey on people's desperation. It cost me thousands of pounds to have some electrodes stuck on Mevlit's head before he was given vitamin tablets. He'd soon scoured the streets to score more heroin because he was in such severe withdrawal. After signing a testimonial as he left the clinic to say that he was no longer an addict, Mevlit walked back into the kitchen at Berry Hills Farm and looked at a roll of tin foil lying on the side.

'I don't need this any more, do I?' he said with a smile.

Addicts use tin foil to take heroin. When Mevlit said those words, I knew that the treatment had been useless.

'I'm going out,' he said and I could not breathe as I watched him leave for God-knows-where.

It was more awful than I'd ever imagined. What I didn't realize then was just how much lower we would have to go before Mevlit and I finally glimpsed light again.

Chapter 20

Mevlit had been back at home for about two weeks when the phone rang one night. I'd just cooked dinner for friends, desperate to cling on to some kind of normal when there wasn't such a thing any more – because I'd reluctantly started giving him money again after realizing that the rehab hadn't worked. I knew I would continue to do so until I found another way to help him.

'My son is a heroin addict, my son is a heroin addict,' I'd think to myself, hearing the words rushing around my brain and trying to get them to sink in, torn between terror and utter hopelessness.

Each night when I got home from Pall-Ex, I continued to go on the internet and read everything I could find. Why hadn't the treatments worked? What else did I need to do? Surely there was something that would help Mevlit? After a lifetime spent problem-solving in business – and occasionally walking away from situations which I knew could never be put right – I was tormented because I couldn't find an answer. I knew that many people around me wanted me to give up on Mevlit but I never could.

I'd learned a little more during those sleepless nights spent reading, and the simple answer is that addicts are forever searching for the perfect high they get when they take heroin for the first time, the feeling of absolute bliss that engulfs them. That's the sensation they search for again and again, not knowing they will never find it. Soon they are addicted.

But although I had agreed to fund Mevlit's drugs again, I'd insisted on putting a limit on the amount of money I gave him.

'You have to try and cut down while we decide what to do next,' I'd told him. 'I'll give you so much but no more.'

But just a few days ago, he'd come downstairs rattling and I'd known immediately that there was going to be trouble.

'I need money,' he'd snarled.

'No. You've had enough.'

'But I need it.'

'No.'

'I'm going out.'

It was often his answer. Like all addicts, Mevlit knew exactly how to manipulate those around him to get what he wanted and how frightened I was every time he left the house.

'Where are you going?' I'd yelled one afternoon as I walked out on to the drive after Mevlit when he stormed out of the house. 'Come back here. You're not going out. Just talk to me.'

Without a backwards glance, he'd walked up to the brand-new Mercedes I'd just bought and started kicking it.

'Just give me the fucking money!' he'd roared and there was nothing I could do as he smashed his foot again and again into the side of my car.

Each day now was a battle: with Mevlit, with Ed and with myself as I forced myself to carry on working, trying to keep my business together – and throwing bloody dinner parties.

As my mobile rang, I got up to answer it, knowing Mevlit would be on the other end of the line.

'You've got to come and get me,' I heard him scream.

'Mevlit?'

'Quickly. I'm going to get stabbed.'

'What do you mean?'

'You've got to come, Mum.'

'Where are you?'

He shouted an address before the line went dead and I looked at my friends.

'I have to go. Mevlit needs me.'

Ed, who was there that night, looked at me angrily.

'If you go to him then you're mad,' he snapped.

I didn't have a choice and so I left my husband and guests as I went alone to pull my son out of a drug den. I didn't think for a second about where I was going or what kind of people would be there. I just had to get Mevlit. But ten minutes after pulling my car out of the driveway, I saw a blue light flashing behind me. I stopped and wound down the window.

'Where are you going?' the police officer asked.

'To pick up my son.'

'And have you been drinking?'

'I've had one small glass of wine and a couple of sips of another.'

'In that case we need to breathalyse you.'

'But I'm not over the limit. I'd never drive over the limit.'

'And so I'm sure you won't mind helping us, will you?'

I got out of the car as the officer went to get a breathalysing machine. Then he walked back to me and told me to blow into it. I must have done it three or four times before the officer turned to me.

'You're over the limit,' he said.

'But I can't be. I've only had a glass and a couple of sips. I've told you.'

'Well that doesn't seem to be the case.'

The officer walked around the car before stopping to stare at the number plate.

'Private reg?' he sneered. 'You won't be driving this for a while, will you, love?'

I was one point over the legal limit for alcohol and absolutely devastated when I was convicted for drink-driving. My reputation in the transport industry was built on being a stickler for standards and I would never have got behind the wheel if I'd thought for a moment that I was over the limit. Since the age of twenty-one, I'd never driven less than 1,000 miles a week or had so much as a speeding ticket. Now I felt utterly ashamed as I stood in court to be told that I would be banned from driving for nine months.

Mevlit had been pulled out of whichever drug den he was in that night by a friend who was at the dinner party, who'd agreed to go and get him after I'd rung home to explain what had happened. Meanwhile, I'd been taken to a police station and as I sat waiting to find out what was going to happen to me, I'd cried and cried, feeling utterly heartbroken about how low I'd been brought and how alone I felt. My husband hadn't come to help me and my son was God-knows-where. When I got home, though, and told Mevlit what had happened, he just looked at me blankly.

'It was your own fucking fault,' he spat.

There were moments over the next month that Mevlit was at home when I felt like I was hovering above my life, looking down at it but unable to believe what was happening and powerless to stop it. When I went away for the weekend, I got back home to find that every DVD and television in my house had gone.

'Where are they?' I asked Mevlit.

'We've been burgled.'

'Really? So shall I call the police?'

There was a moment's silence before he started to walk away.

'You didn't leave me with any money,' he hissed.

An outhouse filled with expensive bottles of wine was emptied and the money used to buy drugs; a petrol card Mevlit had been given to fill up his car was used to fill up other drivers' tanks in return for cash; and everything that was worth anything and wasn't bolted down went missing – from jewellery and designer clothes to a Chanel handbag and joints of meat from the freezer. I soon put locks on all the doors in the house to try and keep things safe. My home was a prison, but the worst of it was realizing that Mevlit hadn't just started stealing from me – he'd been doing it for years.

It's as if the foundations of your life start to crumble as you look back and try to find the signposts to what started your child on drugs. You pick through the past, examining every moment as you try to find the key. I remembered a day when Mevlit was about fourteen and I'd caught him taking an emerald ring from a safe in my bedroom. He was with a friend and insisted he was the one who'd made him do it so I'd believed him. I had no reason not to, and after giving him a severe dressing-down I told him that there would be even bigger trouble if I ever caught him doing anything like it again.

I hadn't, and thought that was the end of it. But now I wondered if he'd been stealing from me even then.

There were other odd things which had gone missing in more recent years but I'd never suspected Mevlit of stealing for a second. I'd thought it was a cleaner I'd had. But now I felt sure that my own son had been thieving from me for longer than I wanted to admit. He even took money out of Mum's purse.

Mevlit's lies and deception seemed to know no bounds and I began to realize that he'd drawn people I knew into his web, forced them to keep his secrets after he'd threatened to reveal theirs. I felt as if there was no one I could trust. It made me feel very alone, utterly powerless, and so I determined to do the one thing I could: help catch the people who were supplying Mevlit and other kids like him. I knew who some of them were because they'd turned up at the house demanding money for his debts, or I'd seen them when I went to rescue him from houses that I now knew were crack dens – even going back to one after pulling Mevlit out because he'd left his ruddy dog behind.

I was so determined to do anything I could to keep him safe that I'd had a tracker device fitted to his car and employed a private investigator to follow him sometimes. But I also contacted the police when I discovered that a regular amount was being drawn out of his bank account on the same day each week and realized it must be paying off a drug debt.

After speaking to the drugs squad in Derby, I was visited by an officer and gave him some numbers I'd copied from Mevlit's phone.

'Is it possible to see the rest?' he asked and I crept up to Mevlit's bedroom where he was sleeping and took his mobile.

The policeman said he'd take the numbers off it and return it the next day. In the mean time, I knew that Mevlit would just think he'd lost his phone.

'We don't have the resources to go after the street dealers, I'm afraid,' the policeman explained as we chatted. 'We need to target the bigger dealers to try and make more of an impact.

'The thing is, for every one we catch, there will always be others waiting to take their place.'

The officer was sympathetic and kind. He didn't judge my junkie son or dismiss my worries and the police used the information I gave them to make arrests. They even found the man who was drawing money from Mevlit's account and told me that he ran his own business – as well as selling heroin on the side.

I was glad he'd got caught and I wanted the rest of those bastards punished too. It gave me a grim satisfaction to know that some of them had been because of me. The police warned me to stop making waves in the end though because otherwise I might end up on a mortuary slab with a tag on my toe. Reluctantly, I listened to them.

But it frustrates me to know that the police have got an almost impossible task. However good the job they do with limited resources, they're fighting a losing battle. The police are never going to stem all the criminality associated with drugs because there are just too few of them and too many of the dealers. That's why I think there's something to be said for decriminalizing drugs and regulating them. Look at Prohibition in 1920s America – the Mob didn't know what to do when it ended and their opportunities for providing bootleg alcohol and committing crimes went with it.

Once again, though, it's down to bloody politicians because no one has got the balls to say that something's got to change. Millions of pounds are going into criminalizing addicts when the money could be used to rehabilitate them. Think of the stigma too – the shame which pushes people further into the secrecy around addiction – just because some drugs, like nicotine, are socially acceptable and some are not. What's the most damaging one of all? Alcohol.

Surely it's time for someone to ask what we're doing wrong when it comes to illegal drugs and to have the courage to try something new. I know it's a controversial point of view that you might not agree with and I certainly can't tell you exactly what should be done. But I'm sure I could come up with a better strategy if I thought long and hard enough about it because the one we have now just isn't working. The problems we have in this country are never going to be solved the way things are.

The one thing you need to know about this time is that Mevlit had told me he wanted to get back in touch with his father, which worried me a great deal. You see, several years before, Hussain's sister Sabiha had told me that he'd been jailed for importing heroin with a street value of £1.8 million six years after we'd finally split. I was utterly shocked because, whatever his failings, I'd never thought that Hussain would get involved in something like drugs. Mevlit was about twelve when I found out and he knew about it all but had never said he wanted to see his dad. All that changed though when he came out of rehab.

It had been fourteen years now since Mevlit had seen Hussain. He was only five when his father had disappeared from our life and I worried that meeting him again – a father who was a criminal because of drugs – would at best be unhelpful and at worst damaging. But I accepted that it was Mevlit's choice and I wasn't going to stand in his way if he believed it might help him.

After hiring a private investigator, because Sabiha hadn't spoken to Hussain since the day he was convicted and didn't know where he was, I was sent Hussain's prison number as well as an address to write to. But a letter soon came back telling us that the prisoner did not wish to make contact. Mevlit took one look at it and ripped it up. I've always wondered since if that rejection only made him worse – and whether the sins of the father were being visited on his drug-addicted son.

Amid the confusion and fear, the sadness and guilt, there was one other feeling which kept bubbling up above all the others: anger. I felt bloody murderous, to be honest, because as much as I tried to understand Mevlit's problems, there was a part of me that just couldn't. How dare he behave like this? How could he do the things he was doing? I didn't think there was anything on earth that could have made me behave as he did.

That's how I was feeling on the day that a woman we'll call Shirley came to see me. She'd started a drug charity after discovering her son was addicted to heroin and now worked to support the families of others with problems.

Her son was on a methadone programme and I wanted to talk to her about the possibility of Mevlit starting one. It's a drug that's used as a substitute for heroin. Under medical supervision, users take methadone instead of heroin and the idea is to wean them off until gradually they become drug-free.

As we sat and chatted, though, I just couldn't concentrate on what Shirley was saying. I knew I should be thinking clearly and discussing the next attempt at getting Mevlit well again, but all I felt was blind rage.

'How could he?' I suddenly exploded. 'I'm outraged at what he's done. The lying and stealing. The aggression and deceit. I try to understand, I really do, but I just don't recognize my own son any more.'

Shirley looked at me as I ranted on. If she told me yet another thing that I didn't want to hear – that I should kick Mevlit out or stop giving him money for the drugs – then I would probably explode. I was trying to find something that would help him and had even gone to Narcotics Anonymous meetings to hear what other addicts had to say, to try and understand it all better. But it was one thing for adults to talk about reaching a higher place. How was a teenager going to do that?

Then Shirley said she understood how I felt and stopped me dead in my tracks.

'You do?'

'Yes. I felt all that you're feeling now when I found out about my son. But if you're going to help Mevlit then you have to understand that the life of a heroin addict is hard. It's a full-time job.'

'What do you mean?'

'Just think of it, Hilary: the cravings and physical symptoms; the money you need and the places you have to go to buy your drugs.

'No sooner does an addict take heroin than they need their

next dose. Think of the worst flu you could ever have and times it by a thousand. That's what an addict feels every time withdrawal starts, which can be hours after their last fix. All they want to do is stave that feeling off. They don't care about anything else. They *can't* care about anything else.'

'But what did I do wrong?' I cried. 'Surely I must have done something? I'm his mother, for God's sake, and he keeps telling me it's my fault. I can't bear it when he does. I can't stop thinking about it.'

'An addict will blame everyone but themselves,' Shirley said kindly. 'But remember that everybody has a path in life that they choose.

'Many heroin addicts have emotional problems that the drugs are masking, but they're not necessarily anyone's fault.

'What you and I think of as normal pressure is too much for them. They can't function in the world as we do. Their lives are based around one thing and one thing only: drugs.

'It's all they care about it and that's why they turn into different people. But the son you love is still there. And if he can find a way to live a drug-free life then he will come back to you.'

I felt a little less angry by the time Shirley left me that day, and glad to know I wasn't alone in feeling as I did. I just wasn't sure if Mevlit was ever going to take the help that was being offered to him.

Mevlit agreed to go on the methadone programme and started it a few weeks after moving out of Berry Hills Farm in July 2006. The lying, stealing, aggression and uncertainty had all got too much for me – as had the visits from police. They'd come once after Mevlit was caught on CCTV talking to dealers and again when he'd failed to return a hire car and the company had reported it stolen. Officers arrived at the house, opened the boot of the car and found syringes and tin foil. I felt so ashamed but Mevlit wasn't at the house and while the police asked for him to go and see them, he refused however many times I told him to.

I had to face facts: we just couldn't carry on as we were. A few months of living with Mevlit's secret had been enough to almost break me. I was hardly sleeping, felt scared and anxious all the time. I just couldn't have coped much longer if we'd stayed under the same roof. I'd never felt so close to the edge but still wasn't prepared to wash my hands of my son. Instead, I paid for him to go into a hotel where me and the people I trusted could keep an eye on him. Robert Benoist, a former lawyer who'd started to work for Pall-Ex and become a trusted friend, was the person I turned to again and again for help with Mevlit.

He stayed for a week at one hotel in Derby before moving into another and it was there that he started on a methadone programme after discussions with a GP. It meant that he had to be taken to a chemist in Loughborough every day, where he was given liquid methadone and watched as he drank it. Robert agreed to take him from Monday to Thursday. I would accompany him on Fridays and weekends.

I can't imagine what my chauffeur Kiran – who I'd employed after losing my licence – must have thought of it all because it was as if the gates of hell themselves opened most days when Mevlit got into the car.

'What time are you coming?' he'd say when he woke up on the mornings that I was due to pick him up. That would be the first of dozens of calls, becoming more and more agitated as time ticked on.

'Eleven-thirty. Just like always, I'd reply.'

'What time?'

'Eleven-thirty.'

'It's too long. Come now.'

'I can't, Mevlit. You have an appointment.'

'I can't wait. Just fucking come and get me.'

We usually had the conversation at least thirty times before I got to his hotel. If I was late on a Saturday, because I always went to see Mum before picking up Mevlit, he'd ring even more. But he'd never let me go up to his room when I arrived and so I had to sit and wait with Kiran until the door opened and Mevlit got in. Then one of two things would happen: he'd either sit completely silently or start screaming abuse.

'Where the fuck have you been? Why did you keep me waiting? And why are you making me do this?'

'Because it might help you to get better.'

'Just leave me alone. What do you care?'

Each time we drove to Loughborough Mevlit would also insist that he was hungry. After stopping to get fast food, he would eat it in a rush and we'd soon have to pull up the car so that he could be violently sick on the roadside.

'Look at me!' he'd shout. 'Why are you making me do this? What a fucking waste of time.'

Sitting beside me, Mevlit would rattle – sweating, shaking and shouting non-stop – until the moment he went into the chemist to get his methadone. Five minutes later, I knew he'd come out a little calmer. But each time I watched him walk inside, I would wonder where my child had gone. It was as if he'd been possessed, and as much as I hated to admit it, there were times when Mevlit frightened me.

Within a couple of weeks, though, it was clear that Mevlit's heroin usage wasn't decreasing – in fact, if anything it was getting worse as he started to ask for more and more money. Some six weeks after starting the methadone programme, Mevlit stopped it and I was at my wits' end. In early September he was cautioned for possession of heroin after being kicked out of his hotel when staff reported him to police. Robert initially hid what had happened from me. He knew how close I was to the edge and simply told me that Mevlit had moved out of the hotel and in with a friend.

The truth couldn't be hidden for ever, though. I knew Mevlit had gone back on to heroin when the requests for money started again, and once more I reluctantly agreed to fund him as I tried to work out what to do next. It scared me more and more though because Mevlit needed up to £400 a day now just to get his fixes. No wonder women are driven to prostitution to fund a habit or young men become serial burglars to pay for their drugs. I understand why they do after seeing what depths addicts will go to in order to fund their habit. It seemed to me that it was only a matter of time before Mevlit got a criminal conviction.

Now that I wasn't living with Mevlit any more, I had enough breathing space to realize for the first time that this was a problem I might never solve. I could offer Mevlit comfort and pay for treatment, I could be tough with him or loving, but I couldn't make him give up, however many chances I gave him. The only thing that would force him to stop was him. But how was he ever going to do that?

The knowledge that I was almost powerless to stop him

killing himself plunged me into the only true depression I've ever experienced. No matter how bad it had got before, I'd managed to pull myself together. But now when I woke each morning, I just wanted to die. I dreaded opening my eyes but knew I had to carry on functioning for everyone else's sake. If it had been down to me, though, I would have given up. I've never been one of those bright-side people. Life's tough and I've always known it. But while my cup had never been full, it had never been empty either. Now I felt as if it was, because my son was beyond my reach.

Looking back at the past, I thought about everything that had happened – Hussain, the times when I hadn't had a penny in my purse, setting up Pall-Ex alone and carrying it all on my shoulders. Then I looked at my present: the son I loved more than anything who was killing himself, the man I'd married believing we'd be happy though we weren't, the people around me who must have known about Mevlit's problems long before I did but never told me. Then I looked into the future and couldn't see one.

I felt as if I was stuck on a wheel that I couldn't get off. The demands of Pall-Ex were relentless as it kept on growing and I was on the edge of an abyss, so close to falling. What kept me going was my sense of responsibility. People relied on me and Pall-Ex saved me in many ways back then because it forced me not to give up. So even though I felt as if I was dying inside, breaking apart piece by piece, I went to the doctor, who prescribed anti-depressants, and I just kept going. Sometimes in life it's all you can do, isn't it? You just keep putting one foot in front of the other.

Chapter 21

It was late 2006 and Mevlit had refused to see me for weeks.
Each time I rang him, the phone went dead. But when I woke
up one Sunday morning after a particularly sleepless night, I
knew I had to see him. It had been too long. I wanted to see
for myself what kind of state he was in.

Robert drove me into Derby because I wasn't sure that I
could go alone, and I found the front door of the flat where
Mevlit was living with a friend unlocked. Walking into the
living room, I looked at him. He was sitting huddled up on
the sofa, staring blankly at the floor.

'Mevlit?' I said as I sat down beside him.

He didn't speak. He just hung his head and my heart almost
stopped as I looked at him. He'd lost even more weight. He
was literally skin and bone. Mevlit's healthy weight had always
been around fourteen stone but by now he must have weighed
about nine and looked like a skeleton. His skin was pale and
spotty, there were shadows under his eyes, his hair was greasy
and his clothes dirty.

'Mevlit,' I said as I reached out to take his hand.

It lay still as I tried to take it.

I looked around the room. With the curtains closed, it was

shrouded in darkness. There were cigarette butts all over the floor, burns in the sofa and carpet. The whole place stank to high heaven.

Tears rushed up in me as I turned back to Mevlit. He wasn't rattling this time. He was out of it. Doped and almost oblivious that I was there. The tears came so thick and fast that I couldn't speak as the two of us sat silently together.

'What am I going to do?' I sobbed when I eventually started talking. 'What do I have to say to convince you that you have to stop this, Mevlit? If not for yourself, then think of me. What life will I have if I lose you? You're everything to me. If you're not here then my life won't be worth a thing.'

He didn't move or speak.

'Please, Mevlit. Listen to me. You have to listen to me. Why are you doing this to yourself? I'm trying to understand. I really am. I know this is an illness but it's different to anything a doctor can cure.

'I'd go to the ends of the earth for you. I'd do anything I could to make you better. But surely you must see that I can't? It's not up to me to put this right. It's down to you. You have to stop, Mevlit. You're killing yourself.'

He still didn't say a word. I had to find a way to get through to him because I knew as I looked at him that I wasn't fighting to save my son from heroin any more. I was fighting to save his life.

'Mevlit, please, please, please.'

I couldn't speak through the tears. I just sat beside him, more scared than I ever had been before that I was going to lose my son to the poison he kept putting into his body.

'Don't you want to get out of this mess that you're in?' I said eventually.

I stared at him, waiting for some sign – however tiny – that he was hearing what I said.

And then it came.

He nodded his head.

'Will you let me try something?' I said. 'Will you trust me?'

He nodded again.

'I've been researching different rehabs, trying to find something new, something that might help you, and I think I might have found it.

'There's a drug called naltrexone and people say it can have really good results. I've found a clinic in Harrogate that will put you on to it but first they'll detox you under sedation. It means that it won't be so painful, Mevlit, that you'll be helped step by step. I want you to try it. Will you?'

Those few seconds felt like the longest of my life as I looked at him and waited. But eventually Mevlit lifted his head and finally looked at me. Pain filled his eyes. Torment.

He nodded his head once more.

I have never found out exactly what Dr Amal Beaini, a consultant psychiatrist at Detox 5, said to Mevlit. All I knew as Mevlit walked out of the room after seeing him was that he seemed to have listened to whatever Dr Beaini had said.

The relief that filled me was cautious. On the journey up to Yorkshire, we'd stopped at some services just past Sheffield and Mevlit had tried to run away. Robert was with me and the two of us had run after him. When we eventually caught up with Mevlit, I could see that he was terrified.

'You're going to die if you don't get treatment,' I said to him again and again. 'You're going to die.'

He'd let me lead him back to the car and sat quietly until

we got to Detox 5. Then he'd gone in to see Dr Beaini and told me when he came out that he would agree to be detoxed before starting naltrexone.

The reason I wanted him to go Detox 5 was because he'd be sedated throughout the withdrawal period and medically supervised. Mevlit 'rattled' within hours of his last dose of heroin – feeling anxious and in physical pain – which is why he medicated himself with another fix. I was pretty sure he'd got past the point of feeling the pleasure of a high by now. He was simply taking heroin to stave off the feeling of going without it and was afraid that a detox would mean even more pain, sweating, muscle spasms and vomiting.

But after being helped through it, Mevlit would go on to naltrexone, a drug that would block the effects of heroin. Even if Mevlit took heroin, he would not feel any kind of high and would be prescribed naltrexone in tablet form for a year – time for him to glimpse what a normal, drug-free life might be like. I knew by now that he'd started experimenting with drugs when he was a young teenager – smoking marijuana at school before moving on to speed and ecstasy, then heroin and crack cocaine. Mevlit didn't know what adult life was like without drugs. Detox 5 would give him the chance of discovering that.

They say that heroin addicts must change the people, the place and the playground. That's why I rented him a beautiful, newly built townhouse in Derby and furnished it for him. He would go there when he left Detox 5 and start building a new life.

I believed he was doing that for all of about four weeks. When Mevlit came home for Christmas and ended up screaming and shouting at me, throwing plates and hurling abuse, as I cleared up the kitchen after lunch I knew that things weren't right. He might be on naltrexone and free of heroin. But he was certainly not free of drugs. I couldn't face talking to him about it on Christmas Day. We had friends over and I wanted them to have as happy a day as possible. But when I did finally tackle Mevlit about my suspicions, he did what he always did: lied and told me there was nothing to worry about.

'I mean it, Mevlit. This will be your last chance. If you don't make the most of it then you won't get another one.'

It was May 2007 and I was standing in the lounge of a house in Burton-on-Trent that Mevlit was now living in with his girlfriend Sam. Unemployed and seemingly as lost as him, I wasn't sure about her at all. But Mevlit had fallen for Sam and they were living in Burton together because he'd had to leave the townhouse I'd rented for him in Derby after leaving Detox 5. The landlord had called me in a rage one day and I'd felt filled with shame as I'd looked at what my son had done to the house: there were holes punched in walls and doors and his dog had defecated all over the bedroom floor and even the mattress. Mevlit and the bloody Hound of the Baskervilles had ruined the place. Between the two of them, I'd had to replace every door, fill in walls, put in a new carpet throughout and even repair skirting boards and the garden fence because the dog had chewed anything it could get its teeth into.

It had cost me £9,000 to put right and I'd refused to give Mevlit any more cash after that. I'd had enough of funding his addiction and having all the chances I'd given him thrown back in my face. I'd pay his rent and utility bills to keep a roof over his head but that was it. Mevlit's ability to manipulate me was breathtaking, though: he'd tell me he needed to go to the dentist and so I'd give money to him, or he'd simply steal from my home again if I refused. By now I had a safe and all my jewellery went into it. Instead he stole whatever was worth anything – from expensive cigarette lighters to cameras. He'd even go into my bag and take my cash card while I was showering.

He must have lasted on the naltrexone tablets for all of four months, and I knew then that he was back on heroin. Soon he began to lose weight again, his skin taking on the familiarly washed-out tone, his mood getting more and more dark. God knows how or why Sam put up with him but she did. She loved Mevlit more than he deserved to be back then. But I was almost at the point where I couldn't bear to look at him. I was angry, disappointed, let down yet again by all his promises and lies.

'Are you back on heroin?' I'd asked a few minutes before as I stood looking at him.

For once, he'd admitted the truth. Maybe he'd seen in my eyes that this time I wasn't going to fall for his lies. I didn't scream or shout. I did not have the energy to fight him any more. He needed to understand that my mind was made up.

'I will send you back to Detox 5,' I said. 'Because if anyone can make you better it's them. We know the naltrexone worked for a while. You just have to keep taking it. But this time you'll have the drug implanted into your stomach rather than take it in tablet form. Do you agree?'

He nodded.

'Because this is it, Mevlit. Do you hear me? The final time. I will help you once more and then you've had all your chances. If you mess this one up then I will not help you again.'

A couple of weeks later, Mevlit went back to Detox 5 to have a naltrexone implant fitted and has been clean of heroin ever since. Don't go looking for a fairy-tale ending, though, because you know there are none of those in this book. Heroin addicts don't just come off the drug and snap back into normal life. They have to relearn it, and that takes time. They might continue to use other drugs even when they are clean of their preferred one.

But step by step, we are living each day and I know how lucky we are. Many parents never experience the comfort of seeing their child start to get well again. Mums and dads who think their children are finally clean get that awful call to tell them their son or daughter is dead from an accidental overdose after relapsing in secret. Or they know their child is back on drugs and have to face the fact that there is nothing more they can do to help them. Or they keep fighting their addiction – and get dragged down for ever into the abyss.

We take each day now as it comes but there is still a part of me that cannot quite believe I will never get that phone call I once dreaded every second of the day. But in the five years since Mevlit came out of Detox 5 for the second time in May 2007, the fear inside has faded just a little. He's still with Sam, she's stuck by him through everything and I've realized that I got her wrong at first. In fact I've come to respect Sam a great deal, because I can see that she wants to better herself in life and is working hard at college to do that. The two of them are happy together and I can only pray that Mevlit continues to be well.

Chapter 22

You might be forgiven for thinking that the rest of my life had stopped during all of Mevlit's problems but it didn't. In August 2006, I'd bought the Edward VII wing of Rangemore Hall, the most beautiful property in Staffordshire. The wing was built especially for a visit from Edward VII in 1902 and boasted a ballroom, the King's original bathroom and a grand sweeping staircase. All that and he only stayed for the weekend! But while I should have felt like a princess in a castle, I rattled around Rangemore most of the time, worrying about either Mevlit or Ed.

Meanwhile Pall-Ex continued to grow, our profits increasing year on year as our volumes did, and we moved more than two million pallets in 2007. How? By doing what we'd always done and constantly innovating our product. By then, we had about eighty-five members in the network and were working on the future launch of new projects including Retail Plus, which would allow companies like Asda, B&Q and Body Shop to use Pall-Ex hauliers to transport goods from their distribution centres into our hub and back out to individual stores.

The same year, Eco Drive was launched, an initiative which underlined our commitment to the environment by collecting and recycling our customers' cardboard and shrink-wrap. I wanted to champion the fact that the logistics industry did not necessarily mean dirty trucks and hairy lorry drivers who were each as environmentally unfriendly as the other. Transport is a vital part of everyone's life and Pall-Ex takes its responsibilities to the environment seriously.

Plans were also well under way for the construction of a new northern hub in Carlisle, which opened in 2008 – the year that I finally divorced Ed on grounds of unreasonable behaviour. I'd first filed for divorce two years before that, but we'd reunited. The relationship was as stormy as it ever had been though, and when I learned that Ed was shagging the seventeen-year-old maid at the house I'd bought in Marrakech, I'd decided that enough was enough.

'I'll speak to you soon,' Ed said the last time we saw each other.

'I'll never speak to you again in this life or the next,' I told him.

All I can say is that I felt two things when our marriage finally ended: relief and worthlessness. There was a lot to keep me busy though because we were deep into negotiations for the first Pall-Ex European franchise, which would start trading in Italy in 2009. Just as I'd once known I'd have to upsize the Gotham hub to keep growing Pall-Ex, I now knew the company would have to expand into Europe. Every successful business is on a growth curve, you see, which will one day peak, and only intuition can tell you when you're nearing it. As early as 2005, I could see that Pall-Ex would one day start to plateau in the UK. I'd had one competitor when Pall-Ex started, who'd told me he'd show his arse in Sainsbury's if I succeeded – he never did – and now there were nine other pallet networks competing with me for business. It was time to find new opportunities.

The European model was simple: master licensees would pay for the use of our intellectual property, like IT systems and our member service agreement, plus management advice on how to set up their network. Italy seemed like a perfect place to start because the logistical demographics were identical to the UK's and everything from car parts to ceramics and clothes is exported from Italy to the UK, so Pall-Ex Italia would mean more freight for my members to transport when it arrived on British soil. Sounds simple enough but it was a long, complicated and draining process to find the right partner and I was knee-deep in it by the summer of 2008. So quite where I found the time to start a TV career, I'll never know. But somehow I did.

I refused when I was first approached to take part in the Channel 4 show *Secret Millionaire* because, with everything that was happening with Mevlit and Ed, I just didn't have enough time. Then they asked me a second time and I decided it was a chance to deliver money straight into the hands of the people who really needed it. I've never had much truck with the kind of charities that spend so much money on staff and administration you wonder how donations ever get to the people they're meant to be helping. *Secret Millionaire* appealed to me.

The idea of the programme is simple: millionaire benefactors go undercover in deprived communities to find out if there's anyone there that they'd like to give money to. I hadn't even seen the programme and didn't give the being-on-telly bit a second thought. It just sounded like a chance to do something very different to being a businesswoman and so I accepted.

I had no idea where I was going when I was picked up for my first day of filming in June 2008. All I'd been told was that I had to dress down for the occasion because jewellery and an Alexander McQueen jacket might get me noticed. So after packing my best Primani, I was put on a train to Rochdale Station, where I got into a taxi and was told that I was going to the Falinge Estate.

'Full of stabbings and drugs,' the driver said dismissively.

I didn't take too much notice. I'd been born and bred in working-class areas. Just how different could this estate be?

Make it about a million miles. Getting out of the taxi, I was greeted by shouts of 'Fuck off' from hoodie-wearing teenagers who started snarling the moment they saw the camera. Apparently GMTV had recently filmed on the estate and hackles were still up. The spotlight was on Falinge, you see, because of the huge unemployment there. Two years after I visited, the estate and the surrounding area would be named Britain's worst welfare ghetto because 84 per cent of people there claimed benefits.

Getting out of the taxi, I looked around at the low-rise blocks of flats jostling for space with high-rises. Litter blew in the wind and the whole place seemed shrouded in grey. Then I took another deep breath when I saw the flat where I was going to live for the next ten days: it was basic, bare and just this side of grotty. I knew I wouldn't be eating at home while I was in Falinge. Or having a bath.

This was a world away from the places I'd known as a child, where people lived cheek-by-jowl in tiny terraces but their front steps were always scrubbed and nets whiter than white. As I stared out of the flat window at a boarded-up shop, I didn't feel surprised that so many people here seemed to have given up. It was bloody depressing. If I'd been born and brought up on an estate like this, I'd have been damned sure to get off it as soon as I could.

The sheer scale of the unemployment problem in Falinge was brought home to me the following morning when I walked outside and saw that most of the curtains in most of the flat windows were still drawn. No one was getting up for work and it was clear that unemployment on this scale must go back to the cradle. If all children know is parents who never work, then how can they learn how important it is, not just for money but a sense of self? Falinge seemed like the kind of place that had been lost and now it was on its knees. How on earth was I going to make a difference?

'So what do you want to do?' I asked the young bloke sitting in the pub as the camera whirred beside me.

'Get a council flat,' he said. 'I'd be really happy then.'

I'd come to the pub to ask for a part-time bar job to supplement my meagre income while I was filming *Secret Millionaire*. I was going to have to live on the equivalent of the dole, and £56 a week wasn't going to stretch very far. At least I only had to do it for ten days though. What about the women bringing up children alone? What would they do if they needed new school shoes? Or the elderly people living on a tiny state pension who lived in fear of the gas bill dropping on the mat? Anyone who thinks that a life on benefits is cushy should think again. Of course there's some who drain the system and they should be cut out of it. Not everyone who's unemployed has a right to an income from the state as far as I'm concerned.

But I know from experience that those who do deserve help are only just scraping by.

'Do you live in the area?' I asked the man.

'Yes. In a hostel.'

'Why are you there?'

'I've just come out of rehab.'

'Drugs, was it?'

'Nah. Alcohol.'

I stared at the pint glasses littering the table he was sitting at with friends.

'So the rehab didn't work then?' I said to him.

Blokes with a belly full of ale inside them weren't going to get a penny of my hard-earned cash.

We're told not to judge a book by its cover, though, and it took me all of about twenty-four hours in Falinge to realize that my first impressions didn't tell the whole story. Statistics and headlines aren't all there is about a place. You have to meet the people behind them, and I soon discovered a small army who were the beating heart of the estate.

Take the elderly lady I met in the local butcher's who invited me back to her home for a cup of tea and a fag. She didn't know me from Adam but immediately offered help when I told her I'd moved back to the north-west after living down south.

'Why did you come here, love?' she asked.

'Because I've just got divorced and the rents are cheap.'

She gave me another Ginger Nut as she refilled the teapot and clucked soothingly at me until it was time to go.

Or the regulars I got to know after getting a job in the Hunter's Rest when Mary the landlady saw that I could still pull a good pint. Men and women who laughed and joked, were knitted into each other's lives, just like the punters I remembered from all those pubs all those years before.

Then there were the staff working at a centre for children with learning disabilities, and a hospice where the TV production team had set up a couple of placements for me as a start to finding something or someone to donate to. Both were wonderful places where Falinge's most vulnerable residents were cared for. But they were also well supported, and I wanted to find someone who really needed my money.

I soon found her, and her name was Sheila Acton. I'd heard about Sheila as I went about the estate, chatting over fences to anyone and everyone to explain that I'd just moved to Falinge and was keen to do more than just sit on my tod each evening. Sheila had set up the Syke Community Base eight years before and now everything from pensioners' lunches to mum-and-toddler groups and IT classes were held there. Anxious to find out more, I got on a bus for the first time in thirty-three years and went to see Syke for myself.

Laughter and chat filled the air from the moment I stepped through the doors and walked into a large room where the Golden Girls and Guys Club was in full swing. After being served a three-course lunch, they were going to have a game of bingo and I was pretty tempted to sit down with them. I couldn't help but think of my parents as I chatted to some of the pensioners. If they'd lived somewhere like Falinge then a club like this would have meant the world to them.

I had no idea as I talked to Sheila that she'd taken one look at my manicured fingernails and wondered if I was really who I said I was: a divorcee who'd moved back to the area and was taking part in a documentary about people relocating.

'No one could afford nails like those on benefits,' Sheila

would later say, but that afternoon she didn't give away a thing.

Sheila explained to me all the work that Syke was doing for the community before telling me that it was now under threat. The centre had lost its funding three months before and seventy-year-old Sheila, who'd retired in 1998 after two strokes, was now doing thirteen-hour days just to keep the place going.

'We'll have to close by October if we can't find any new money,' she said sadly.

As I looked around at the Golden Guys and Girls, I wondered what they'd do without the lifeline that Syke was providing.

'How much do you need?' I asked.

'Sixty-two thousand pounds.'

It was a lot of money and I was anxious that mine would help long-term. I needed to know more so I told Sheila that I'd love to come back and help out.

Syke interested me because of Sheila and her extraordinary energy. If she'd gone into business then I'm sure she'd have given me a run for my money. But the other person I wanted to find in Falinge was someone working with youngsters about Mevlit's age. As I'd walked around the estate and got to know people, seen the teenagers hanging around street corners and the smaller kids watching them, I'd thought to myself that if Mevlit had been tempted into heroin with all he'd had in life, God knows what the young people here would do if they were offered an escape route like hard drugs.

It makes me bloody angry, to be honest. The north of England that I grew up in was full of bustling communities built on jobs in mills, mines, engineering and manufacturing. But generation after generation of politicians have allowed manufacturing and production to die and drained skills out of the system by doing away with tax breaks for apprentice- ships. Great swathes of our country – from the mining areas of Wales to the mill towns of the north-west – have been disen- franchised and left with the slow rot of mass unemployment, crime and drug use.

It's no exaggeration to say that there'll be no Great left in Britain in a decade if we don't watch out. Politicians haven't been improving our lot, they've been crisis-managing for years. As far as I can make out they're far too preoccupied with all their deal-making – or should I say fiddling? – to think of the consequences for the people who elect them, and too bloody weak to stand up to all those European bureaucrats whose petty regulations are making business suffer. Skills have been drained out of the system, jobs lost, and who are the people worst affected by all this? Kids. It makes my blood boil today just as much as it did when I got to Falinge.

There was a more personal reason too for wanting to help those kids. Deep down I was still reeling from all that had happened with Mevlit and the feelings it had left inside me. He was a bit like a newborn chick as he tried to negotiate a life without drugs, and was constantly on the phone. As the mum of an addict there's only one thing that fills you during the moments when you stop worrying about the here and now: guilt. Even now that Mevlit was clean of heroin, I couldn't stop going over and over it, what I'd done or hadn't done that somehow must have put him on the path to his addiction. I was his mother, after all. Surely I must have failed him in some way?

Mevlit himself had told me that he'd paid the price for my business success and I knew he had in some ways. If there was anything I could do in Falinge to stop another child going down the path he had, then I wanted to do it. Maybe I could atone.

Women really do rule the world, don't they? Men might when it comes to politics and business – the head of this or that – but it's the thousands of women, not just bringing up families but holding their communities together and giving them a good kick up the backside, who are just as much of a powerhouse in this country. I met another the day I walked into the Back Door Music Project, where I was greeted by a woman with a shock of bright red hair. Just like Sheila, Carol Moore was a ball of energy and filled with relentless enthusiasm for the community project she'd set up to provide young aspiring musicians with a place to develop their skills.

From the instant you walked in, you knew that Back Door was the kind of place where kids would love to be. There were live music nights for them to take part in and mixing desks for them to practise on, free music-technology training and a small kitchen that Carol was hoping to turn into a bit more of a café. I loved the place and had no doubt that kids who might otherwise be hanging around on the streets would come here. Just like Syke, though, money was a constant worry and Carol ran Back Door in between doing her day job at a bank.

The problem for me as the days passed in Falinge was realizing that if I was going to give money there, it would be the kind of investment I'd never made before. I couldn't go through the books or the balance sheet of either Syke or Back Door with a fine-tooth comb to get a proper idea of the financials. Hilary, the divorcee at a bit of a loose end, couldn't go sniffing around too much. I'd told both women that I'd had some business experience through jobs in the past and had a quick look at the books. But I couldn't ask too many questions or I'd blow my cover. I just had to see for myself, get a feeling.

I'd always relied on gut instinct in business but had made sure to back it up with black and white figures. Now I had to do something different and so I did the only thing I could: spend as much time as possible at Syke and Back Door, just seeing how things were run, getting to know the people and Carol and Sheila in particular. By the end of the week I knew what I was going to do: donate double what I'd originally thought I would. As well as giving a £2,000 cheque to a single dad I'd met called Sean, who volunteered at Syke, was an absolute gem and ran a local football team that the money would be useful for, I was going to donate larger sums to both Back Door and Syke. Sheila in particular, you see, had turned my financial instincts on their head because while I wouldn't have invested in Syke commercially, I knew in my bones that she would make the place work if she had the money she needed.

And so at the end of my time on the Falinge Estate, I ditched the baggy sweaters for my normal clothes and went off to see Carol.

'You look posh,' she said as I walked into Back Door.

'Well, there's something I need to tell you,' I said.

She looked at me and I knew she had absolutely no idea what I was about to say.

'I'm a businesswoman,' I told her. 'And I'm a millionaire. There's something I want to give you.'

The look on her face when I handed her a cheque for £70,000 – enough to pay for a new kitchen and her wages for the next three years – was priceless. I told Carol that it was time to give up her bank job and put her all into Back Door.

Then it was off to Syke, where Sheila burst into tears as I told her who I was and handed her a cheque for £62,000.

'And there's another one just for you,' I said as the stress of the past few months flooded out of her. 'It's for two thousand pounds, and I want you to have a holiday. You deserve one.'

It was the best day of my life. Giving something to people for whom it meant so much was wonderful, and knowing the money was getting directly to the people who needed it made it even more rewarding. I felt like Father and Mother Christmas rolled into one – with a dash of the Tooth Fairy, the Good Fairy and Tinker Bell thrown in.

I didn't just donate to be a good Samaritan though. I firmly believe that doing something for charity is about getting out as much as you put in and that's what happened in Falinge. I not only learned for myself how much good work was going on there but was also reminded of how close-knit and kind-hearted communities like that are. The people of Falinge had welcomed me, they were open and kind, givers of the kind of true northern hospitality that I remembered from my childhood. I will never forget my time there.

So while there's something to be said for living in a huge house in a posh place, I'd say there's as much joy to be found in a million other places. Maybe more. I left Falinge knowing that many of the people there had a sense of belonging that I'd never had. I'll always treasure the hidden gold I discovered. I'm still involved in both projects today.

I'd almost forgotten that my stay in Rochdale was going to be shown on TV by the time *Secret Millionaire* was screened in September 2008. In fact, I'd gone out for dinner with a friend the night it was shown and was infuriated to find that I couldn't get through to Pall-Ex the next day when I phoned.

'What's going on?' I said when the phone was finally picked up, ready to chew someone's ear off because I always insist that calls are answered within three rings.

'People are ringing about *Secret Millionaire*,' came the reply.

'Why?'

'Because they want to talk to you.'

'Why?'

'Some want money, others just want to meet you, and a few men are asking to take you on a date.'

I didn't understand what all the fuss was about, but there was a lot of it. I'd got stacks of letters by the time it all died down and most were written by people who wanted me to help them financially. As tempted as I was to give when I read some of their stories, I knew I couldn't.

Then there were the offers of marriage – eleven, to be exact. One was from a man who told me that he was sixty-seven with the body of a thirty-five-year-old and owned a bungalow in Hastings. Another was from an elderly gentleman who sent me a six-month itinerary detailing what we'd do each day if I agreed to be his wife.

We will go bowling on Wednesdays, he wrote. *You can bring your servants.*

I even got letters from prisoners about to be released who wanted to meet me. I didn't take them up on the offer.

I was deeply concerned when Mevlit told me he wanted to try and contact his father once more, in late 2008. He'd been so hurt the last time that I wasn't sure I wanted him to try again in case he faced another rejection. I was also still worried that a father who'd been involved with drugs was the last thing Mevlit needed as he started to rebuild his life without them. But if he was going to learn to stand on his own two feet then he had to make his own decisions. I told him I'd help him with a letter and we sent it off to the Prison Service.

I was at my house in Marrakech when my mobile rang.

'Hello, Bobos,' a voice said.

It was Hussain; seventeen years since we'd last spoken, I didn't feel anything when I spoke to him again. Not happy. Not sad. So much water had gone under the bridge that I realized all the love – and the hate – had gone.

'I'd like to see Mevlit again,' he said as we talked. 'If I send you a visiting order will you bring him to see me?'

Whatever had happened between us, I'd never stopped Hussain from having a relationship with his son, and so I took Mevlit to see him at a prison in Sheerness. A modern building surrounded by fields, we didn't see too much of it because we went straight from the car park into a reception area, where we waited with other visitors. Then we were ushered into security, where my handbag was given a thorough check and Mevlit had his photograph taken. I knew he was a bag of nerves as he followed me into the visiting room and I felt so much for him – seeing the father who was a stranger after so many years apart. I felt quite calm though as we walked into a room full of tables and chairs, a bit like a canteen. I scanned the faces as I looked for Hussain – for the man who'd been in his late forties when I'd last seen him.

'Hilary?' I heard a voice call and I searched the room again to find Hussain.

Then I realized that a hunched old man was looking at me. Was that really him?

'Hilary!' he said, and Mevlit and I walked towards him.

I was shocked by the man I sat down opposite. Hussain seemed so much smaller than the huge figure who'd loomed in my head for so long. His hair was white and he only had one tooth left in his head. He looked so feeble. Mevlit was quiet, unsure of what to say to the stranger sitting in front of him, and so I started chatting to Hussain as our son tried to take it all in.

'What happened?' I asked Hussain. 'Why did you do this?'

He raised his hands as he shrugged his shoulders before starting to cry and all I could think as I looked at him was: 'What a waste of a life.' There were reasons why I'd fallen in love with Hussain. Good ones. But the bad inside him had brought him to this: not one but two prison sentences for drug importation.

'They were right to lock me up the first time,' Hussain told us. 'But not the second.'

I felt exhausted by the time we left and questions filled me. Had Hussain been involved with drugs even back when we were together? Was it yet another thing I'd been too blind to see? I soon quietened my worries though. I would never get answers and I'd grieved for Hussain for years. The past was another place and it should be left that way. From then on, Mevlit and Hussain started to speak on the phone and I chatted to him occasionally too. I still do. I'm not one to carry bitterness. I don't like dwelling on bad blood. Mevlit is happy to have his father back in his life and that is good enough for me.

So after a brief step into the TV spotlight and getting back in touch with Hussain, I went back to running Pall-Ex, thinking that life would go back to its usual pattern. Little did I know.

Chapter 23

'So have you written to Fred Stevens?'

'Yes, Hilary.'

I stared up at Adrian's face. What had he just said?

'Have you written to Fred Stevens?'

'Yes.'

Another pause. Words were rushing round my head but none of them would come out of my mouth. I had to speak.

'Have you written to Fred Stevens?'

'Yes, Hilary. I've just told you that I have.'

Frustration snapped inside me. Then rage. What did Adrian mean?

'No,' I snapped.

'I did, Hilary.'

Adrian was speaking to me like he'd speak to a child. I looked at him. I couldn't think straight. Had I really asked the question before? I didn't know. I just wanted the answer.

'Have you written to Fred Stevens?'

It was then that I saw it in his eyes. As Adrian looked down at me sitting in a wheelchair, my left hand useless and curled into a claw, a shell of the woman he'd known for years after my body had been wrecked by a massive stroke, I could see just one thing in his eyes: pity.

How dare he?

There are bits of what happened to me after I had a stroke on 9 February 2009 that I can't remember. Chunks of time that are lost in a haze of drugs and not knowing, black spots in my memory I'll never get back. But what I know is that I went to bed with a terrible headache after throwing a dinner party at Rangemore one Saturday night and couldn't find it in me to pack a suitcase for a business trip to Turkey the next day. My head was throbbing and my mind was like cotton wool. People often say they can't think straight and I truly couldn't. As pain shot down my left arm, I went to bed hoping that the migraine or whatever it was I had would be gone in the morning.

But when I woke up on the Monday morning, I realized that I had no sensation in my left hand and little feeling in my face. Robert, who in between being both my employee and friend often stayed over at Rangemore because work never stops for me, took one look and called the doctor. Within twenty minutes an ambulance had arrived and it was three months before I went home again.

I didn't really understand what the word 'stroke' meant when the doctors at Queen's Hospital in Burton first told me I'd had one. Weren't strokes the kind of thing that only the elderly had? I was fit and well. I'd worked eighteen-hour days for as long as I could remember. In the early days of Pall-Ex, I'd had surgery on torn ligaments in my knee and also on my back after damaging it when I fell down some stairs at a service station on the way back from a meeting. I'd been back at work within days of both operations. But now I was lying in a bed almost unable to speak. My speech had been slurred when I'd woken up but I couldn't talk at all by the time I had a CT scan a few hours after reaching hospital. It would be more than a week before I started to speak again, and until then the only things that came out of my mouth were strange, strangled sounds. The stroke had affected the whole of my left side, you see: I was deaf in my left ear, my peripheral vision had gone in my left eye, my left arm hung limply and my leg was the same. I still insisted on being wheeled outside into the hospital grounds for a fag though. Stupid, wasn't I?

The clearest memory I have of those first few days is lying in bed, trying to remember how to spell the word 'the'. All that my mind could curl itself around was that one tiny word: the, the, the. Somehow I knew I should be able to spell it but couldn't. The letters wouldn't come to me.

After two days in intensive care, I went on to the stroke unit. It's the place where they try to get broken bodies whole again, or at least as whole as they ever can be if the stroke has caused permanent brain damage, as it had in my case. All the nurses were lovely and did their best with me but I was too poorly to do much with because, as well as the stroke, I was in a lot of pain due to a problem that had developed three months before.

There's been a lot of rubbish written about me and one of the things people seem to be constantly asking is if I've had plastic surgery. Let me say now that I haven't had a facelift or cheek implant (those hamster cheeks were with me from birth). I've had a bit of Botox in my forehead; some collagen in my lips, which to be honest I thought was a waste of time and then a tummy tuck, which was what was causing me so much trouble by the time I had the stroke.

I don't see anything wrong with plastic surgery and the reason I had the operation was because to be honest I felt ruddy useless after my marriage to Ed failed. Ugly. Another failed relationship. Don't forget I'd also ballooned by three stone all those years before when I was put on to pig insulin for my diabetes, and although I'd lost most of the weight by now, I hated the bit of saggy skin that having a child and losing weight had left behind on my stomach. It wasn't that bad but my self-esteem was at such a low ebb that I felt it was, and my view is that if you can improve yourself then do something about it if you want to. Just don't get addicted to plastic surgery, at least not if you don't want to end up looking like something from Madame Tussauds.

The reason I was in additional pain after the stroke was because I'd developed post-operative complications after having the tummy tuck at a private hospital in November 2008. An infection had set into the incision and what had been a straight line about two inches in diameter across my stomach when I came out of the operating theatre soon started to open up, the skin red and angry. Nothing the doctors did could heal it and as the infection bedded in, the incision turned into an open wound the size of a saucer and the skin started to die. For months before the stroke, I'd been going back to the hospital to have the wound regularly re-dressed but it hadn't worked and the pain was so bad that I'd sometimes had to work from bed at home. I was on tramadol and even two further operations to cut away the infected skin hadn't sorted out the problem.

That was why I wasn't fit for intensive physiotherapy after

the stroke, but it didn't worry me because I was sure I didn't need it. That's the thing about being stubborn: sometimes it stands you in good stead and sometimes it makes you refuse to see reality. I simply wouldn't accept how ill I was. On my first night in hospital, I fell out of bed and was found dragging myself along the floor with my good arm. When people insisted I should rest, I got angry with them and demanded the phone to make a business call.

Something inside me just wouldn't let the information sink in. I was the person who'd always looked after everyone, the sole shareholder of a multi-million-pound business, a doer. I had been all my life. I was damned if I was going to allow my body to let me down. I'd been told that the recovery period for a stroke of the magnitude I'd had would be several years. I convinced myself that I'd be back to normal as soon as I left hospital.

'You sound very slurred,' someone might say when I phoned them from my room on the stroke ward.

Bugger them, I'd think.

Or I'd stare at the laptop that I'd insisted be brought in to me and wonder what to do with it. My poor PA Deena got phone call after phone call in which I'd repeat myself, or hiss down the phone in rage when the words I wanted to speak wouldn't come out. I will never forget her patience and kindness. All the while, Mum was jamming up the hospital switchboard with so many calls that they had to ban her from phoning. She visited me once, the day after the stroke, but wasn't well enough to come again because her health was getting worse and Mevlit could hardly bear to come into the hospital. The three of us were the terrible trio.

I was an awful patient to be honest but somehow still

managed to get on like a house on fire with the nurses. The second series of *Damages* was being shown on TV at the time and I was addicted to the exploits of Glenn Close's devilish Patty Hewes. So on Sunday nights I'd send someone off to the canteen with money to buy all the staff a bacon butty – or a bacon barm cake as us Boltonians call it – and the nurses would be in and out of my room watching the show. They were worth their weight in gold.

I must have been in hospital nearly two months before I had a physio session and never had any more because the following day a surgical doctor came to see me, took one look at my wound and put me into an ambulance straight back to the private hospital where I'd had the tummy tuck. The wound was worse than ever and I was operated on for a third time to try and finally cure the infection with a skin graft from my thigh. By this time, quite frankly, I felt as if I'd been run over by a truck and you might have expected that after all that had happened I was due a little nursing TLC. Instead, as I recovered at the private hospital, I realized that the head nurse not only looked like a reincarnation of Eva Braun, she had the personality of Nurse Ratched too.

When it came to me and my disobedient ways, it was all she could do not to straitjacket me as I insisted on smoking and went on an online shopping spree because I soon got bored. As box after box arrived from ASOS, my room filled up with catsuits, jackets, tops and shoes that I couldn't try on so why I was buying them I'll never know. But Nurse Ratched/Braun would walk in and purse her lips before sighing and walking out again.

It was only when I realized that she'd got a soft spot for Robert that I found a way to warm her up a little.

'I think he has a crush on you,' I'd say whenever he left, and I was sure I could see a tiny crack in her icy veneer.

I was right. Nurse Ratched/Braun was soon buzzing around me like my very own good fairy and doing all she could to make me feel comfortable. I don't think she ever did work out that Robert is gay.

And so, almost three months after first going into hospital, I went back to Rangemore and thankfully the wound finally seemed to be healing. As far as I was concerned, the effects of my stroke would do the same. I was utterly convinced that I would be fine again and refused to consider for a second that I would never be in the same health that I'd once enjoyed.

Mevlit put his arms underneath mine.

'I'm just going to lift you, Mum,' he said softly.

I stared at the motorized wheelchair I'd bought so that Mum could get up the stairs at Rangemore. Now I was the one who was going to be using it. Desolation washed through me as my son lifted me on to a contraption that should have been used for my elderly mother. I didn't say a word as I was slowly manoeuvred up the stairs and looked at my left arm lying limply in my lap.

There were so many moments like that when I went back home, as the truth of what had happened started to hit me. It's strange how your mind will let so much go before some insignificant detail almost overwhelms it. For instance, I'd switched off when I was lifted in and out of the bath in hospital. I'd even managed to convince myself when I got home that everyone was overreacting when they told me that Renata and Aneta, the housekeepers I'd employed at Rangemore, needed to stand outside the shower when I insisted on standing up for long enough to have one.

But it was as I sat on the bath afterwards trying to dry myself that it all hit me: I realized I wasn't even strong enough to put on my own knickers any more. One hand was steadying me, the other was useless, and I felt exhausted by the effort of standing up for just a few minutes.

I pushed the thought away and covered myself in a towel as I called Aneta.

'Come on,' she said softly as she walked in to find me. 'There's no need for modesty, Hilary. I'll help you. It isn't a problem.'

It was to me. I felt utterly humiliated by having to be dependent on people for almost everything and the feeling wasn't limited to my personal life. Professionally I felt mortified by the meetings I insisted on having at Rangemore with Adrian (don't forget that Britain was in the grip of the worst recession for decades and Pall-Ex had to be carefully steered through such troubled waters, however healthy our bank balance was) when I'd see the sympathy in his eyes.

I insisted on working, though – even if dictating a single email finished me off. For years, I'd dictated everything to Deena each morning – firing off scores of messages without a single written note. Now my brain just couldn't absorb information or retain it. An hour's meeting would send me to bed for the rest of the day and while I slept and slept, I never felt any stronger. The frustration I felt was like nothing I'd ever known. I was the fireball, the one who would work twenty hours a day, the one who told people to burn the midnight oil because that's what I paid them for and could always last longer than any of them. Now I was nodding off during meetings and it horrified me.

I could accept not being able to stand upright for more than a couple of minutes without falling over, or the fact that I had to sleep for hour after hour just to get through a day. It was the mental exhaustion that I resented most. Thank God I can laugh at myself and had enough sheer willpower to force myself not to give up. I did as much work as I could and my colleagues were extraordinarily patient and kind. I'm grateful they were because I'm not sure I'd be here today without Pall-Ex. The business forced me to keep my brain active and, just as it had with Mevlit, it saved me.

Life certainly wasn't easy for the people looking after me, though. The frustration and exhaustion I felt, the pain which filled me as I tried to use muscles that were atrophying because my brain wouldn't send the proper signals to move them, made me explode with rage almost without realizing I was doing it. When Renata and Aneta did my hair and make-up, I'd complain if anything was out of place.

'I look like a ruddy clown,' I'd cry.

Or when Robert took me out to the shops for half an hour just to relieve the boredom of lying in bed, I'd snap his head off if he dared leave me sitting in my wheelchair while he went to look at something.

'What do you think you're doing?' I'd roar. 'Leaving me here like a sack of bloody potatoes.'

Given my increasing frustration at having to rely on others so much, it's only natural that I grabbed the chance of a bit of independence when it came. It happened after one of my trips with Robert to Marks & Spencer in Fosse Park, Leicester, when I'd noticed an elderly woman driving around the store in one of those motorized buggies and asked him to book one for me.

'Freedom at last,' I thought as Robert helped me into the buggy a few days later.

It was only when I looked at the hand controls that I realized there might be a problem: I needed both hands to operate them.

'A mere detail,' I thought to myself.

I'd driven all my life without having an accident. What could possibly go wrong in a motorized buggy? I'd just use my right hand. Two minutes later I was careering through the food department sending boxes of biscuits flying, but, drunk on my first taste of freedom in months, I didn't take a blind bit of notice.

Heading for the lingerie department, I heard Robert calling out as he ran after me.

'Please stop, my dear!' he cried. 'Hilary, my dear!'

I didn't listen. Bras and pants went flying as I carried on and concerned members of staff joined Robert in the chase.

'I will not be beaten!' I thought as I found myself at the end of an aisle, unable to turn around.

With that, I accelerated the buggy towards a sock display and started trying to batter myself through it.

'Hilary! Please!'

Deaf to Robert's cries, I only admitted defeat when a gaggle of M&S staff surrounded me like a ring of steel. But after I'd been put safely back into my wheelchair and was being pushed sedately through knitwear by Robert, I realized I might not be too safe behind the wheel any more. The place looked as if a herd of cattle had been driven through it. All I can say is that the people looking after me had the patience of saints.

What I found almost harder to cope with than my dependency though was the realization that Mum was struggling to understand what had happened to me almost as much as I was. She was eighty-three by this time and couldn't seem to comprehend that the daughter who'd been a rock was little more than useless. Gary and Stuart were still living in Bolton, while Mum had moved to Nottingham to be nearer to me. With their own jobs and families, they were busy with their own lives and I'd always been the one who mostly looked after her.

Now Mum had always required a lot of attention. I remember one long phone conversation I had with her when I took a trip to the Sahara Desert on holiday and she insisted on talking me through the plumbing problems she was having with her toilet. We were always on the phone and I visited her at least once a week. But after my stroke I just couldn't, and she got more and more demanding.

'I need a new bed,' she'd cry when she rang Rangemore at 7.30 a.m. and Renata or Aneta would pick up the phone. 'Let me speak to Hilary.'

When they tried to explain that I was sleeping, her rage would increase.

'I have to talk to her,' she'd shout and they'd gently explain that I'd ring her when I was awake.

'I want those girls sacked!' Mum would scream down the phone when I called her back. 'Do you know what they did? They refused to let me speak to you, Hilary.'

'I'm sorry, Mum.'

'And so you should be. The bed you bought me is awful. I need a new one. Today.'

I just wasn't strong enough to argue so I'd do what I could

to calm her down, knowing that she wasn't being unkind. She was elderly and frail and needed me when I couldn't be there for her. She didn't understand.

'You're too busy to see me, I suppose,' she'd snap when I phoned.

'No, Mum. I'm just not strong enough.'

'But why not?'

'Because of the stroke.'

'Well you can get in the car, can't you? You've got a driver, haven't you?'

Nothing I said made a difference and it tore me apart.

By the time I went to my villa in Spain for a holiday in July 2009, I was strong enough to work for a day on the phone from home, but then needed two days off to recover. Still in a wheelchair when I went out but able to walk around at home, I also had a bit of movement back in my arm. The improvements had come about after visits from a neurophysiotherapist to Rangemore. I'd started to regain some use of my leg and arm because the exercises I'd done had strengthened my muscles a bit. I could now put a little weight on my left leg, and bend my arm but not lift it.

I was lucky to be able to afford that kind of help. Others, sadly, can't, which is why I now support two charities that do such great work: the Stroke Association and the Princess Royal Trust for Carers. Both help not only those who are directly affected by illness but the people around them too, and I'm proud to do what I can. It's not just adults who care, but children too, and strokes don't affect only the elderly. I've seen children and young mothers who've been affected by them and it's tragic that lives with so much potential are blighted in this way. The courage and strength I've seen has never ceased to amaze me.

I'm also proud to be able to do something for Princess Anne because I love the royal family. They're the greatest ambassadors Britain will ever have as far as I'm concerned and I would be horrified if a politician ever became our head of state. Can you imagine any of that lot working so hard when they're used to taking a holiday every few weeks? The only one of them I really like is John Prescott, and that's because he's got such a good sense of humour and did a lot for the transport industry. Princess Anne and her family do an amazing job for us all and, having seen her at work, I know she has a capacity for it that I've seldom seen equalled. She is an amazing woman and I take my hat off to her.

So by the time I got to Spain, I'd managed to convince myself that the worst was behind me and was happy to meet up with my cousin Janet and her husband George, friends Stephanie and Tony and my niece Jade. Robert was there too and it felt like a bit of normality at last.

But about a week into the holiday, I was sitting on my bed one afternoon when I got up and started shuffling in circles. I couldn't go in a straight line however much I tried to.

'Lie down, Hilary,' Stephanie told me. 'You're tired. You need to rest.'

As she told me to empty my mind, I was filled with the strangest feeling I've ever had. It was as if I was falling, plunging who-knows-where even as I lay on my bed. And then everything went black.

I'd had a serious seizure because I was at greater risk of having one following the stroke. Then I had another at the hospital in Benidorm where I was taken, and the doctors had to start my heart again after it stopped twice. I remember nothing about it of course and the first I knew was when I woke up two days later strapped to a bed. Apparently I'd been sedated because I'd been so agitated at first that I'd somehow managed to wriggle out of bed and Robert had found me crouching behind it, trying to pull out the drips that had been fed into my arms.

They couldn't keep me sedated for ever, though, and if I wasn't a model patient when I was in a UK hospital, then I became the patient from hell in a Spanish one. I'd hide the sleeping tablets the doctors gave me because all I wanted was to get back to work. I'd smoke out of the window and refuse to listen when I was told to stop. My Spanish doctor should have been awarded a humanitarian medal or something for putting up with me.

'Get my passport!' I'd cry when Robert came to see me. 'Get me a plane ticket. I've got to get home.'

'But you're ill, Hilary. You need to rest.'

'I don't! Can't you see, Robert? I don't need to be here. I'm fine.'

'You're not, dear,' he'd say in his usual calm tone.

'I am! Get me my credit card!'

Like I said, the patient from hell. My already weak body had been further shocked by the seizures and I left hospital three weeks later with an additional problem. The muscles in my oesophagus had already been affected by the stroke but the problem had got worse and I now found it hard to eat solid food. I was given orders not to fly and told to rest at my villa for at least six weeks before even thinking of going back to the UK. As you might have guessed, I didn't listen to any of the advice I was given because within a week the phone rang at the villa and I picked it up.

It was Sue, the woman who was looking after Mum at Rangemore. I'd asked for her to be taken there from her flat in Nottingham when I was told that she wasn't feeling well. Over the past year, one thing after another had started to go wrong with Mum's health. She had problems with her kidneys, heart and feet and I wanted her to be at Rangemore if she was feeling poorly.

'She's getting worse, Hilary,' Sue said. 'I'm going to call the doctor.'

Then she handed the phone to Mum, whose voice was small when she spoke.

'Hello, love,' she said. 'How are you?'

'I'm OK, Mum. Just resting. How are you feeling?'

'Not too good.'

'Well, Sue's going to call the doctor and we'll make sure you're OK. She's going to ring me later to let me know what he said.'

'OK.'

She paused for a moment before speaking again.

'Come home, Hilary. Please come home.'

I knew then that something was very wrong. When Mum was taken into hospital, I was frantic with worry.

'She needs me,' I kept saying.

'And your health wouldn't stand the trip,' came the reply.

But when I spoke to a doctor who told me that Mum was deteriorating, I knew I had to get back to England. However I did it, I had to be with Mum. But no airline would fly me so I knew there was only one thing for it.

'We're going to have to drive,' I told Robert.

'But Hilary, my dear! You've only just got out of hospital yourself and you know what the doctors said. You shouldn't risk it. You might have another seizure. It will take more than a day of non-stop driving to get back to Rangemore.'

'Then that's just what we'll have to do, isn't it?'

It took twenty-seven hours and I phoned constantly.

'I'm on my way,' I kept telling Mum. 'I'll be there soon.'

I could hear from her voice that she was hanging on to see me and I was determined to get back to her. Mum perked up a little when I arrived.

'Why travel all that way, love?' she said in a whisper as she lay looking up at me from her bed.

But the next day she fell unconscious and died two days after I reached her bedside. I was alone with her at the end.

'Wake up, Mum, please wake up,' I pleaded with her.

But she never did. My mum had left me, and whatever age you are when that happens, nothing can prepare you for how it feels.

Chapter 24

I was back working full-time at Pall-Ex by the end of 2009 and by then had finally started to accept that I was never going to fully recover from the stroke. Specialists I'd seen after the seizures had told me that I would never be able to drive again because my peripheral vision was permanently affected, as was my hearing. Today I still have little feeling in my left hand, I haven't regained full movement of my left arm and I am unsteady on my feet if I have to stand or walk for too long.

Don't think I've had a terrible accident if you see me in a wheelchair at an airport. I'd just rather not show myself up by collapsing on the floor. Better to take the safe option than become the laughing stock of Heathrow or Gatwick. Today I have a wonderful assistant called Magda who is my left hand for me. She helps me to dress and does my make-up and hair as well as a million other things. I couldn't be without her. But while I don't have the energy I once did and still get very tired, it doesn't mean I'm not permanently working. I just have five meetings a day instead of ten, but push myself to keep going because somehow my body manages to recharge itself and fight another day.

Stroke or no stroke, though, I had to get stuck back into

Pall-Ex because the main challenge facing the business in 2009 was doing all we could to withstand the continuing recession. It was the only year in our history when our profits dipped, after pallet volumes dropped by more than 200,000. But we were better off than most because we had significant saved profits, which gave us a buffer against testing times, and I'd also taken early action to withstand the worst.

A recession for a company like mine doesn't necessarily spell disaster. The deeper a country goes into one, the less freight there is to move and the fewer full loads there are on lorries. That means companies will use a hub to transport the goods they have, because at least their vehicles will then take a full load back when all the hauliers' goods are shared around the network. It makes more economic sense than running their vehicles for their sole use.

Even so, I'd known long before the recession had officially started that trouble was coming and had responded by cutting costs at Pall-Ex (mostly in personnel by making some redundancies and not replacing people when they left) while investing in marketing and sales. I also put money into special projects like our European expansion, and took on a team of hand-picked MBA graduates to work on this. They were headed by our home-grown talent Anand Assis, who joined us as a graduate and is now a Pall-Ex board director, and between them the team could speak eight languages ranging from Mandarin Chinese to Polish. They were key to driving our European project forward.

Having the confidence to reinvest like this for the future – as well as making necessary cutbacks – was what helped me to steer my business forward during tough economic times. I can safely say that the negotiations to expand into Europe were the most testing I've ever known. As well as the sheer mechanics involved in setting up a new pallet network and finding the right partner to work with, there are cultural, social, economic and demographic factors to take into account – as well as different legal systems. But today, despite all the problems in the eurozone in late 2011, the European arm of Pall-Ex is performing outstandingly well. Our Romanian network launched in November 2011 and France followed in January 2012.

But while 2009 was a challenging year, it was also the one in which I was recognized with my industry's biggest honour – the Sir Robert Lawrence Award from the Chartered Institute of Logistics and Transport. By then I'd been invited to Buckingham Palace to meet the Queen after being recognized for special achievements in industry, and received many awards for what I'd done in business. I'd also started to speak about my life and work to everyone from charities to business leaders in the UK and abroad. But the Sir Robert Lawrence Award meant so much because I was the only woman to have ever won it. It was a true honour to be recognized by my peers.

I never thought for a second that I'd end up having a second career in television when I was approached by Channel 5 to do a series called *The Business Inspector*. I just thought it would be another one-off project – this time a four-part series – and it interested me because the producers wanted me to go into small businesses and turn them around. I knew filming would be tiring, but I was keen to give it a go because more than 99 per cent of the British economy is made up of SMEs – small- and medium-size enterprises – which turn over £3,100 billion a year. They're vital to our economy and I'd always felt passionately that any business of any size should be professionally run. That's why I wanted to do *The Business Inspector*, and I'd enjoyed *Secret Millionaire*, so why not?

Just how haphazardly some companies are administrated was a shock even for me, though, when we started filming in January 2010. Donna Coventry and Ann Scott, who ran Leaf It Out florists in Milton Keynes, had such a loose grip on their costings that they were in line to lose £14,500 that year.

'Who's funding these losses?' I asked.

Donna and Ann were. And so were other relatives, including one of their mums. The pair of them got short shrift from me. What right did they have to play with their loved ones' money like that? The bank of Mum and Dad should be insolvent by the time a child reaches eighteen as far as I'm concerned, unless there's a very good reason for it not to be. Losing money doing flowers isn't one of them.

After going to see the mum in question, I gave Donna and Ann some straight talking: it was time for them to factor in fixed costs like rent, heat and light into their prices and get a lot more proactive about finding new business. I've said before that if you can market and sell then you can run a business, and the girls at Leaf It Out weren't being nearly creative enough in their approach to finding new customers. By the time I left, they were well on their way to getting them.

It was the same story with many of the businesses I inspected: at Premier Karting in Reading, I advised owner Derek Halpin to get out and start sourcing new clients by leafleting the town centre to advertise an open evening for local people, because bookings for corporate events had dived off a cliff. When I met with Jass Patel, who ran a cocktail bar called Mokoko in St Albans, I told him to get off his high horse and stop buying such expensive spirits because he was throwing away his profits. I even made him do a taste test in the street to prove to him that no one would know the difference, and they didn't.

'Are you selling sex or keep-fit?' I asked Lou Gardiner, who ran Affinity Pole Fitness from an exercise studio just outside Canterbury.

What fifty-something woman was going to swing off a pole to try and get fit? I believed that Lou was making her product too niche – and the same went for Noeline Stevens' dog-grooming business, because hardly anyone knew about it given that it was hidden in the garage at the side of her house in Bournemouth. None of these people were maximizing their chances for new customers and being proactive about finding them.

Then there were all the other basics to running a small business: proper accounting and financial procedures; marketing and selling your product; thinking creatively about how to maximize your customer base – and never, ever forgetting your bottom line. Noeline soon stopped putting her cash takings into a tin that she and her husband dipped in and out of after meeting me. Donna and Ann were under no illusions that they had to get their gross profit margin of 11 per cent far closer to the 32 per cent that most florists work on by the time I left. Jass Patel, who was paying himself £15,000 when I went to see him so might as well have been working far less hours on a Tesco check-out, had forgotten that the core of any business is its costings versus profit – not its brand of vodka.

Passion alone doesn't create profit. It's all about your bottom line. And business isn't rocket science, whatever some people might say. Of course, the bigger your business gets, the more scientific you have to be about financial projections and logistics. But if you're starting out then it's about knowing your product and keeping your costings tight. Remember that ink I used to syringe into the photocopier back at Pall-Ex?

I've often been asked what makes the ideal entrepreneur, and I'd say it's a mix of creativity and commercialism. You have to have a sound grasp of business essentials, but if you have creativity then you have intellect, which means you can nurture it to learn new things like basic business sense. Innate good business sense is not enough on its own. Trust me: accountants make lousy entrepreneurs.

Every piece of advice I gave on *The Business Inspector* was basic. It was just common sense with a bit of straight talking thrown in. I finished filming the series pleased that I'd done my best to turn each business around and went back to Pall-Ex. Soon, though, I'd be sitting in one of Britain's five most famous business seats after entering the *Dragons' Den*. So did I breathe fire when I did? You can be the judge of that.

I was on the way to my first day of filming for *Dragons' Den* in May 2011 when I told Kiran to stop the car. Next thing I knew, I was being sick with nerves on the pavement. It wasn't the TV cameras I was worried about though. It was the dragons themselves. It was all very well filming solo for *Secret Millionaire* and *The Business Inspector*. But how was I going to keep up with Duncan Bannatyne, Peter Jones, Deborah Meaden and Theo Paphitis?

The run-up to that morning had been like something from a spy film. When the BBC had first approached me, they didn't say what series they had a spot to fill for. There was just all this talk about opportunities and screen tests and I ended up doing a day's filming at a bakery in Wimbledon with no idea what I was being considered for. Then came the call to offer me *Dragons' Den* and I knew I couldn't refuse. I'd always watched the show and enjoyed it.

It seemed like the perfect shopping trip to go looking for investment opportunities, and I'd already put money into businesses outside Pall-Ex – including an event company that I'd worked with on *The Business Inspector* called Wow Table Art. I'm always on the lookout for opportunities and it would give me no greater pleasure than to find a business that I could help turn into a household brand.

The other reason I wanted to become a dragon is because of something that had happened years before. You'll remember the problems I had when I first started trading at Wymeswold and thought there was business planning permission on the site before discovering there wasn't? Well, I'd made another mistake even earlier, after the planned date for Pall-Ex to go live had got pushed back ten weeks during the BT phone line fiasco. I hadn't budgeted for the delay, was already paying staff and rent, so I'd had to borrow some money from an investor to tide me over.

He was introduced to me by my hairdresser's fiancé and I simply trusted that he'd be the sort of person I'd want to do business with. Don't forget that back then it was far harder to research people's backgrounds because there was no internet. I was green though and the deal turned very bad after I realized that the man and his associates were not the type of people I wanted to have any links with. I repaid the money in full via a solicitor plus substantial interest and they also signed a legal document called a compromise agreement saying that the matter was at an end. But it was a very distressing time for me and I'd learned some lessons the hard way. Maybe by getting involved with companies right at the start of their life via *Dragons' Den*, I could help other budding entrepreneurs avoid the same fate.

Thankfully my fears about my fellow-dragons proved groundless. They were pussy-cats really. All of them welcomed me on board and even put up with me when I held up the filming of those opening shots in which we're all super-imposed standing on the top of buildings looking like executioners waiting on the scaffolding.

'Keep a straight face,' the cameraman kept telling me, but I just couldn't.

And so filming started and I found myself stuck in the most bloody uncomfortable chair known to man, on a set at Pinewood studios that was so freezing it made my feet turn to ice within minutes of sitting down. All I could think as I stared down at them was whether the delicate shade of blue they were turning would show up on camera. And as for that chair . . .

'Can I buy my own?' I asked as I got up from it feeling about 150.

'Noooooo!' came the reply. 'They're iconic.'

In the end I had to get one of those heated wheat bags and hide it behind me during filming to ease my back pain. I got used to it in the end but the one thing I never got over was that I had to wear the same thing day in, day out during weeks of filming. I'd been planning a mega-wardrobe until I was told that we had to look the same all the time because the sequence of would-be investors viewers see trooping into the den doesn't necessarily correspond to when we see them.

I had to have two changes of exactly the same outfit and all

I'd thought as I'd picked what to wear was that I didn't want to look too sombre. So I'd brightened up a black dress with a cream jacket I'd had made by the dressmaker I work with to design my clothes. Let's face it, that jacket and its shoulder pads are so me: stuck in the eighties. But I had no idea it would get such a reaction. Twitter was afire with talk of my jacket when the first episode of *Dragons' Den* was shown.

But what seemed to attract even more attention – and to be honest it baffled me – was the way I straight-talked. As you know, I'm made that way and after years in haulage, my tongue has got even blunter than the one I was born with. Believe it or not, though, I was quiet as a mouse when filming first started because being the new dragon reminded me of growing up and going to all those new schools. I felt like I didn't fit in and was too scared to say much. But I soon realized that I wasn't going to get a look-in if I didn't speak up.

'Bugger it,' I said to myself. 'Just be you, Hils.'

And so I was. Which is why I told Alan Sharrock, the owner of Miruji Health and Wellbeing, who came to see us with a massage chair that played audio to help people do everything from slim to stop smoking, exactly what I thought of him. The dragons had asked question after question but we just couldn't get a proper answer.

'How ridiculous of you to come here and pitch to investors without that information when by God, man, it's your job to have it,' I roared at him. 'I still haven't got a clue how your turnover's broken down or the state of your balance sheet.

'You're talking to potential investors. It's your *job* to come on and make us aware. Forget the Miruji experience. We're on Planet Earth in *Dragons' Den*. You would make my foot itch, mate. I'm not amused. I'm angry. I'm out.'

Alan wasn't alone. Other would-be investors who didn't listen to what was being said soon got short shrift too.

'Why weren't you prepared?' I told a man who was looking for investment in his signage business. 'And how do you hope to grow your business when you can't even motivate yourself to do what should have been the biggest pitch of your life?

'How do you expect someone to invest in you, the product or your company? I'm out.'

When three young guys came in to show us Barmate – a device which held a pint pot steady to allow bar staff to carry on serving and save time – I told them what I thought.

'I was pulling pints illegally from the age of seven and to be honest if I'd got bar staff who couldn't add up an order, open a bottle, pour a spirit and deliver a pint then frankly I would think they were badly trained. I'm out.'

And there was also the man who wouldn't stop talking over us all as we asked him about his idea to revolutionize selling houses online.

'God gave you one of these and two of these,' I said to him as I pointed at my mouth and then my ears. 'So use them wisely.'

The thing is, you can immediately tell the people who are being disingenuous with the facts – and those who aren't. That said, I still wasn't prepared for Glen Harden from Kent, who came into the den with his son stripped naked to the waist. He wanted investment in his UV Body Sculpture – a tanning device which allowed users to define their muscles.

'He's a right little pudding,' Glen said as he showed us his son's buff body. 'It's all down to selective tanning.'

When we asked him about a business plan, he told us: 'I ain't got a clue.' Then I suggested that the salesman working for his existing business manufacturing kitchens and bed-rooms also tried to sell the tanning device and he told me that his brother was the salesman.

'So why doesn't he sell your product?'

'You've got to meet him,' Glen said. 'We check for a pulse and regularly don't find one.'

I was sure the whole thing was a joke by the time Duncan asked him what happened to the product if people tried to use it in a stand-up sunbed and Glen told us that it just fell off. It wasn't.

Everyone from popcorn makers to a man who'd invented a device to stop splashback in the toilet trooped in to see us. There's no end to the weird and wonderful ideas that people have, and I found it encouraging that so many wanted to give business a go even in such difficult economic times.

Moments before someone came into the den, the same call always went up: 'Dragons. Eyes on stairs.' Then Peter would start tapping his pen like the death march until people appeared. Some of them were like frightened rabbits, while others were far too cocky. But you can soon sort the wheat from the chaff because instinct tells you if the product is good and the people behind it are too.

I didn't mind if would-be entrepreneurs couldn't pull every financial detail out of their brain as questions were drilled at them by the dragons. Being in front of us must be daunting I'm sure. I was more interested in getting a feel for the person and their product, because there were three things I was looking for: low-cost growth that didn't require investment, something generic that could be franchised out, and an inno-vative product that would fill a gap in the market. Not every investment I was interested in had all those factors of course but all those elements were important. The most important one of all though was simple: would I get on with the people I invested in? If I didn't think I would then I didn't invest.

At times, though, I had to make sure my head ruled my heart. Take seventy-one-year-old Wendy Thompson, a former chartered physiotherapist from the Isle of Wight, who came in to show us a health swing. She'd developed it after her husband had a stroke and it was designed to help users strengthen and mobilize their muscles through non-weight-bearing exercise. I had a go and thought it was a good idea.

But I also knew that the £50,000 Wendy wanted would be a drop in the ocean and so I told her that however much I wanted to, I couldn't invest. Neither did any of the other dragons. But after the programme, I put Wendy in touch with the Stroke Association and one of her swings is going to be trialled in the newly built Bromsgrove Stroke Rehabilitation Centre. The health swing won't make Wendy a millionaire, but I hope she'll have the pleasure of knowing how many people she's helped.

There were also times when I just didn't think my nerves could stand the pressure of an investment: most particularly in the case of Rodrigo Perez, the human cannonball. He and his wife Lois had met while performing in a circus in Mexico and now wanted £30,000 for 10 per cent of their business. Rodrigo told us that he was building himself a new cannon which would revolutionize things but I knew I wouldn't be able to live with myself if anything happened to him. I'd have been on the phone to Lois every time he shot out of his cannon just to make sure he'd survived the fall.

In the end, I invested in four businesses: Duncan and I offered on a company producing children's balance bikes called Kiddimoto and I invested alone in Bob's Box – a thing that Deborah accurately described as a big bingo blower. It's a game aimed at the corporate and private event market which allows users to climb into a huge Perspex box and try to grab balls as they fly through the air before pushing them down a tube. Sadly, neither of those investments came off because the process that people have to undergo after coming out of the den with an offer often throws up problems which mean that an investment cannot proceed.

The two investments that I'm working on today though are Duvalay and Shoot It Yourself. Duvalay is a memory-foam mattress developed for the caravan market by Alan and Liz Colleran. I could immediately see that the potential was far larger than Alan and Liz had considered: planes, lorries and prams, to name a few. I also bought a share of Shoot It Yourself, a wedding-videography company run by Andrea McDowell and Rebecca Baldwin. Both had worked in television and come up with the brilliant idea of hiring out cameras so that guests could shoot footage of the day for the bride and groom. Then it's edited to make a truly professional but personal memento. Once again I could see huge potential for other markets and possibly even franchises.

I wasn't up against any other dragons for either of those investments. In fact, I didn't even listen to what the others had to say when it came to Shoot It Yourself. I was convinced that both businesses had huge potential and that was enough for me. But when it came to making offers against other dragons, I usually lost. Most of the time, I took it on the chin. It's business after all and I was a new dragon who no one knew. Some of the time, though, I thought the people who turned me down were bloody stupid.

You might have seen all this for yourself on screen if you watched the series. What you probably didn't know is that for some of the series I was wearing camouflage make-up to cover up the bruising on my face after having a bad fall on set. And I'm sure you didn't realize Johnny Depp came into the den. He was filming at Pinewood at the time and is apparently a big fan of the show. He seemed like a very nice guy when I met him.

But that's the thing about *Dragons' Den*. Everyone from Hollywood A-listers to a bloke who believed that hot dogs made out of haggis would make his fortune wants to be part of it. And I'm very glad that I am too.

Epilogue

So you've heard about my childhood, growing up and the career that didn't get off to a flying start. Then there's the story of how I built Pall-Ex, my entry into the *Dragons' Den* and my personal life. There haven't been many dull moments, have there? But perhaps there's one more thing I need to tell you: I got married for the third time in March last year. I know, I know: I'm terrible at picking blokes. But I really hoped this one would turn out better than the others.

His name is Phillip and I met him when I was selling the first house I'd bought in Spain, after buying a new villa just down the coast. Phillip was living in Spain and had a background in the building trade, so I asked him to be in charge of the project to get the house ready to go on to the market. We got on as we worked together but I didn't think any more of it because I'd all but given up any thoughts of meeting a man after my stroke. To be blunt: I'm partially disabled, attractive enough but not one of life's great beauties, and thin as a stick because of all the problems I've had with eating after the seizures.

I didn't think I was exactly what most men were looking for

and I'd given up any thought of a relationship to concentrate on my work and animals. Let's face it: pets are more reliable and don't answer back; you can feed them whatever you want and they'll eat it; and they only need one bath a week so they're very economical. My Teacup Yorkshire terriers, Micha, Mixie and Dixie, are the loves of my life – as is my American cocker spaniel Charlane, who's nicknamed Marilyn because she's blonde and dizzy. Then there are my horses Bessie, Sky, Gentleman, Minnie Proctor and Arthur Channon, who I used to ride but sadly can't any more. They have a good life though. In fact Gentleman, who is a former show jumper, starts each day with a bacon barm cake and a cup of tea.

Anyway, decent single blokes don't just hang off trees, do they? Not long before the stroke, I'd joined one of those dating agencies, and what a load of rubbish it was. All I met was a bunch of midde-aged tossers who were after someone else's money. I was even told that some of them were paid to meet the women who'd signed up because they didn't have enough eligible men on their books. I made a couple of good friends out of it but that was it. So I'd say to any woman of my age to be very cautious about those kinds of agencies and who you might meet.

I was just happy paddling my own canoe, getting stuck back into Pall-Ex as we worked on our European network expansion, and thought that was my lot. I was content with that. But things changed between Phillip and me after he came over to the UK to do some work at Rangemore. It was the night of the International Freight Weekly Awards, at which I'd won Freight Personality of the Year, and Phillip had escorted me because we'd become friends by then but after some people had come back to the house following the ceremony and didn't leave until 3 a.m., I just burst into tears. All we'd talked about was work and, exhausted after such a long day, I had one of those moments when I wondered if there was anything in my life but that. Phillip and I got chatting and that was the moment when our friendship started to become something else.

We married at Rangemore about a year after we met, on 28 March 2011 because it's a significant date for me: my mother's birthday, the day I joined the WRAF and the day the Pall-Ex hub opened. I really thought it was a good omen to get married on that day. What I didn't realize then is that you both come with a lot of baggage when you get married in middle-age. Past relationships, children, ways of doing things, the list goes on, and sometimes it's hard to work through all of that. I also hadn't appeared on *Dragons' Den* by the time we got married and life really changed when it was aired a few months later. It's bloody hard knowing that a third relationship has gone down the pan. What on earth can I say? I feel hurt, angry and just a little bit bewildered because I can't seem to get it right with men, just like Mum said, and it's a chink in my armour that I have difficulty accepting. But for now I'm just taking life one day at a time. What will be will be.

The world went mad after *Dragons' Den* was shown. Apparently I'm a celebrity now, although I'm not sure quite what that means other than having to buy a new dress every time I go to an event. I like clothes, but my outfits take a lot of thought and it's bloody time-consuming.

I had no idea what was going to happen after I entered the den though. My other television work hadn't caused much of a stir but suddenly Twitter went mad and I became the second most Googled celebrity of the summer. Everyone from *Hello!* magazine to *Grazia* and *Heat* wanted to talk to me, and people like Graham Norton, Radio 1's Greg James and Alan Titchmarsh wanted to interview me. T-shirts were printed with I LIKE DEVEY YOU MOVE, and even a phone ringtone was created from my voice. Comedians imitate me, and I got one of them – Vikki Stone – to perform at the last Pall-Ex Christmas do. She raised the roof.

The first time I realized that life might have changed a bit was when a girl came up to me as I sat in Luton Airport.

'Are you real?' she said.

'Of *course* I'm real,' I replied with a laugh.

Then, when I was sitting outside a café in Spain, I realized that people were stopping to take pictures of me. When I nipped out without a scrap of make-up on to go to the nail bar I use in London for manicures, some paparazzi started snapping too. I just laughed. I don't quite understand what the fuss is all about, to be honest, but I have to say that I've enjoyed the rest of it. It's nice to make people smile by stopping to have a chat or signing something for them. I genuinely like people, you see, and I'm still Hils. Always have been, always will be.

So what of the future? Well there's Pall-Ex, of course, and our European expansion. We're in negotiations to start operating in Germany, Poland, Turkey and Benelux. I won't rest until I realize my vision: to be the biggest pallet network in Europe. As you know, failure isn't an option and I honestly love my work: I've had a lot of betrayals along the way but I've also been demonstrated a lot of loyalty which has more than made up for them. Then there are my other business investments and the people I work with on those. I'm thrilled that Wow Table Art is on the up and up and believe that Shoot It Yourself and Duvalay will be household names one day.

But there's more to life than business, and part of me really thinks that I might end up in politics some day. I want to make a difference and I think I might be able to. Listen to Cameron or Miliband and all that's coming out of them is a stream of words that the man or woman in the street can't understand. Does the average person know what the inter-branch lending rate is? No. Where's the common-sense talk that would get everyone far more involved in the running of our country?

The thing is, people in Westminster make politics a mystery when it shouldn't be. Running a country is like running a business: you have a balance sheet – and it should balance. Take the NHS: it's just too big and being stretched too far, and no one is brave enough to say that. It makes you wonder why the politicians are where they are, because if they can't run the NHS then how can they run our country? The UK is a business, and in terms of the economy, if you've got a deficit then you've got a cost-cutting exercise to do. The people in power would have known years ago what was going to happen. Analysts are paid to study demographics and we've got sufficient historical data to provide an accurate statistical analysis. But they chose not to tell us. Maybe I'll go into politics and sort them out.

I'll never stop pushing myself in other directions, you see. For now, there's more *Dragons' Den* and a two-part series for the BBC in which I'll meet women politicians, chief executives and ordinary people to examine whether there's a glass ceiling that stops women from rising to the top or not. I don't believe there is. I've proved that a manicured fist can smash

341

any glass ceiling just as well as a hairy one, haven't I? There *are* sacrifices to make, though – even if you don't know you're going to have to make them. But as difficult as mine have been at times, most particularly my feelings of guilt during all of Mevlit's problems, he tells me today that he would have died without my help and I'm so proud that he's well again.

I'm proud of what I've achieved too. Materialistic success doesn't mean much, to be honest, but my sense of professional pride and love of family and friends really do. Most of the time I'm too busy to stop and look back but, on the odd occasion I do, I often think of what my dad would have made of it all. I don't think Arthur Channon Brewster would have been that surprised. He saw the drive in me as a child and taught me to apply it well. So what would he say if he was here today?

'You've done well, our Hils,' I like to think. 'It's a job well done.'

And so it will be, until I start pushing up the daisies. For now, there's so much more to do.